The Homeowner's Guide to
MANAGING
A RENOVATION

Tough-As-Nails Tactics for Getting the Most from Your Money

SUSAN E. SOLAKIAN

STERLING

New York / London
www.sterlingpublishing.com

STERLING and the distinctive Sterling logo are
registered trademarks of Sterling Publishing Co., Inc.

Remodeling Cost vs. Value Report, p. 9,
used by permission, © Hanley Wood LLC

Library of Congress Cataloging-in-Publication Data

Solakian, Susan.
  The homeowner's guide to managing a renovation : tough-as-nails
tactics for getting the most from your money / Susan Solakian.
       p. cm.
   Includes index.
   ISBN 978-1-4027-2754-2
1. Contractors—Selection and appointment—Amateurs' manuals.
2. Dwellings—Remodeling—Planning—Amateurs' manuals. I. Title.
   TH4815.4.S65 2008
   643'.7—dc22   2008003797

10   9   8   7   6   5   4   3   2   1

Published by Sterling Publishing Co., Inc.
387 Park Avenue South, New York, NY 10016
© 2008 by Susan E. Solakian
Distributed in Canada by Sterling Publishing
c/o Canadian Manda Group, 165 Dufferin Street
Toronto, Ontario, Canada M6K 3H6
Distributed in the United Kingdom by GMC Distribution Services
Castle Place, 166 High Street, Lewes, East Sussex, England BN7 1XU
Distributed in Australia by Capricorn Link (Australia) Pty. Ltd.
P.O. Box 704, Windsor, NSW 2756, Australia

Book design and layout: *tabula rasa* graphic design

Printed in China
All rights reserved

Sterling ISBN: 978-1-4027-2754-2

For information about custom editions, special sales, premium and
corporate purchases, please contact Sterling Special Sales Department
at 800-805-5489 or specialsales@sterlingpublishing.com.

CONTENTS

Acknowledgments

This book is dedicated to my father—a design engineer from whom I inherited my curiosity about how things work.

Special thanks go to Joel Luper, RA, who created all the great architectural drawings and illustrations, to Jeff Evans, RLA, for the landscape designs, and to John Duncan for the specifications—all of which will make your learning experience easier and more pleasurable.

Thanks to Dave and Peggy Mackowski, owners of Quality Design and Construction, Inc., and Terry Ashe, Executive Director of Firm Foundations Community Services, who shared photos of construction work in progress.

And many, many thanks to all the homeowners and contractors who allowed me to photograph their homes and their work so that you, the reader, would be able to envision what we're going to talk about.

Introduction

You're ready! You want to remodel! You want to live in a space you love. You have in your hand exactly what you need. I've spent more than twenty years coaching property owners through all sorts of major remodeling projects, and I'm going to share everything I know with you—in plain and simple English.

Planning, designing, and executing a substantial home remodeling project are not for the faint of heart. Remodeling is not for the romantic, the disorganized, or the undisciplined. Making sound financial decisions about your home requires that you toughen up a bit and become a student of the real estate market, of basic home design principles, and of construction project management strategies.

The Homeowner's Guide to Managing a Renovation is not for do-it-yourselfers. Amateur design and construction can actually lower the value of your home. What you will learn here will help you successfully plan and execute a major home remodeling project using professional designers and contractors. It will guide you through the project one step at a time—from planning, to finding and working with a great architect, to selecting great contractors and letting the job out for bid, negotiating a contract, monitoring the work in progress, controlling payments, dealing with disputes, and enforcing your warranty.

It will also ensure that you get what you want without exceeding your budget!

1960s home

1960s home

1970s home

1970s home

The Homeowner's Guide to Managing a Renovation will not only teach you the principles of remodeling project management—it will also give you the chance to work on an entire, complex, make-believe home renovation that will double the size and completely change the character of a little brick ranch.

By the time you finish learning the basics of project management in Part 1, you'll be ready to manage Our Project in Part 2. And by the time you've completed Our Project, you'll know how to use this book like a roadmap and you'll manage your own job like a pro!

Learn . . . practice . . . go for it!

Remodel? Or Move and Remodel?

The real estate market is not what it used to be, and I'm not referring to the ups and downs of the interest rates over the years.

At least half of all American homes were constructed before 1972.

That means that half of the homes standing today are more than thirty-five years old.

At that age, many of a home's original materials and services, such as plumbing connections, cabinetry, windows, siding, and roofing, have reached the end of the line and need to be replaced.

All the good lots are taken, and with so many older homes on the market, the Big Question has changed. We used to ask ourselves, "Shall we remodel or move?" Now the question is, "Shall we remodel—or move and remodel?" For the first time in history, remodeling expenditures in the United States exceed new construction costs, and that trend is expected to continue into the foreseeable future.

It's time to stop being afraid of remodeling.

It's time to learn to take care of what we own.

DEPT. OF HOUSING & URBAN DEVELOPMENT - AMERICAN HOUSING SURVEY
Population & Housing Data by US Region
Source: http://www.census.gov/hhes/www/housing/ahs
Data represents census est. for the year 2005, based on real numbers from year 2000

	US TOTAL		NORTHEAST		MIDWEST	
List of states in each survey region Source: http://www.census.gov/popest/			CT, ME, MA, NH, NJ, NY, PA, RI, VT		IL, IN, IA, KS, MI, MN, NE, ND, OH , SD, WI	
Census population estimates for 2005	**Qty**	**%T**	**Qt**	**%T**	**Qty**	**%T**
Total US population, and % by region	296,410,404	100%	54,641,89	18%	65,971,974	22%
Owner-Occupied Housing by Region	**72,238**	100%	12,964	18%	17,889	25%
				9%		
Year Structures Built						
2000 - 2004	4,239	6%	394	9%	885	21%
1990 - 1999	11,432	16%	1,152	10%	2,462	22%
1980 - 1989	9,672	13%	1,400	14%	1,729	18%
1970 - 1979	13,359	18%	1,766	13%	2,923	22%
1960 - 1969	9,187	13%	1,612	18%	2,325	25%
1950 - 1959	8,696	12%	1,949	22%	2,456	28%
1940 - 1949	4,643	6%	1,003	22%	1,215	26%
1930 - 1939	3,192	4%	807	25%	979	31%
1920 - 1929	2,799	4%	956	34%	975	35%
1919 or earlier	5,018	7%	1,951	39%	1,977	39%
Median Construction Date	**1972**		**1959**		**1965**	

	US TOTAL		SOUTH		WEST	
List of states in each survey region Source: http://www.census.gov/popest/			AL, AK, DE, DC, FL, GA, KY, LA, MD, MS, NC, OK, SC, TN, TX, VA, WV		AR, AZ, CA, CO, HI, ID, MT, NE, NM, OR, UT, WA, WY	
Census population estimates for 2005	**Qty**	**%T**	**Qty**	**%T**	**Qty**	**%T**
Total US population, and % by region	296,410,404	100%	107,505,413	36%	68,291,122	23%
Owner-Occupied Housing by Region	**72,238**	100%	26,699	37%	14,686	20%
Year Structures Built						
2000 - 2004	4,239	6%	2,017	48%	943	22%
1990 - 1999	11,432	16%	5,327	47%	2,553	22%
1980 - 1989	9,672	13%	4,379	45%	2,163	22%
1970 - 1979	13,359	18%	5,499	41%	3,171	24%
1960 - 1969	9,187	13%	3,388	37%	1,862	20%
1950 - 1959	8,696	12%	2,624	30%	1,667	19%
1940 - 1949	4,643	6%	1,451	31%	974	21%
1930 - 1939	3,192	4%	830	26%	576	18%
1920 - 1929	2,799	4%	508	18%	360	13%
1919 or earlier	5,018	7%	674	13%	417	8%
Median Construction Date	**1972**		**1977**		**1975**	

PART ONE

Basic Principles of Remodeling Project Management

ONE

Facing Facts: Remodel, or Move and Remodel

Establishing the cost of moving is pretty easy: purchase price plus 20 percent of the purchase price for moving costs, Realtor's fees, an interior paint job, new window treatments, and some new furniture equals the total cost of the move.

But cost is not the only consideration. What about the impact on your family?

Everything will be turned upside down. Everyone will have to adjust. There will be new friends, new neighbors, maybe a new job; new streets, new stores, maybe even a new climate. These are very big adjustments. The physical move will be over pretty quickly, but the impact of the relocation will linger for years.

I'm going to assume that if you are unhappy enough with your current home to consider giving it up, you would have to do a substantial remodel in order to feel good about staying there.

Planning and executing a substantial remodeling project can take a year, but during that year you will have the comfort of familiar surroundings and the support of your friends and neighbors; your kids won't get uprooted; and although the work will take a little longer, the result will be all positive!

That's something to consider.

The Remodeling Alternative

Most homeowners who want to start a remodeling project have some idea of what they want to do, but they don't know what that might cost. The first thing most folks do is call a contractor. Don't do that.

Imagine that you are that contractor. Your prospective client stands in the middle of the living room and waves her arms around describing her dreams: " . . . and maybe this or maybe that . . . "Then she turns to you with a rueful smile and asks what you would charge her. How would you price that project description? You would have three choices. You could low-ball the price, hoping to get your foot in the door; you could give her a price that was high enough to cover everything you think she'll end up doing and hope for the best; or you could give her a "no, thank you" price—one that was so high she wouldn't want to hire you.

None of these prices will be helpful to the homeowner. And if you (the homeowner) consulted several contractors, you would wonder why you were getting such a wide *range* of prices.

Getting Started

While most owners think they know what the architect and the contractor are supposed to do, it's been my experience that they rarely know what their own job is!

Your job, as owner, is to provide a well-thought-out Master Plan and then to ensure that everybody follows it. Since you'll be paying all the bills, you automatically become the CEO, and you have all the executive responsibilities.

What will that entail, and how do you get started?

Your first instinct was right; you need to get some idea of what your dream project might cost you.

Reliable information about the cost and the return value on common remodeling projects is at your fingertips. For the past twenty years, *Remodeling Magazine* has published a nationwide study of the investment value of twenty or more common remodeling projects. Construction data are collected from sixty U.S. cities, independent appraisal firms calculate the returns, and the numbers are aggregated by city and region, as well as nationwide. Excerpts from the 2004, 2005, and 2006 Remodeling Cost vs. Value Reports are included on page 9.

You can order a copy of the current report on *Remodeling Magazine*'s Web site, http://remodeling.hw.net.

The return value is expressed as increase in equity value—not market value—of the home, and assumes that the home is sold within a year of the time the paint dries. Note that very few projects return 100 percent of the cost. Let's talk about this for a minute.

The numbers you'll find in these charts are really helpful, but they miss the point. Most of us *don't* spend lots of money on a remodel, because we want to increase our equity value before we sell. The real value of a remodel is *intangible*; the whole point of going to all this trouble and expense is to create a home you will love to live in. So when you see that a family in Milwaukee spends $7,000 on a new deck but gets only 85 percent back in increased equity, don't get discouraged. Consider the more important, *intangible* return they'll get from having such a great place to relax and socialize with their family and friends—and know that the 85 percent financial return is not, by a long shot, the whole story.

We can now conclude at least two things about planning to remodel: first, the longer you plan to stay in the house, the greater the overall return you'll get on your investment; and second, if you're planning to sell, spruce up (the type of work you see on reality home design television programs) but don't bother to remodel unless it's the only thing that will make the home marketable.

If you think about it, since the reason you plan to remodel is so that you can tailor this home to suit you, the more you tailor it to your own tastes, the less likely it is to suit someone else and the less a buyer will be willing to pay for the details you love best. Did that make sense? Remodeling is something you do for yourself—not for a prospective buyer.

WORKING ON HISTORIC PROPERTIES

Work on buildings with national historical significance is regulated by the National Parks Service, a division of the Department of the Interior, through representatives in every state known as state historic preservation officers (SHPOs). The state is the clearinghouse for a tremendous amount of information about remodeling older homes. There is no cost or obligation for the assistance furnished through your state preservationist. As a matter of fact, your home doesn't even have to have historic significance for you to get technical assistance from the state.

If you're working on a home that is fifty years old or older, you can get all the information you need with one phone call. The SHPO can tell you whether or not your property is of interest to the federal government, and if it is you must follow the guidelines that they provide you. If you will be required to follow the federal guidelines, the state will help you at every step.

It is also possible that your property has some significance to the town or county you live in, in which case you may be governed by a set of rules set by a local preservation commission. The state preservation office can also connect you to a local commission if that's necessary.

None of the historic authorities are inflexible. Contemporary design may be welcomed as long as the scale and character of the neighborhood are reflected in the new structure.

Generally, projects are reviewed with some consideration for economic and technical feasibility too. The preservation standards are not applied unreasonably.

If you find you have a conflict between what you need to do to comply with the building code and what the preservation guidelines will allow, the state will even help you negotiate with the municipal inspections department to reach a compromise.

Preservationists can often help property owners find cost-effective, preservation-sensitive solutions to remodeling challenges. By discussing your project with them before you begin your design, not only will you be able to incorporate some of their wonderful ideas, but you will also ensure that your plans will be approved when the state or your local commission reviews them. A historic project that has not been formally approved will not receive a building permit.

REMODELING COST vs. VALUE REPORT - 2004, 2005 and 2006
Costs and values are nationwide aggregates unless a specific region is indicated.
Prepared annually by *Remodeling Magazine*   Available at www.costvsvalue.com

PROJECTS	2004 Cost of Work	2004 Resale Value	2004 Percent Return	2005 Cost of Work	2005 Resale Value	2005 Percent Return	2006 Cost of Work	2006 Resale Value	2006 Percent Return
Kitchen, Minor Remodel	$15,273	$14,195	93%	$14,913	$14,691	99%	$17,928	$15,278	85%
Kitchen, Major Remodel, Midrange	$42,660	$33,890	79%	$43,862	$39,920	91%	$54,241	$43,603	80%
Kitchen, Major Remodel, Upscale	$75,206	$60,367	80%	$81,552	$69,194	85%	$107,973	$81,896	76%
East	$76,315	$62,324	82%	$82,528	$70,718	86%	$109,364	$80,621	73.7%
Midwest	$77,809	$55,131	71%	$45,237	$36,691	81%	$110,241	$73,511	66.7%
South	$70,380	$61,593	88%	$41,133	$36,329	88%	$103,137	$82,508	80.0%
West	$77,807	$62,496	80%	$45,242	$45,353	100%	$110,623	$91,547	82.8%
Bathroom Remodel, Upscale	$25,273	$21,629	86%	$26,052	$24,286	93%	$38,165	$29,529	77%
Bathroom Remodel, Midrange	$9,861	$8,887	90%	$10,449	$10,727	102%	$12,918	$10,970	85%
East	$10,348	$10,842	105%	$10,978	$11,446	104%	$113,472	$11,167	89.2%
Midwest	$10,501	$7,829	75%	$11,047	$9,885	90%	$13,534	$9,857	72.8%
South	$8,572	$7,918	92%	$9,293	$9,596	103%	$11,545	$10,321	89.4%
West	$10,394	$9,708	93%	$11,025	$12,340	112%	$113,514	$12,837	95.0%
Bathroom Addition, Upscale	$41,587	$33,747	81%	$47,212	$40,488	86%	$60,535	$44,041	73%
Bathroom Addition, Midrange	$21,087	$18,226	86%	$22,977	$19,850	86%	$28,918	$21,670	75%
East	$22,195	$20,477	92%	$24,010	$21,959	92%	$30,141	$21,516	71.4%
Midwest	$22,542	$16,627	74%	$24,157	$17,998	75%	$30,530	$19,985	65.5%
South	$17,942	$16,847	94%	$20,055	$17,648	88%	$25,248	$20,407	80.8%
West	$22,596	$19,896	88%	$24,560	$22,481	92%	$30,853	$25,409	82.4%
Master Suite Addition, Upscale	$134,364	$104,200	78%	$137,891	$110,512	80%	$176,268	$128,096	73%
Master Suite Addition, Midrange	$70,245	$56,257	80%	$73,370	$60,460	82%	$94,331	$68,458	73%
East	$73,439	$74,914	83%	$75,959	$64,419	85%	$97,355	$70,086	72.0%
Midwest	$74,914	$51,926	69%	$77,343	$57,592	75%	$99,479	$62,481	62.8%
South	$60,729	$51,418	85%	$65,037	$52,977	82%	$83,273	$62,522	75.1%
West	$60,729	$51,418	85%	$77,640	$69,425	89%	$100,611	$81,236	80.7%
Home Office Remodel	NIC	NIC	NIC	$13,143	$9,569	72.8%	$20,057	$12,707	63%
Attic Bedroom Remodel	$35,960	$29,725	83%	$39,188	$36,649	94%	$44,073	$35,228	80%
Basement Remodel	$47,888	$36,457	76%	$51,051	$46,010	90%	$56,724	$44,685	79%
Family Room Addition	$52,562	$42,347	81%	$54,773	$45,458	83%	$74,890	$53,519	72%
Sunroom Addition	$31,063	$22,002	71%	NIC	NIC	NIC	$49,551	$32,854	66%
Deck Addition	$6,917	$6,000	87%	$11,294	$10,196	90%	$14,728	$11,307	77%
Window Replacement, Midrange	$9,127	$7,839	85%	$9,684	$8,681	90%	$10,160	$8,500	84%
Window Replacement, Upscale	$15,383	$12,875	84%	NIC	NIC	NIC	$13,120	$11,109	85%
Siding Replacement, Midrange	$6,946	$6,445	93%	$7,239	$6,914	96%	$9,134	$7,963	87%
Siding Replacement, Upscale	NIC	NIC	NIC	$10,393	$10,771	104%	$13,149	$11,573	88%
Roofing Replacement	$11,376	$9,197	81%	$11,164	$9,456	85%	$14,276	$10,553	74%
National Average Return on Remodeling Costs			**80%**			**86%**			**78%**

TWO

Project Planning

2.1 OBSTACLES AND OPPORTUNITIES

Good investment decisions are based on anticipated *future* outcomes. Take a good look at your property and its surroundings and decide if this is the right time, the right neighborhood, and the right property to invest in.

Do Some Research

Whether you're about to buy a fixer-upper, you just moved in, or you've lived in this house a good long time, it may help to have another look at some of the details on your deed and property survey. Both documents are available in the office of the registrar of deeds at your local county courthouse. If there are covenants (restrictions) on the deed or easements (restricted areas) on your property that would limit you in some way, you need to know this before you begin work.

• *Learn the Value of Comparable Properties.* Find out what comparable homes in your neighborhood have been selling for. Over-improving your home would be a big mistake. How much financial elbow room do you have between the current value of your home and what the market value of homes that are like yours will be when you've finished the project you're planning? You want to upgrade, but you don't want to create a white elephant.

• *Assess the Surrounding Neighborhood.* Find out how your neighborhood is changing. You may think you know because you've lived there for a while, but it can't hurt to look more carefully before you invest in an expensive remodel.

Talk to a few good Realtors. You can get great insights from community leaders, local newspaper columnists, PTA presidents, school board members, executives from the local chamber of commerce, and others with insider knowledge of local politics.

Ask them all what neighborhood changes they anticipate. Are businesses (and jobs) moving into or out of town? What is the standard of living in your area, and how is it changing?

• *Talk to the Inspections Department.* Every prospective remodeler ought to find out what permits are being issued for big commercial developments. Suppose a great big shopping mall was built out near the highway. Would downtown become a ghost town? It wouldn't be the first time, and what would happen to your property value?

• *Look at the Local Government's Five-Year Plan.* Contact your local planning department personnel. Find out if your street is about to be closed, paved, or widened or if the town is planning to build a firehouse or a grammar school on the corner. Where will the new community center be built?

- *Check Zoning and Land Use Ordinances.*
Local zoning codes dictate setbacks, on-street parking rules, and housing density parameters—how a property can be used. Any change in zoning regulations will affect you, but the one you have to watch out for is something I call "zoning creep." When the town leaders decide to move the edge of the commercial district an additional two blocks in your direction, it won't be long before the house next door becomes a hair salon or a dentist's office. Find out what's in the long-range plan. Find out how your city council plans to manage growth.
- *Call the State Department of Transportation.*
Get information about new highways that are only in the planning stages now. What would happen if they built a new highway two miles away from you? What if you found out they were going to add an exit off the interstate that would direct lots of new traffic through your neighborhood? It often takes ten years or more for the planners to get their ideas on paper. Snoop around a bit.

Get a Good Home Inspection

If you decide that remodeling would be a good investment, start your planning process by getting a really *thorough* home inspection. Small problems that you *can* see can hide much more important problems that you *can't*. The home inspection report will tell you what needs repair. It will also uncover problems that might have become surprise costs if the contractor found them after the work started.

You may need to hire more than one inspector. For example, if you need to assess special equipment—such as your furnace— you'll get more accurate information from a

Vines entering house under siding will rot siding

Weather-damaged porch

Porch ceiling indicates roof leak above

Cracked wall plaster indicative of house settling

Heaving pavement may indicate a leak in the main plumbing line

trained technician than you would from even the best home inspector. The same would be true for hazardous materials and for termites; let specialists have a look.

Where do you find a good professional inspector? Strategies for finding the best professionals in your area are described in Section 3.1, "Hire the Best," in Chapter 3, but here's a preview. Try asking for referrals from professionals in related fields who would be apt to see home inspection reports on a regular basis and who know which inspectors do consistently good work. Call mortgage bankers, Realtors, property insurance claims adjusters, or commercial property managers. Ask each for a short list of inspectors he or she uses on a regular basis. The names of the very best inspectors will appear on more than one of the referrals lists; these are your strongest candidates. Call a few of them. Briefly describe your plan and ask them how they would approach their inspection so that the report gives you the most helpful information. A short conversation can tell you a lot about how these people do business and what you might expect in the final report.

Take a Photo Inventory

Before you disturb anything, you'll want to document the existing conditions around your home. Take pictures of everything: the view from the street, including the properties on both sides of you; all your exterior walls; every interior space; all the architectural details, inside and out; and any valuable items or collections you may currently have on display. Label each photo (e.g., 123 East ABC Street; June 6, 2008; master bathroom). Keep one set out to work with, and store a second set for future use.

ENVIRONMENTAL HAZARDS

Before or during demolition, remove or encapsulate any materials that are hazardous to your health.

GET PROFESSIONAL HELP

To find out which hazards might typically be found in a building like yours, call your state department of health and human services. They will provide you with sound advice and lists of licensed consultants who can help with the details.

Briefly describe your building, your neighborhood, and your plans for renovation. Find out what the licensed consultant thinks you ought to test for.

The consultant can identify hazards, sample the materials that appear to be suspicious, and get those samples to a licensed laboratory, then translate the lab results into a report written in plain English, and provide you with a scope of work and some cost estimates for the treatment or removal of the toxins.

FOLLOW THROUGH

Save the assessment report, incorporate the consultant's suggestions into your renovation plan, and have any hazardous materials treated or removed when you remodel. Your environmental consultant should be able to coordinate this process for you. If you are working on your own home, you will be required by law to leave the property during the remediation work period. If you are renovating an income-producing property, you must notify your tenants of your work plan and temporarily relocate them.

When the remediation work is finished, ask the consultant to return to your property and test it again. The purpose of this test is to confirm that there are no hazards left. The resulting report is called a "clearance report." If you are a landlord, share the clearance report with your tenants so that they feel safe when they return.

KEEP RECORDS OF EVERYTHING

Because of the risks and liabilities involved in handling toxic materials, I suggest you make notes of all telephone conversations, and keep all brochures, correspondence, lab results, risk assessments, remediation plans, contracts, and a copy of the clearance report forever.

Keep the original copy of the clearance report with your property deed. The law requires that when you sell your property, you disclose whether or not you know of any hazardous conditions. If your property is free of hazards and you can prove it, you may be able to sell for a higher price.

In addition, as more and more landlords are faced with lawsuits brought by families with children permanently brain-damaged by elevated blood-lead levels, insurance companies are beginning to require that you prove you have a hazard-free rental unit before they'll renew your liability insurance on that property. Your clearance report will provide the documentation you'll need to lower those liability premiums.

Have your property sampled and cleared at the end of the remodel whether or not you included abatement work in your contract. You never know what you've stirred up; a clean bill of health will bring you peace of mind.

These pictures will serve several purposes:
- Sometimes you'll see things in these pictures that you overlook when you're busy with daily routines. This will help you determine your design goals (in Chapter 3, "Design").
- You will have documented your pre-construction conditions, which will be useful in case of damage or dispute.
- If you choose to increase your insurance coverage for the duration of the contractor's work schedule, these photos will provide a pre-construction inventory for the insurance agent.
- When you're finished with this project, you can take "after" photos of the same areas and see quite clearly how you have improved your space.

2.2 DETERMINING WHAT MATTERS MOST

You can create a cost-effective, high-impact Master Plan if you focus on what's important right away. By doing this, you won't waste time and energy fiddling with ideas that won't make a significant difference in the look or function of your home.

Uncover Fundamental Problems

The free and foolproof way to begin your project planning work is to decide what you like and what you don't like about what you have. This couldn't be simpler, but it's very important; it will provide the foundation for the entire project. Be deliberate and thorough; don't rush. This guide leads you through a process that moves smoothly from one step to the next; the quality of thought you put into your first list will determine the quality of your finished project.

Put Your Subconscious Mind to Work

Somewhere in the back of your mind you've got a list of things around your home that bother you. You need to remember what those things are now and start writing them down.

Walk around your home and look at it the way a Realtor or an interior decorator might. Make notes about everything that seems out of scale or out of balance, unattractive or unsuitable. Ask yourself:
- Where do you spend most of your time, and why? Where does the rest of your family spend most of their time, and why?
- If you entertain a lot, where do your guests always seem to settle in? Would you like that to continue, or do you want to redirect them by changing your floor plan?
- Which activities need separate spaces, and which can share spaces with other activities? Could you redesign an area that doesn't get much use so that it's more flexible?
- What about the relationship between the inside and the outside areas? Where is the best natural light, and how would you like to use it? If you have a view, are you taking advantage of it?

If you love something—the privacy and quiet of the home office, for example—make a note about that. If there's something you wish you had—a mudroom or a place for that wonderful portrait of your great-grandfather—note that too.

Do you need a desk in the kitchen, a coat closet near your front door, a linen closet in the master bath, a place to toss the mail when you come home in the evening? If so, make a wish list.

For the next few days, let your subconscious operate independently. Keep a

HOW LONG DO THINGS LAST?

(Note: time frames given in years)

Windows

Aluminum and vinyl casement	20–30
Screens	15–20
Window glazing, glass	20
Wood casement windows	20–50

Gutters and Downspouts

Copper	Lifetime
Galvanized metal	15–30

Shutters

Aluminum, interior	35–50
Aluminum, exterior	3–5
Vinyl or plastic, exterior	7–8
Wood, interior	Lifetime
Wood, exterior, depends on weather	5

Hardscaping and Landscaping

Asphalt driveways	10
Brick and concrete patios	24
Concrete walks	24
Gravel walks	4
Swimming pools	18
Sprinkler systems	12
Tennis courts	10
Wood fences	12
Wooden decks	15

Finishes

Ceramic tile, high-grade installation	Lifetime
Drywall and plaster	30–70
Exterior paint on wood and brick	7–10
Interior wall paint (varies widely)	5–10
Interior trim and door paint	5–10
Sealer, silicone, and waxes	3–5
Wallpaper	7

Floors

Carpeting (varies widely)	11
Marble	Lifetime
Oak or pine	Lifetime
Slate flagstone	Lifetime
Terrazzo	Lifetime
Vinyl sheet or tile	20–30

Doors

Exterior, protected by roof overhang	80–100
Exterior, unprotected/exposed	25–30
Folding	20
Garage doors	20+
Garage door opener	10
Interior, hollow core	15–20
Interior, solid core	30+
Screen	20

Millwork: Finish Carpentry

Stairs and trim	50–100
Disappearing stairs (attic access)	30–40
Closet shelves	Lifetime

Cabinetry

Kitchen cabinets, stock	15–20
Medicine cabinets and bath vanities	20

Countertops

Ceramic tile, high-grade installation	Lifetime
Granite	20+
Laminate	10–15
Wood/butcher block	20+

Appliances

Compactors	10
Dishwashers	10
Disposals	10
Dryers	14
Exhaust fans	20
Freezers, standard	16
Microwave ovens	11
Ovens, gas	14
Ranges, electric	17
Ranges, gas	19
Refrigerators, standard	17
Washers	13
Water heaters	10

Insulation

	Lifetime

Rough Structure

Basement floor systems	Lifetime
Framing, exterior and interior walls	Lifetime

Electrical

Armored cable (BX)	Lifetime
Conduit	Lifetime
Copper wiring	100+

Home Security Systems

Intrusion systems	14
Smoke detectors	12
Smoke, fire, intrusion systems	10

Plumbing

Faucets (depends on quality)	13–20
Gas hot-water heater	15–20
Private septic systems	15–25
Sink, enamel over steel	25–30
Sink, enamel over cast iron	25–30
Sink, china	25–30
Water pipes, galvanized	30–50
Waste lines, cast iron	75–100

Bathroom Fixtures

Cast-iron bathtubs	50
Fiberglass bathtub and shower stalls	10–15
Shower doors, average quality	25
Toilets	50

Heating and Air-Conditioning

Boilers, hot-water or steam	30
A/C, central unit	15
A/C, window unit	10
A/C compressor	15
A/C, rooftop	15
Burners	21
Dampers	20
Diffusers, grilles and registers	27
DX, water and steam coils	20
Electrical coils	15
Fans, induction or fan coil units	20
Fans, axial	20
Fans, centrifugal	25
Fans, roof-mounted, ventilating	20
Furnace, forced-air	15
Furnaces, gas- or oil-fired	18
Gas chillers	12
Heat exchangers, shell-and-tube	24
Heat pumps	10
Heaters, units, gas or electric	13
Heaters, radiant, electric	10
Heaters, hot water or steam	25
Heaters, baseboard	20
Humidifiers	8
Molded insulation	20
Pumps, sump and well	10
Water heaters, electric	14

Footings and Foundation

Concrete block	100
Concrete, formed and poured	200
Termite proofing	1–3
Waterproofing, bituminous coating	10

Masonry

Chimney, fireplace, and brick veneer	Lifetime
Brick and stone walls	100+
Stucco	Lifetime

Siding

Aluminum	20–50
Steel	50–Lifetime
Vinyl	50
Wood (depends on maintenance)	10–100

Roofing

Asphalt and wood shingles and shakes	15–30
Asphalt composition shingle	15–30
Asphalt overlag	25–35
Built-up roofing, asphalt	12–25
Built-up roofing, coal and tar	12–30
Clay tile (depends on climate)	50
Slate (depends on grade)	50–100
Sheet metal (depends on application)	20–50+

notepad with you while you're at work or doing your daily chores; you will be reaching for it pretty regularly.

Make a List of Basic Repairs

You got a great home inspection, and that will give you a good list of what needs repair. But you need to look at upcoming repairs too—what may be reaching the end of its life cycle and will need repair in the next year or two. Have a look at the chart "How Long Do Things Last?" and add to your list the repair or replacement of things that are about to need work anyway.

Imagine the Environment You Want Before You Lay Out a New Floor Plan

Forget about the walls. If you have been doodling floor plans on a piece of graph paper, you're missing out on a great opportunity. It's time to engage the imaginative side of your brain.

When you think about your new space, imagine surrounding yourself with the things you love; then surround *those* things with walls and windows. Was that clear? Create your environment first, and then your enclosure. Let's talk about this process again; it's important. Stand in the middle of your (imaginary) kitchen, and—in your imagination—place your china, your saucepan, your refrigerator, and all the other kitchen things right where you want them to be without regard for existing walls or windows. Once that's done, you will see where the walls and windows have to be in order for this kitchen to work properly for you. Did that help? Now sketch that kitchen, and you will have the kitchen you want.

Interior furnishings, and the sizes and shapes of the rooms you design, are the yin and yang of home design. They have to work together. If you know the dimensions of your most important art or furniture pieces and you give your architect a list of them, the two of you can ensure that your favorite things will be the highlights of your new spaces.

Think about how you want to live now, how you will probably want to live in ten years, and how much space you would like to dedicate to each major activity in your home life. If you understand yourself well—your health, your priorities, your interests, and your need for privacy or your love of entertaining—the walls will end up where they need to be.

Don't Forget Curb Appeal

What about improving the outside of your home? The *equity* value may not change if you do a little landscaping, for example, but the *market* value will, and so will the way you feel when you come home after work every day.

You might want to consider adding some design elements that would distinguish your home from the others in your neighborhood. Grab your camera and go for a walk. Take pictures of homes with distinctive exterior features that you could incorporate into your own redesign plan. Look for inviting front entries, window and door styles and the pattern they create on the exterior walls, porches and decks and where they are placed, and landscaping that frames and complements the home. Go treasure hunting. File these photos. We'll talk about them in a minute.

Prioritize Your Design Challenges

When you think you've identified all of your likes and dislikes, and you've documented all your wishes on paper, begin to turn this scatter-shot list into a cohesive Master Plan. Start by listing the categories of at-home activities that are most important to you.

Let's say that you have listed your primary activity areas as (1) *Cooking, Eating, and Entertaining*; (2) *Beds and Baths*; and (3) *Family-Time Space*. Your list must suit *your* needs—this is only an example. Start with a fresh piece of paper with these three (or your own three) activity titles as your three column headings.

Now rewrite every item on your lists—*What I Like, What I Don't Like, What I Wish I Had*—under one of these headings. For example, you might want to hang great-grandfather's portrait in the formal dining room; put that note under *Cooking, Eating, and Entertaining*. The plasma TV should probably go into a family entertainment area under *Family-Time Space*. The fact that you hate the master bath because it's only 6 feet square should become a note under *Beds and Baths*. You get the idea. If you have additional concerns that don't fit under any one of your three or four high-priority areas, make a list of those items under the category *Miscellaneous*. You aren't going to spend a lot of money on these problems.

Once you've sorted all this out, look carefully and you'll probably see that the reason you're not happy with your current space is that things are out of balance. There are groups of activities that require more space than you can currently give them, and there are spaces in your home that are not used very often that could be put to better use.

Once you have identified areas that are underutilized and activities that need a place to happen but don't have one, you will have set your design challenges.

You have gotten off to a great start. By doing a little deliberate thinking, you have created a short list of specific *design challenges*, and the solutions will provide you with

maximum return on your remodeling dollars. That's exactly what you need to know!

Consider Every Possible Solution

Find a sturdy cardboard box that is deep enough to hold a big pile of pictures. We'll call this your *Design Ideas Box* (see pages 18–23).

Now begin looking for solutions to each of your design challenges.

Don't feel that you're limited to design or materials styles that resemble what you already have. The reason you're doing this remodel is to achieve a *change* . . . and you will be working with a designer who will pull all of your various ideas together for you. Don't worry too much about the details at this point.

Get out and go shopping. What are your best resources for design ideas? An obvious place to start is the local home improvement center. What about an oriental art store? How about model home tours? What about attending a home and garden trade show, visiting a local commercial nursery, cutting pictures out of magazines, going to art galleries, or looking through architectural design portfolios on the Internet?

Do an exhaustive search for solutions of every sort for each of your design challenges. For example, if your kitchen is dark and depressing, you might consider doing something about both the light and the layout. Let's think about brightening it up first. You could
• Add a window or a skylight,
• Replace your solid back door with one that is half glass,
• Add some under-cabinet task lighting,
• Install a brighter fixture in the center of the ceiling,
• Hide some indirect lighting in the crown molding or a ceiling tray,

Deck with roof

Landscaping

Porch rail

Landscaping

Deck chair

Open plan

Kitchen

Kitchen combos

Bath

Appliances

Lavatory

Appliances

Wood flooring

Cozy arrangement

Chinese cabinets

Area rugs

Chairs

Chandeliers

Light fixture

Knobs

Light fixture

Front entry

Sunroom

Sunroom

Sunroom

Sunroom

Sunroom with deck

COST-EFFECTIVE REMODELING STRATEGIES

In Chapter 1, I shared excerpts from the *Remodeling Magazine* annual Cost vs. Value Reports for 2004, 2005, and 2006. They covered the big projects. Here are a few more tips about working on smaller ones. Statistics have been drawn from nationwide studies of home appraisals done for the National Association of Home Builders, *Consumer Reports*, and others.

- Take care of maintenance and repairs first. They will pay you back in reduced *future* maintenance costs, and a home in good condition will appraise at a higher value than one that gives the impression that it might have even more problems than the buyer can see.
- Redesign the space you have before you consider building an addition. Transform little-used spaces. Open up rooms that are too small for the activities that take place in them. Connect inside and outside living areas to create bright and friendly environments and an illusion of larger interior spaces.
- Waterproofing a basement to provide extra storage space, a workshop, or a family entertainment area may pay you back in full, with interest.
- Repainting, especially the exterior, may do the same.
- Replacing visibly deteriorated finishes such as your roof will return nearly 100 percent of your costs, but *invisible* improvements, such as new plumbing or a new septic tank, may not pay you back at all. Faulty services and systems would certainly show up on the home inspection and lower the market value though; fix them if they're broken.
- Updating a kitchen or bath in a thirty-year-old home will probably increase the value by 70 to 90 percent of the cost. If the house is relatively new, this work may not add much to the value.
- If you have only one bathroom, adding a *second* bathroom will pay you back about 90 percent, but adding a third may not be such a good investment unless the home has four or more bedrooms.
- If you rearrange the floor plan and *improve* the layout, you'll probably recover about 50 percent of your investment. This is tricky. Who gets to decide if the layout has improved?
- Installing energy-efficient windows and doors will return 30 to 50 percent of the cost. If your windows aren't badly deteriorated, repair them and recapture 70 percent of the repair costs.
- For the most part, standard windows sell better than exotic ones. In high-priced neighborhoods, buyers will care about the quality of window but still tend to prefer the standard shapes and sizes.
- Nobody wants to pay for exotic landscaping unless they can afford to pay others to do the maintenance—too much work.
- A swimming pool may scare more buyers than it attracts because of liability and upkeep issues—even if the house is in an area where pools are common amenities.
- Amateur design can actually lower the value of your home.

Here's a great example of a super-cost-effective design that is also a knockout!

The goal of this project was to open a pass-through between the kitchen and the dining area so that the hosts and the guests could talk but the guests couldn't see the dirty dishes in the sink. If you look at the pass-through in the "after" shot, you'll see that this is a house full

High-impact kitchen remodel—kitchen after

of windows with an open floor plan. Even if the designer had cut a pass-through as the owners requested, the "before" kitchen really didn't look like the rest of the house. What a great idea it was to install the lighted glass display cases over the pass-through. It was a relatively inexpensive detail, but it integrated the style of the kitchen with the style of the rest of the house, added more light to the kitchen, provided a fantastic, eye-catching focal point, and lit the cooktop too. Notice that although a few of the kitchen cabinet doors were removed, the remainder of the room was only painted; nothing was changed except the area around the range. This is why you hire a great designer. Would you have thought of this?

High-impact kitchen remodel—kitchen before

- Put a lamp on the kitchen table, or
- Use reflective finishes to bounce the existing light around the room.

There are seven ideas. See if you can come up with six more in the next two minutes. Be bold. Consider everything!

How about building a greenhouse-style breakfast nook? Does that sound crazy? It might be really wonderful, and you would add space and brighten up the area with one stroke.

Challenge yourself to think creatively. You're just brainstorming; it's all free so far! The only mistake you could make now would be to stifle your imagination.

When you think you're done, you should have *at least* a dozen ways to solve every design challenge you've identified. Each solution ought to change the look of the space in a different way. Money is no object right now. Your architect will help you find materials that look like what you want but fit into your budget. Your only limitation is that you must stay focused on the areas you've determined need the most work; don't wander off.

Incidentally, write notes on everything you throw into your ideas box. When you meet with your architect, you'll want to remember why you cut out a picture of a candy-pink kitchen. Your note will remind you that you really liked the sink faucet.

The Wine-and-Design Party

Ah, but we've overlooked a very important resource, haven't we!

It's time to tap into the creative talents of your friends. Invite them to a wine-and-design party. Serve something tasty along with a nice bottle or two of wine, and talk a little about your remodeling plans. As your friends get

more comfortable, they'll start to have a good time with this discussion and you'll begin to get some great suggestions. As the party progresses and the wine vanishes, the ideas will get better and better.

Never say no. Don't discourage any suggestions. The best ideas will come when you're all just having a great time.

Write each idea on a separate piece of paper with a bit of detail or a little sketch that will put it in context, and put all the ideas in the ideas box. Do not disregard the ideas you think are a little over the top. You wouldn't believe what a great designer can do with a crazy idea.

2.3 THE MASTER PLAN

There is a Remodeling Master Plan lurking inside your ideas box. All you have to do is sort out which solution you like best for each of your design challenges, and tie them all together. Don't throw any ideas out, though. They may not get into your initial plan, but they may still come in handy. We'll talk about this in a minute.

In this section you'll learn how to express your Master Plan on a single piece of paper by using a tool I call the "Task Abstract List."

The Task Abstract List

The Master Plan is not a document the contractor will build from; it serves only as a quick summary—an outline—of the elements in your design, but it must be expressed in a way that your architect and later your contractor will understand and in a way that will allow you to keep track of your costs from the day you develop your preliminary plan until you hand your contractor his last check, in one seamless paper trail. Here's how to get started.

- First, lump together groups of similar tasks. For example, include the installation of all new drywall, no matter where it's located, in one line item. That's the "task" part of your list.
- Second, shrink the description of that work to as few words as you can without forgetting what the phrase refers to. That's the "abstract" part.
- Third, organize all of your task abstract phrases into a single list, in a particular order.

The sequence of the tasks on the list is the same as the sequence of the work on the project site—demolition is first; framing, drywall, and finishing follow that; and the three services—electric, plumbing, and HVAC (heating, ventilation, and air-conditioning)—are listed last because workers from these three trades are on and off the job site pretty regularly, right up until the end. An illustrated construction work sequence and a glossary of construction terms appear at the end of this section and may help you understand the process and some of the terminology if you've never done construction before.

There is a descriptive title for each type of work that you will do. Here is the list of work categories. Get comfortable with this list. You're going to use it a lot.

Work Categories

000	Hazard Remediation
100	Demolition and Site Work
200	Foundation and Structure
300	Exterior Envelope
400	Doors and Hardware
500	Windows
600	Interior Finishes
700	Painting
800	Plumbing
900	HVAC
1000	Electrical
1100	Alternates

When the time comes for you to begin work on your own project, set up the Task Abstract List for your Remodeling Master Plan on a computer spreadsheet, if you can, so that when you complete your first plan, you can *copy it* onto a blank worksheet and ask a cost estimator to fill in some numbers for you. When the estimator is done, you will *copy* that same list again (without the cost estimates), and turn it into a Bid Form so that the contractors can price the items just as the cost estimator did. When they're done, you'll *copy* and expand the spreadsheet to compare the bids. You will use the Task Abstract List from the time you create it until the time you finish the job. If you never destroy any of your spreadsheets, you will have an unbroken paper trail that starts with your preliminary plan and ends with the calculation of the contractor's last check. If you ever need to remember who knew what when—if you ever have to deal with a dispute—you will be very glad you employed this strategy. It will save you a lot of trouble.

Alternates

Did you notice the item "Alternates" at the bottom of the list of work categories?

You're going to put your *first-choice* solution for each design challenge into your Master Plan. Your second- and third-choice solutions will go into the Alternates list as optional, alternative ways to achieve your goals. They may come in handy if you have to make adjustments quickly once work begins. Make a list of *all* of your alternative solutions, under the heading *Alternates*, in the same work-category order as the first-choice items are listed in the plan. The Alternates list should be long and imaginative, including ideas that are more expensive and less expensive, fancier and plainer, than those you've included in your preliminary plan.

Think of Alternates as players sitting in the dugout waiting for you to put them into the game. For example, we talked about how to get more light in your kitchen. Let's say that you've included under-cabinet task lighting in your plan. You might also consider a large window, a greenhouse-style breakfast nook, or a half-glass rear entry door, any of which would add light to your kitchen, but each would cost more or less than your first choice and would give a very different feel to the space once it was finished. Keep them in the list of Alternates for now.

Included on page 30 is a sample Task Abstract List for a small kitchen remodel. Try to imagine what this project might look like. We're going to refer to this little project now and then.

Create a Preliminary Cost Estimate

Are you getting a better picture of what your project will entail? Before you finalize your Master Plan, you'll need to know that you're planning something you can afford. Before you pay a cost estimator to give you real numbers, let's see if you're even in the ballpark.

Included on page 31 is a Preliminary Cost-Estimating Chart that you can use to determine what your predictable construction costs will be. (We'll deal with the unpredictable costs—the surprises—a bit later.) You won't need to have a completed a Master Plan list, but you will need to have a pretty good idea of the level

of work you want to do: Are you renovating a rental property and limiting your work to major repairs and a paint job, or are you ready for that spa-style bathroom and lots of fine woodworking? Here's how to figure out roughly what your dream may cost you.

- Calculate the total number of enclosed, heated square feet (s.f.) in your current home.
- Find your level of work and the age and condition of your home.
- Multiply the cost per square foot that best matches your project by the number of square feet in your home, and, voilà, you have a first-cut construction cost estimate.

If you're planning to build an addition, you have to use the new construction costs at the bottom of the chart. Multiply the number of square feet in the addition by the cost you think is appropriate and you'll have a guesstimate of the cost of that addition.

If you're going to both remodel your existing home and build an addition, do both calculations and add them together to find your total predictable construction cost.

Please remember that this chart can't possibly be right for everyone—so many costs depend on your local market—but it will help you keep your expectations within range of reality.

You now have your first rough cost estimate. Did it turn out to be what you expected?

Estimate the Resulting Return

Forget the cost estimate for a moment. Let's test the *value* of your plan and calculate a probable rate of return.

To set a responsible cap on your remodeling costs, you'll need to know both the as-is value of your home and the after-remodel value that assumes you complete the project as you've planned it.

Both Realtors and appraisers can provide you with information about real estate values. To get an educated guess of the possible after-remodel value, you'll have to provide your Realtor or your appraiser with a copy of your Master Plan in the Task Abstract List format so that he or she will know exactly what your project will entail.

Ask three or more real estate pros for their best guess of the current market value of your home as it stands, and for their best guess of what it might be worth if you did your dream remodel. Take the average of their numbers. Subtract the average estimated current value from the average estimated after-remodel value to determine the probable tangible return on this investment. Compare this return with your *cost estimate*. For example, if your Realtors think your home is worth about $250,000 as it stands today, but that it might be worth $310,000 after you finish the project you described to them, then you could anticipate getting back about $60,000. If your estimated cost of doing the work is $100,000, then you would be looking at about a 60 percent return on your investment. Even considering the intangible returns of this great remodeling project, you may not be happy with 60%; you might want to weed out some of the less important work you had planned to do in order to get a higher return—or you might not care because you intend to live in this house for the next twenty years

and will get such joy from the changes you plan to make that getting money back at resale just isn't important to you. This is entirely your choice, but let's be sure you're making an informed decision.

What *percentage* of your costs will you get back? If you really care about your tangible return, refer to the Remodeling Cost vs. Value Report in Chapter 1 and see if you've beaten the national average.

To increase your return, you must be able to achieve the same increase in value but spend less money doing so, or you can spend the same amount of money but put it into different kinds of work so that you get a higher assessed value when your project is finished. If you need to cut costs, ask the pros what they would cut out of your project; then refer to your list of Alternates for less expensive design ideas that still address your most important deficiencies. Ask for another quick assessment. See whether or not you've hit your target.

While you're considering less expensive design alternatives, remember that the reason you're doing the remodel in the first place is for the *intangible* return, and don't give up anything that is important to you. You don't want to waste money, but there's no point in just prettying up a space that makes you unhappy.

This exercise will educate you about the value of the work in your plan, and it will give you a good idea of what a reasonable remodeling budget might be.

Sample Task Abstract List: Small Kitchen Remodel

Sec	Item	Task List
000		**Treatment of Household Hazards**
	001	Test for hazards and provide lab report
100		**Demolition and Site Work**
	101	Remove and discard all existing cabinets and countertops
	102	Remove sheet vinyl flooring and subfloor
200		**Foundation and Structure**
	201	Repair floor framing under sink cabinet
	202	Install new subfloor; match level of adjacent rooms
300		**Exterior Envelope**
	301	Repair siding at kitchen entry door
400		**Doors and Hardware**
	401	Install louvered bifold doors at laundry closet
	402	Replace pantry door and hardware
	403	Replace kitchen entry door with half-glass door
500		**Windows**
	501	Replace single window over sink with two windows
	502	Install new skylight over breakfast nook
600		**Interior Finishes**
	601	Install new tile flooring
	602	Install new ABC cabinets with door style #1
	603	Install new man-made countertops
	604	Furnish and install new refrigerator, dishwasher, washer-dryer, and disposal
700		**Paint Preparation and Painting: Interior and Exterior**
	701	Patch drywall walls and ceiling
	702	Prime and paint walls, ceiling, and trim
	702	Prime and paint repaired siding and kitchen entry door
	703	Paint new interior doors and windows over sink
800		**Plumbing**
	801	Install new double-bowl, stainless-steel sink and faucet
	802	Replace all plumbing under sink; add shut-of valve
	803	Replace water heater in pantry
900		**HVAC (Heating, Ventilation, and Air-Conditioning)**
	901	Install new range hood with exhaust to exterior
1000		**Electrical**
	1001	Install 4 new outlets over countertop backsplash
	1002	Upgrade circuits to kitchen appliances to carry new load
		Total Master Plan
1100		**Alternates**
	A1	Repair existing window over sink
	A2	Hang new Tiffany-style chandelier in breakfast nook
	A3	Upgrade cabinet door to style #3
	A4	Install (less expensive) XYZ Cabs
	A5	Install new stone countertop
	A6	Relocate new water heater into attic
	A7	Install unvented range hood with light
	A8	Install lighting under all wall-hung cabinets
	A9	Replace 2 fluorescent ceiling fixtures

PRELIMINARY COST-ESTIMATING CHART

Level	Scope of Work	Age of Home	Condition of Home / Extent of Work	Cost per Square Foot
1	**Repair and Spruce Up** Repair exterior trim and gutters Replace damaged windows and doors Repair plumbing leaks Replace heating and air-conditioning unit Replace floor finishes Paint interior and exterior	<25 yrs	Good / Simple Fair / Moderate Poor / Extensive	$15–$25 $20–$30 $25–$40
2	**Repair and Remodel** Repair plumbing leaks Replace heating and air-conditioning unit Replace damaged windows and doors Paint or reface kitchen cabinets Replace floor finishes Paint interior and exterior	<25 yrs	Good / Simple Fair / Moderate Poor / Extensive	$20–$30 $25–$40 $35–$40
3	**Substantial Remodel** Replace heating and air-conditioning unit Replace damaged plumbing pipes Repair foundation or framing Repair exterior wall finishes Replace damaged windows and doors Replace damaged wood trim on exterior Remove or build new interior walls Replace cabinets and countertops Replace floor finishes Paint interior and exterior	<25 yrs	Good / Simple Fair / Moderate Poor / Extensive	$35–$60 $40–$80 $50–$100
4	**Substantial Remodel** Replace heating and air-conditioning unit Replace deteriorated sections of plumbing Replace electrical panel and some wiring Remove hazardous materials Repair foundation and framing Repair exterior wall finishes Replace windows and doors Replace roof and exterior trim Remove or build new walls Replace damaged drywall or plaster Replace damaged subfloor and floor finishes Replace cabinets and countertops Paint interior and exterior	25–40 yrs	Good / Simple Fair / Moderate Poor / Extensive	$50–$100 $65–$150 $80–$200
5	**Rehabilitation** Replace heating and air-conditioning unit Replace entire plumbing system Replace entire electrical system Remove hazardous materials Repair or replace exterior walls, windows, and trim Repair foundation and floor framing Replace subfloor and floor finishes Strip interior to framing Replace all drywall, and wall and ceiling finishes Replace all millwork, cabinets, and countertops	35+ yrs	Good / Simple Fair / Moderate Poor / Extensive	$60–$150 $70–$200 $80–$250
6	**New Addition**	N/A	No plumbing w/bath w/kitchen Kitchen and bath only	$100–$150 $125–$200 $250–$300 $250–$350
7	**New Deck on Foundation with Steps & Rails**	N/A		$20–$30

THE CONSTRUCTION WORK SEQUENCE

Whether you're building a doghouse or a skyscraper, the construction *process* is always the same. The details may change, but there will always be three pretty distinctive phases of work.

PHASE 1—TAKING THINGS APART...

Setup: The very first thing the contractor will need is his construction permit. With that in hand, he can set up a temporary electrical panel on a pole in your yard, hook up a temporary water supply, and get a large steel container and maybe some temporary toilets on-site.

Demolition

Temporary power pole

Demolition: When you remove old wall and floor finishes, you uncover things you never dreamed of. This is the time of greatest risk for unanticipated costs. We will talk shortly about how to handle these costs.

Surprise mold behind bathtub

Site work

Site Work: Right after demolition, trees and tree limbs are removed, trenches are dug for electrical or plumbing services to run to an outbuilding or to the connections to the street, and the site is graded for a foundation for the new addition.

PHASE 2—
PUTTING THEM BACK TOGETHER AGAIN . . .
Foundation: Whether you are building an addition or remodeling an older home, you will work on foundation walls, footings, and piers before you build above them. If the foundation isn't plumb and sturdy, nothing that sits on top of it will be either.

Structural Framing: When the mortar is dry, the foundation is ready for floor framing and the layer of plywood subfloor that will stabilize it. The outside walls and any interior load-bearing walls (walls that carry the weight of the second floor and the roof above them) will be laid out and constructed, with cross-members along the top of the studs to carry the ceiling framing, which goes in next.

Weathering-in: Exposing wood framing and sub-floor to rain or snow is not a good idea, so once the structural framing is up, the contractor will "weather-in" the structure by covering it entirely with rigid sheets of plywood or another similar material, and then covering that with a moisture barrier made of a thin sheet of plastic or plastic derivative. Roof finishes, windows, and exterior doors complete the weathering-in process and ensure that the inside work will remain clean and dry.

Foundations, floor, and structural framing

Weathering-in

Weathering-in windows and doors

MEP Roughing: MEP stands for the basic services in your house—mechanical (heating and air-conditioning, also known as HVAC), electrical, and plumbing. Roughing includes the ductwork, wires, and pipes that run under the floors, above the ceilings, and inside the walls. By the time MEP roughing work is finished, you ought to be finished with about 40 percent of the project, and the likelihood of finding any more surprises is very low.

MEP—mechanical roughing

MEP—electrical roughing

MEP—plumbing roughing

PHASE 3—
APPLYING THE FINISHING TOUCHES

Exterior Finishes: As soon as he is able, the contractor will install all of the exterior finishes: brick, siding, trim around the windows, and so on, to seal the structure, and will install insulation inside, in between the wall studs, to prepare for drywall.

Finishes

Finishing drywall and trim moldings

Interior framing for non-load-bearing walls, closets, stairwells, and so on is next. Hot on its heels are the HVAC, electrical, and plumbing subcontractors bringing smaller branch lines into the interior walls, for example, running plumbing to the location of a new sink or tub.

Interior Finishes: Finish work includes installing drywall and taping and spackling to make the walls and ceilings ready for paint; installing new floor coverings and new interior doors and trim; painting; and installing cabinets and countertops.

Interior finishing—floor and wall tile

Interior doors

Interior finishing—cabinetry

HVAC finishes

Plumbing finishes

Electrical finishes

MEP Finish Work: Once the walls are painted, and after the cabinets are installed, the heating and air subcontractor, the electrician, and the plumber finish all their work. This includes installing grills at duct openings and hooking up the new thermostat; installing light fixtures, and switches and outlets with cover plates; and installing final plumbing hookups, fixtures, and hardware in bathrooms and kitchens.

Paving, Hardscaping, and Landscaping: The last tasks the contractor will do include paving the driveway, laying stone pavers on the front walk, putting up a fence, constructing brick or stone planting beds, laying sod, planting bushes and flowers, and completing all of the other outdoor tasks.

Paving

Hardscaping

Landscaping

At this point your project is considered "substantially complete." The remaining work includes final details such as paint touch-ups, tightening screws in hinges, and submitting all of the paperwork you have requested, such as operating manuals and a list of subcontractors and vendors in case you need a repair in the future.

When you look at the work headings on the Task Abstract List, you will understand how the list reflects the order of work on the project. That will be extremely helpful when you're monitoring the contractor's work and preparing payments.

Substantially completed

GLOSSARY OF CONSTRUCTION TERMS

AMPERE (AMP) A unit measure of electricity.

APERTURE An opening, such as a window or the space inside a pipe.

ASBESTOS A naturally occurring mineral fiber sometimes found in homes built before 1960, when it was banned as a home-building material. Asbestos is harmful, possibly deadly, if inhaled or ingested.

AWNING WINDOWS Windows with hinges at the top, allowing them to open out and up.

Awning windows

BASEBOARD Usually wood or vinyl trim strips installed at the bottoms of the walls, around the perimeter of a room, to cover the intersection of wall and floor materials.

Baseboard

BASEBOARD HEAT A heating system with the heating units located along the baseboard trim. The system can run on either electricity or hot-water steam.

Breaker box

BREAKER BOX A metal box that receives the main power cable from the power source at the street and distributes electricity to the circuits inside the house. Each circuit is anchored in a breaker that will cut off the current when the power flow is uneven or excessive.

BUCKLING Unnatural bending as a result of unbalanced pressure or contact with a substance, such as water, that causes swelling and deterioration.

BUILDING CODE A body of law that regulates building design, construction, rehabilitation, repair, and materials, for the protection of public health and safety.

Buckling porch deck

CASEMENT WINDOWS Windows that open on hinges secured to the side of the window frame. Casement windows often require the use of a small hand crank to move them into the open or closed position.

CAULKING A rubbery filler material, similar in consistency to toothpaste, that is used to seal small openings such as those between a tub and its surrounding finishes.

CIRCUIT BREAKER A mechanism that interrupts the flow of electricity to an electrical circuit if the demand for power on that circuit becomes excessive or unbalanced.

CLASS B DOOR A door with a fire-resistant rating of one to one-and-a-half hours, as determined by the Underwriters Laboratories Classification; in other words, a class B door ought to be able to withstand fire on one side of it for one to one-and-a-half hours before it allows the fire to spread into the next room.

CPVC The abbreviation for chlorinated polyvinyl chloride, the chemical makeup of a specific type of plastic.

CRAWL SPACE Shallow space between the underside of the first-floor framing of a house and the ground beneath it.

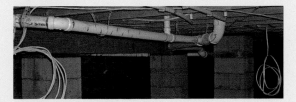

Crawl space water pipes

CUTOFF VALVES Valves used to shut water off, generally located under sinks or behind bathtub and shower access panels. These valves stop water flow to one fixture instead of cutting off all water to the house.

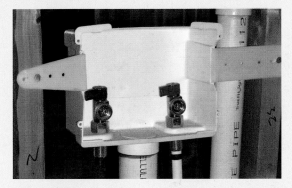

Cutoff valves

DAMPER An adjustable vent that regulates the flow of air inside a fireplace flue or ductwork from the furnace or air conditioner.

DISPOSAL A device that grinds food sufficiently to allow it to enter drains without clogging them.

DORMER A small shedlike structure with a window that projects through a sloping roof.

Dormer

GLOSSARY OF CONSTRUCTION TERMS

DOUBLE-HUNG WINDOWS Windows that open when the sashes slide up and down in side tracks.

Double-hung windows

DRYWALL A gypsum-board material used as a surface finish for walls and ceilings, sold in 4 x 8 sheets in a variety of thicknesses.

Drywall

DUCTWORK A network of tubes or channels, like tunnels, that distributes heated or cooled air from centrally located HVAC equipment through the entire house.

Ductwork

EAVES The section of the roof that overhangs the walls of a house.

Eaves

EXHAUST FAN A fan that extracts air from the interior of a home.

Copper flashing at roof

FLASHING Sheet-metal strips used at the intersection of roof angles and around chimneys to provide a water-tight seal.

FLUE A tubular chamber over a fireplace or furnace that directs heat, flames, smoke, and other gases into the outside air.

FOOTINGS Formed-concrete cubes set in the soil that support the rest of the foundation and the weight of the house above them.

FORCED-AIR FURNACE A machine that heats the air that circulates through the ducts of a house.

FOUNDATION The part of the structure upon which all other construction is built, generally either a concrete slab or a number of piers (brick or block columns) on formed-concrete footings.

Foundation wall

FUSE BOX A metal box that receives the main power cable from the power source at the street and distributes electricity to the circuits inside the house. Each electrical circuit is anchored in a fuse that will break the flow of power if it becomes uneven or excessive.

GROUND FAULT INTERRUPTER (GFI) An electrical circuit that is wired to shut down if any switch, appliance, or outlet comes in contact with ungrounded electrical conduits, for example, wet hands. GFIs are now required by the building code in bathrooms and kitchens and wherever else an outlet could be exposed to moisture.

GUTTERS AND DOWNSPOUTS A network of channels that diverts rainwater from the roof down to the ground and away from the foundation of a house.

Gutters and downspouts

HEARTH The floor of a fireplace.

Hearth in fireplace

GLOSSARY OF CONSTRUCTION TERMS

HEAT EXCHANGER A combination of heating coils and fans that warms the air to the temperature set on the thermostat, then pushes that air through your ductwork.

HEAT PUMP A reverse-cycle refrigeration unit that can either heat or cool the air that circulates in your home.

Heat pump

HOT-WATER HEATING SYSTEM Machinery that heats water to the boiling point, then pumps the steam through a network of pipes in your home to heat the spaces they pass through.

HVAC Acronym for heating, ventilating, and air-conditioning.

HVAC

INSULATION material used to prevent or reduce the exchange of heat or cold between environments with two different temperatures.

JOISTS Horizontal framing members such as timbers, beams, or bars that support floors, ceilings, and roofs.

LATH Strips of wood used as a base for the installation of plaster. Wire-mesh screening can also serve this purpose.

MASONRY Building materials made of natural or artificial mineral products, such as stones, bricks, cinder blocks, or tiles, usually requiring mortar or cement as a bonding agent.

Masonry

MEMBERS Units of lumber or steel that make up the structural framing of a building.

Members (framing)

MORTAR A cementitious bonding material used in the construction of brick or stone walls.

MOLDING Strips of decorative wood used to frame the edges of architectural details such as cabinetry, windows, and doors and to conceal the intersections of walls and floors or walls and ceilings.

PARAPET WALL A low wall or railing along the edge of a roof, balcony, bridge, or terrace. Parapet walls provide decorative detail to the exterior of a building, safety for occupants, and control of rainwater flow.

Molding

Parapet wall

PARQUET FLOORS A wood floor with an inlaid pattern of different tints and grains.

POINTING Repairing or touching up deteriorated mortar between bricks or blocks by removing and replacing any damaged material.

POLYBUTYLENE A polymer that is used to create a type of plastic pipe.

R-VALUE A measurement of the ability of insulation to slow the transfer of heat or cold. The higher the R-value, the greater the insulation power.

RADIANT-HEATING SYSTEM An electrical heating system that distributes heat through cables usually installed in baseboard panels or under floor finishes.

RADON A colorless, odorless gas known to cause cancer that is emitted from soils, rocks, and water as a result of radioactive decay. State departments of the environment and natural resources can help identify and treat a radon problem.

RAFTER The structural member or beam that supports the roof and that spans the distance between a load-bearing wall and the ridge beam at the peak of the roof.

Rafters

GLOSSARY OF CONSTRUCTION TERMS

REGISTERS Wood or metal decorative grilles, often with adjustable fins, that are set at the point where ductwork releases treated air into a room.

RETAINING WALL A masonry wall constructed to restrict the movement of soil or water.

Retaining wall

SASH The frame that holds the glass in a window or a door.

Sash

SETTLING The gradual sinking of a heavy object into the material beneath it. A house built on raw land—soil that has not been properly compacted—may settle over time, causing the structure to sit out of square.

Settling

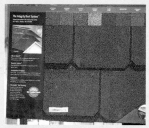

Shingles

SHINGLE A thin piece of wood, metal, slate, or composite minerals laid in overlapping rows to cover the roofs and walls of buildings.

Siding

SIDING Exterior wall-finish materials such as wood, Masonite, vinyl, and aluminum.

SILL A narrow, horizontal, decorative platform beneath a window or a door usually slanted toward the outside of the home to provide rainwater runoff.

SLAB A concrete platform with a smooth top surface that usually sits at ground level.

SUMP PUMP An electrical pump, usually installed in the basement or crawl space, to prevent water from collecting there. The pump empties water from a collection area such as a well or pit and pumps it through channels or pipes to the outside of the house.

THERMOSTAT A device that controls the temperature and circulation of air coming from the HVAC unit.

THRESHOLD A narrow, horizontal, decorative trim piece beneath a door.

UREA FORMALDEHYDE (UF) FOAM INSULATION Foam insulation that is usually blown into an existing wall cavity. There is some disagreement among regulators as to whether or not this form of insulation releases formaldehyde gas in quantities that might be hazardous to human health. State departments of the environment and natural resources can provide guidance.

WATER HEATER
An apparatus that heats water and usually also stores the heated water for later use.

Water heater

WEATHER STRIPPING
A thin length of felt, rubber, or other dense, compressible material that, when attached to the framing surrounding a door or window, provides a seal that results in reduced energy loss.

WINDOW WELL A cutout in the ground around a basement window that may be located wholly or partly below the surface of the yard. These wells allow light and fresh air into the subterranean space and are usually equipped with a lining that extends above the edge of the yard to prevent groundwater from entering the basement through the window.

BIBLIOGRAPHY
Appraisal Institute. *The Dictionary of Real Estate Appraisal*. Chicago, IL: Appraisal Institute, 1993.

Boyce, Byri N., ed. and comp. *Real Estate Appraisal Terminology*. Rev. ed. Cambridge, MA: Society of Real Estate Appraisers, Ballinger Publishing, 1984.

Flexner, S.B., editor in chief, and C.H. Leonore, managing editor. *The Random House Dictionary of the English Language*. 2nd ed., unabridged. New York: Random House, 1983.

Friedman, Jack P., Jack C. Harris, and J. Bruce Linderman. *Dictionary of Real Estate Terms*. 2nd ed. Hauppauge, NY: Barron's Educational Series, 1987.

Home Ownership Partners. *Maintenance and Educational Manual*. Louisville, KY: Home Ownership Partners.

Old House Web. www.OldHouseWeb.com.

R.S. Means. *Means Illustrated Construction Dictionary*. New unabridged ed. Kingston, MA: R.S. Means, 1991.

2.4 THE BUDGET

Remodeling costs are predictable.

That is, you know you'll have surprises even if you don't know just what they will be. And you know you'll have to pay some fees to the designer and maybe an engineer, and a fee to the banker when he makes you a loan. As long as you anticipate these costs, you can set a budget that you can stick to. This is how to stay in control.

Allowing for "Soft Costs"

You have already paid for a home inspection, a pile of home and garden magazines, and a wine-and-design party. As you move the project along, you'll have to pay for an appraisal, loan closing fees, design fees, and perhaps fees for legal advice. These non-construction costs are called "soft costs." You're going to set aside 10 percent of your Total Project Budget for soft costs. Don't worry if you haven't determined what your Total Project Budget will be just yet—we can back into that number in a minute.

How you spend your soft-costs budget will depend on the kind of project you're doing. Use the Wild-Guess Soft-Costs Estimates Chart opposite to see what some of these fees might be. Fees vary by region and depend to a large extent on the strength of your local economy, so don't expect these numbers to be exact.

Sample Budget Calculations	Sample Numbers
Total Project Budget	$100,000
Less 10 Percent for Soft Costs	$10,000
Total *Construction* Budget	$90,000

How to Use the Wild-Guess Soft-Costs Estimates Chart

Construction professionals price their services based on the following four variables:
- The size of the house
- The condition of the house
- How much work you want done
- How much time you will need from them

The estimated fees on this chart reflect these variables. Only one column of numbers will have any meaning to you. You must determine which column that is.

- Figure out whether your home has less than (<) or more than (>) 3,500 square feet of enclosed, heated space. If it's less than 3,500 square feet, use the estimates on the top of the page; if it's more than 3,500 square feet, use the estimates on the bottom.
- Determine the *condition* of your home. The easy way to define "condition" is that a home in fair to good condition can be lived in comfortably, although it may need some repairs, while a home in poor condition has roof leaks, plumbing leaks, bouncy floors, cracks in the walls, and other problems. (Poor condition and dilapidated condition are not the same. A dilapidated house is not habitable and generally speaking is not a good candidate for remodeling.)

  If your home has less than 3,500 square feet of heated space and is in fair to good condition, you have narrowed your focus to only two columns on this chart.
- Your last qualifier is the size of the project, your Total *Construction* Budget. Do you expect to spend less than $80,000 or more than $80,000 on construction by the time your project is finished? (We'll figure that out in a minute.)

WILD-GUESS SOFT-COSTS ESTIMATES CHART

SIZE OF HOUSE	Less Than 3,500 Square Feet			
CURRENT CONDITION	FAIR - GOOD		POOR	
TOTAL CONSTRUCTION BUDGET	<$80,000	>$80,000	<$80,000	>$80,000
Home Inspection	$250	$350	$300	$400
Environmental Consultant's Fee lab work and 2 reports	$1,000	$1,000	$1,000	$1,000
Architectural Design	$5,000	$6,000	$6,000	$7,000
Design by Spec Writer	$2,000	$2,000	$3,000	$3,000
Professional Cost Estimate	$250	$300	$400	$450
Loan Closing Costs	$1,000	$1,000	$1,000	$1,000
Attorney	$150 per hr	$150 per hr	$150 per hr	$150 per hr
Engineer	$100 per hr	$100 per hr	$100 per hr	$100 per hr
Remodeling Coach	$50 per hr	$50 per hr	$50 per hr	$50 per hr

SIZE OF HOUSE	More Than 3,500 Square Feet			
CURRENT CONDITION	FAIR - GOOD		POOR	
TOTAL CONSTRUCTION BUDGET	<$80,000	>$80,000	<$80,000	>$80,000
Home Inspection	$450	$550	$600	$650
Environmental Consultant's Fee lab work and 2 reports	$1,500	$1,500	$1,500	$1,500
Architectural Design	$7,000	$8,000	$9,000	$12,000
Design by Spec Writer	$3,000	$3,000	$4,000	$4,000
Professional Cost Estimate	$400	$450	$500	$600
Loan Closing Costs	$1,000	$1,000	$1,000	$1,000
Attorney	$150 per hr	$150 per hr	$150 per hr	$150 per hr
Engineer	$100 per hr	$100 per hr	$100 per hr	$100 per hr
Remodeling Coach	$50 per hr	$50 per hr	$50 per hr	$50 per hr

Now you have identified the only column of numbers that represents the fees you will probably pay to your consultants, and none of the other columns are relevant.

You'll notice that in some cases there are hourly rates. These professionals know they can't predict the amount of time you'll need from them. If you multiply their hourly rate by the number of hours you guesstimate you'll need, you can plug in numbers for all your anticipated soft costs on the budget sheet that follows.

You will adjust your soft-costs budget as you learn more about what you will and won't need in the way of support from consultants, but do not allow the combined value of these commitments to exceed 10 percent of your Total Project Budget.

Setting Aside Money for Surprises

You just deducted 10 percent of your Total Project Budget for your anticipated soft costs, so the remaining 90 percent can go toward construction costs, but not all of it can be committed to the Initial Construction Contract.

Eighty percent of the Total *Construction* Budget (72 percent of the Total Project Budget) can be used for your Initial Construction Contract, but every remodeling project is full of surprises: you're about to open up spaces you have never seen. The older your home and the more humid your environment, the more surprises you can expect to find, so the remaining 20 percent of the Total Construction Budget (18 percent of the Total Project Budget) will be set aside for unanticipated costs. This is the "Oops" contingency, and it is designed to keep you safe and sane when you face the inevitable.

Sample Budget Calculations	Sample Numbers
(1) Total Project Budget (TPB)	$100,000
(2) Less 10 percent for Nonconstruction (Soft) Costs	$10,000
(3) Total *Construction* Budget	$90,000
(4) Less 72 percent of TPB for Initial Construction Contract	$72,000
(5) Leaves 18 percent of TPB for Unanticipated Costs	$18,000

If you used the Preliminary Cost-Estimating Chart to determine what your predictable *construction* costs would be, you would know the answer to line 4 first, but you could figure out your Total Project Budget (line 1) by dividing the Initial Construction Contract amount (line 4) by 0.72.

Category of Expense	% of Total Anticipated Expense
(1) Total Project Budget $300,000 ÷ 0.72 = $416,667	100%
(2) Soft-Costs Allowance	10%
(3) Total Construction Budget	90%
(4) Initial Construction Contract $300,000	72%
(5) Unanticipated Construction Costs	18%

Calculating the rest of the allowances once you have the total (line 1) is simple. Multiply the Total Project Budget amount by the percent of that total that each of the other categories represents.

BUDGET FORMULA WITH SOFT-COSTS BREAKDOWN

Find the column on the Wild-Guess Soft-Costs Estimates Chart that fits your project and fill in the blanks.

COST CATEGORY	Percentage of Total Costs	Sample Project Budget	Your Master Plan Budget

Calculate your Initial Construction Contract Amount using the Preliminary Cost-Estimating Chart (Section 2.3)

Number of enclosed/heated square feet	1,800 s.f.	
Condition of the house	Good	
Magnitude of Total Construction Budget	>$80,000	
Estimated cost per square foot for construction	Constr$ = $40/s.f.	

Find estimates for your soft costs and fill them in below but do not exceed your soft-costs budget

COST CATEGORY	Percentage of Total Costs	Sample Project Budget	Your Master Plan Budget
Total Project Budget	100%	$ 100,000	$_____
(minus)			
Soft-Costs Allowance	10%	$ 10,000	$
Home Inspection		$ 350	
Environmental Consultant's Fee		$ 1,000	
Designer's Fee		$ 6,000	
Professional Cost Estimate		$ 300	
Loan Closing Costs		$ 1,000	
Attorney's Fee - Document Review		$ 150	
Remodeling Coach		$ 1,000	
Other - 1		$ -	
Other - 2		$ -	
Other - 3		$ -	
Total Anticipated Soft Costs		$ 9,800	
(equals)			
Total Construction Budget	90%	$ 90,000	$_____
Initial Construction Contract Allowance	72%	$ 72,000	$_____
Contingency for Unanticipated Costs	18%	$ 18,000	$_____

Category of Expense	% of Total Anticipated Expense
(1) Total Project Budget $300,000 ÷ 0.72 = $416,667	100%
(2) Soft-Costs Allowance $416,667 × .10 = $41,667	10%
(3) Total Construction Budget $416,667 × .90 = $375,000	90%
(4) Initial Construction Contract $300,000	72%
(5) Unanticipated Construction Costs $416,667 × .18 = $75,000	18%

If you know your limits and you want to spend a certain amount on the entire project and not a penny more, no matter what you include in the project, here is how you would set the amount you would be willing to spend on the Initial Construction Contract (line 4):

Category of Expense	% of Total Anticipated Expense
(1) Total Project Budget $250,000 (Maximum)	100%
(2) Soft-Costs Allowance × .10 = $25,000	10%
(3) Total Construction Budget × .90 = $225,000	90%
(4) Initial Construction Contract × .72 = $180,000	72%
(5) Unanticipated Construction Costs × .18 = $45,000	18%

Now it's your turn. Practice creating a project budget by using the preliminary cost estimate you worked on in the last section. Use your predictable construction cost estimate as your Initial Construction Cost amount (line 4). Now find the remainder of the numbers and set your budget for the project:

Category of Expense	% of Total Anticipated Expense
(1) Total Project Budget $_____	100%
(2) Soft-Costs Allowance $_____	10%
(3) Total Construction Budget $_____	90%
(4) Initial Construction Contract $_____	72%
(5) Unanticipated Construction Costs $_____	18%

If you are uncomfortable with the Total Project Budget, fiddle with your remodeling plan until you've cut out some of the more expensive ideas and substituted some of the less expensive Alternates; then run the numbers again and see what you get.

Lock and Load

We've all heard remodeling horror stories from our friends and colleagues. Almost every one of them says that the job cost them 50 percent more than they anticipated. Can you see where that 50 percent comes from? They didn't anticipate soft costs or surprises, so they were really stressed out when those costs came along and they had to write checks they hadn't counted on. You, on the other hand, will hold money aside for these costs from the start, so you won't have that problem!

You have just created a remodeling budget that you can stick to, one that is based on real information (if not precise, detailed information) and sound choices about what work to include and what to ignore. Good for you. You have set yourself on a path that will result in the successful completion of a cost-effective, maximum-impact remodel that you will love to live in for years to come.

You ought to feel pretty good about this.

Your Planning Is Done!

The cost of your planning work to date was probably about $600 for the home inspection, a trunk full of design magazines, and your wine-and-design party, but you have earned your degree in project planning. Let's look at what you've achieved:

• You understand why you're doing this project.
• You focused right away on work that would be cost-effective, have a major impact on your home environment, and bring you the best return possible.

• You controlled your costs from the start, which has greatly lowered the possibility of cost overruns and the stress that accompanies them.
• You set a budget that you can stick to and set aside reasonable allowances for nonconstruction and unanticipated costs.
• You are prepared to work quickly with a great designer because you have already given careful thought to all of the questions a designer will ask. That ought to save you a few dollars in design fees.
• You have educated yourself about the terminology and costs of construction work, which will allow you to communicate effectively with the project team you are about to put together.

Actually, you know as much about your project as any professional would at this point.

If you're happy with the results so far, this would be a good time to begin shopping for a loan.

Congratulations!

THREE

Design

3.1 HIRE THE BEST

You have already had to find a good home inspector. That was a challenge. But now you need an architect and a contractor, and you can't afford to make any mistakes in these choices.

Hot Tip

The odds of getting the best work (and exactly what you want) from professional consultants go *up* in proportion to the number of times they've already successfully done exactly what you are about to ask them to do. Read that three more times. It's important.

Finding the Right Professional for Your Project

When you're looking for special consultants, always start by calling professionals in related fields for referrals, folks who *use* the services you seek on a regular basis. For example, if you're looking for an architect with years of experience redesigning *older* homes, you might consider calling the historical society, home equity lenders and Realtors who work in or near older neighborhoods, neighborhood association presidents in communities similar to your own, and others who have seen what lots of different architects have done with homes like yours. They can provide you with referrals to the architects who have consistently designed the most successful older-home renovations.

Decide who is in the know. Call and get referrals. After a little networking, you'll notice that a few names pop up on more than one list of referrals. These people, well regarded by some of their most critical clients, will turn out to be your best candidates. You're going to call these candidates, but you're going to prepare some questions first.

Any good recruiter will tell you that the best way to find out who your candidate really is, is to get them to talk about themselves. Devise a list of open-ended questions, not questions that can be answered in one or two words, and test them on your spouse, partner, or a friend. If you were looking for a great contractor, and you asked one of the contractors on your list, for example, "How long have you been in business?" he could easily answer, "Ten years." What would you have learned about him? Almost nothing. But if you ask him how he got started in the business, you would find out what his father did for a living, what his first job was, how long he's been remodeling homes, what other careers he's had, how he met his wife, who his mentor was, and all sorts of other things. You would be able to make a much better assessment of his character and experience from that answer than from the first one.

Conduct telephone interviews to see if the best candidates seem appropriate for your own project. The architect that designed the Taj

Mahal, as fantastic as he may be, may not be the right guy to remodel your basement. When you've narrowed the field to two or three candidates that you think would do the best job for you, make appointments to meet them in their own surroundings, and ask to see examples of their work.

Share just the most basic information about your plan (never share your budget), and see what sort of response you get. Are these candidates good listeners? Did they understand what you told them? What did they ask you? What did they suggest? How did you feel about what they suggested?

When you find a candidate or two you think would do a great job for you, outline what you need from them (we'll get to that in a minute), and ask for a proposal that includes a detailed description of the services they would provide and a fixed price for each service (not a lump sum!).

Professional consultants can help you keep the project moving quickly and avoid costly mistakes, but their time can be expensive. You must negotiate a deal that gets you only what you need for a price that fits into your budget. For this deal to be enforceable, it must be in writing. If a simple letter of agreement won't be enough, you'll need a contract.

The Binding Agreement

Did you know that you can create a binding agreement without securing the other party's signature? A simple letter that I call a "reiterate-and-confirm letter," something attorneys call a "rebuttable presumption," restates your verbal agreement and asks the other party to notify you if he thinks your written affirmation is not correct. If he *doesn't* contradict you in writing, you've got an agreement that will stand up in court.

At the end of this chapter is a sample reiterate-and-confirm letter for you to review. It consists of a standard introduction and a standard closing paragraph that make this letter a contract. The body of the letter is what sets the terms of the agreement between you and the other party (the scope of work, the cost, and the schedule), and it is the way you express the terms of the agreement in the body of this letter that determines whether or not you will get what you want.

He Who Writes the Contract Always Writes It to His Own Advantage

Professional services contracts are available from several sources; there is no law that says you have to sign the one your consultant offers you. You have choices:

- If you use the contract offered by the professional, you can be sure that the contract terms will be in his or her favor.
- The American Institute of Architects has a pretty complete collection of design- and construction-related contracts; there may be something you can use. Call the AIA at 800-242-9930 and ask them to send you their list of documents; then order the one you think might work best for you. These documents are written in complicated, legal language and were prepared by attorneys on the AIA payroll, so guess whom they will benefit most?
- There may be standard contracts available through the national association of whatever kind of professional you're looking for. The difference between this form and the one your expert offers you is that the association's standard is designed to protect the association, not the individual practitioner. Most professional associations have a code of ethics they want their members to observe. This

Sample Reiterate-and-Confirm Letter (Rebuttable Presumption)

Owner's Primary Address

City, State, Zip

Date
Addressee's Name
Company Name
Company Address
City, State, Zip

Re: The Renovation of (Project Address)

(The Subject of the Agreement, e.g., Plumbing Leaks)

Dear (Contractor Name),

(Standard Opening) To reiterate and confirm our conversation of (date), the following is for the record:

(Describe the scope of work) There is a leak in the new plumbing under the house, near the second bathroom.

(Describe when the contractor will take action) You have promised to bring the plumbing subcontractor back early next week to make a repair.

(State what cost or credit you've agreed to) There will be no charge for this repair work, because this repair represents a correction of work that is included in the contract.

(Standard Closing) If this is not in accordance with your understanding, please notify me in writing within five business days. In the absence of such notification, this letter will constitute a formal agreement between us.

Sincerely,

Owner's Name

Contact Phone Number

Note: A telephone response is not the same as a written response. If the contractor calls to object to the arrangement you are proposing, remind him to follow up with a letter within 5 business days or your letter will still constitute the formal agreement.

contract might be broader and a little less one-sided than the one an individual professional offers.

- You can use a standard document as a model and create your own contract. Ask your attorney to review what you've written if you do this. *Scope of work*, *schedule*, and *cost* are the three essential items you must address in any agreement you make. If you leave any one of these three key elements out, you have made a deal that will not be enforceable.

Negotiating a Professional Services Contract

A contract is rarely a take-it-or-leave-it proposition. Read carefully. Discuss your concerns and negotiate so that you get what you need.

- Omit clauses that excuse the professional from responsibility for his or her own errors and omissions.
- Add clear and reasonable standards. For example, if you write into your design contract that the cost of the finished design should not exceed your Initial Construction Contract Allowance, and the designer's cost estimate or the contractors' bids indicate that the designer didn't comply, your design contract ought to stipulate that you won't owe the designer the final portion of the fee until she edits the drawings (for free) so that the market value of the job is the same as or lower than your cost allowance. The contract the designer wanted you to sign would probably not allow that.

Remember that whether you're altering an existing contract or writing your own, your consultant must be willing to sign it. Consultants will walk away from a client who seems unreasonable.

3.2 THE ARCHITECT

If you are planning to redesign a substantial portion of your home, the best designer for you is a licensed architect with years of experience working on similar projects. A good architect has all the skills of an artist, an engineer, and a psychoanalyst, rolled into one.

In the last section we discussed how to network among professionals in similar fields for referrals to the best architects in your area; how to prepare a set of questions and hold telephone interviews with the best candidates; how to meet them in their own surroundings to see how they live and work; and finally, how to create a binding agreement for whatever work you choose to ask them to do. Please use that procedure in this case as in all others.

Once you have selected your architect . . .

Showing Off and Letting Go

It's often difficult for homeowners to share their vision and then let go and allow the professional designer to change it. But if you don't let the designer do her job, you'll be paying a professional fee to have an architect draw your amateur design.

Let's talk about what the design experience will be like for you. Specifically, let's talk about how to balance your need to stay in control with your wish to get the very best design.

Phase 1—Concept Design

Your architect will ask you about your lifestyle and how it is evolving. She will be listening for your preferences and expectations.

When you share your plan and explain how you figured out what your high-priority design challenges were, she'll be astounded that you've been so deliberate in your planning, and she'll grin and roll up her sleeves. You will have just become her favorite client.

Tell her you've brought your ideas box and ask when she'd like to see its contents. Let her tell you when to open that box.

She'll make every effort to understand what you're thinking; she will probably sketch a few quick ideas for you and ask for some feedback. She's testing her own understanding of your style and wishes; she's not making final drawings. If her ideas and yours aren't in perfect synch on the first try, don't be upset. Give her some latitude. Because you have come so well prepared, she's in the uncommon position of having to bring herself up to *your* level instead of the other way around.

She'll ask you what your budget is. Your *design* budget is the same as your Initial Construction Contract Allowance, and not one penny more. It's not the same as your Total Construction Budget (which includes unanticipated construction costs) or your Total Project Budget (which includes these costs as well as all the soft—nonconstruction—costs). Those allowances have been set aside for other purposes. That's a very important distinction.

After you've talked a bit, if you like the way she thinks, ask her to give you a proposal to do three things:

1. Provide an ⅛-inch-scale, dimensioned drawing of your existing floor plan.
2. Provide three or four quick sketches of proposed floor plans that will show what she thinks are the diverse ways to incorporate the ideas in your Master Plan within the constraints of the design budget you've given her. These sketches will begin to define the shapes, sizes, locations, and adjacencies of the major spaces. A concept sketch is very loose, informal, and inexpensive.
3. Provide a preliminary construction cost estimate for *each* proposed floor plan, in the

Task Abstract List format, with a price for each major construction task. (Leave her a copy of your Master Plan in that format as a guide.) Don't expect a lot of detail, and don't expect this very rough cost estimate to be the final cost estimate. You don't know yet what details you may add.

If her fee for this work seems reasonable to you, authorize her to begin work on these three items only. What would constitute a reasonable fee?

Typically the architect charges between 5 and 7 percent of your Initial Construction Contract value as her fee. You have done such great planning that she may spend just as much time designing, but you've cut her standard allowance for meeting time in half; assume you'll pay 5 percent . You ought to pay no more than 20 to 25 percent of her total fee for concept design (design phase 1 of 3), so if your initial construction budget is $100,000 and her total fee is 5 percent of that ($5,000), then 20 percent of that $5,000 is $1,000. That amount, or something close to it, would be perfectly reasonable for the first phase of design work on a $100,000 construction contract.

Formalize your agreement with a reiterate-and-confirm letter and send it within twenty-four hours of your meeting. Include in the body of the letter the scope of work (the three items above), the schedule (when she will have the sketches and their preliminary budgets ready), and the cost for this work only. Don't commit yourself to anything more until you've seen her first ideas.

Reviewing the Designer's Sketches

When you return to look at the concept designs, the architect will ask for feedback.

Don't make any quick decisions. Pay her for her work. Take the sketches and their rough cost estimates home and look at them with an open mind. Allow yourself time to digest *her* ideas.

Then compare what she designed with your own preliminary plan. If she understood your design challenges and goals, there will be some similarities between what she put on paper and what you are envisioning, and—here comes the best part—if you were successful in letting her take the lead once you knew she understood your plan, there will almost certainly be a few "Wow!" ideas there that you never dreamed of.

If you clung to your own plan and redirected her when she offered anything else, you are certain to see nothing new in these sketches. The "Wow!" ideas will have been squelched.

Phase 2—Design Development

If your designer's concepts are far off the mark, or if her tastes and yours are miles apart, thank her, pay her, cut your losses, and start working with another architect. You chose to buy only concept design, and now you're glad you did.

If you like one of the preliminary designs enough to start the hard work, ask for a proposal for design development services. Design development is phase 2 of your architect's work, and the part you've worked the hardest on already—selecting materials, finishes, and colors.

Negotiate a fee and the terms of this agreement (including a stipulation that each design change will generate a revised Task Abstract List that reflects the related changes in costs), create a formal agreement for this work, and begin selecting materials and cabinets. The fee for design development ought to be about 30 to 35 percent of the total design fee, which we decided would be about 5 percent of the value of the Initial Construction Contract allowance. Do the math. What would be a reasonable fee for design development services on a construction contract worth $100,000?

Now your box full of ideas will really do some good.

Discuss the new environment you want to create for yourself and your family, and show your architect pictures of your favorite pieces of furniture or art.

Provide her with a list of your most important design goals and show her your favorite solutions.

Edit your Task Abstract List every time you make a definitive choice or a change to your plan, and keep track of the cost of every line item. Never completely discard any ideas. When you put a new idea into your plan, just move the original idea down into that long (and getting longer) list of Alternates and save it for a rainy day.

When you agree that all of the details have been resolved, ask the designer to make you a copy of the annotated design development drawing with a corresponding final cost estimate. Pay her fee, and take the design home and think about it—live in it. Don't sign off on it until you're absolutely sure it's right for you and complete in every detail.

The deeper you get into the design process, the more difficult (and expensive) it will be to make changes. This is really your last chance to revise anything, so it would be wise to take a few precautions.

Precaution 1: Pull out the lists of what you like and don't like about your house and be sure you're solving all of your problems. Review your home inspection report and be sure that every repair will be addressed. Look at your wish list and see if your architect was able to incorporate at least a few of the new spaces you wanted. See what she did with the spaces you told her you rarely use. Imagine serving a dinner party of eight from the kitchen she's designed. Imagine having six teenagers in the house. Imagine living the next ten years of your life, with all that you expect to happen during that time, in the space she's designed for you. Study this plan for as long as it takes to be sure that you've addressed all of your most important concerns. Make a careful list of design details that still need to change.

Precaution 2: Gather a few good friends and have them critique the drawings. They may spot things you miss.

Precaution 3: Ask for a professional design review meeting. The opinions offered by other design specialists can only add value to your final design. Your architect should have no objections to hosting this meeting. Smoothing out the kinks now will take less time than making changes to the final set of detailed construction drawings.

- *Invite a structural engineer.* He will check the spans of the lumber that hold up the ceiling over the new great room. If you're adding a second floor, he may want to check the size and condition of your foundation piers.
- *Invite a certified kitchen designer.* The kitchen is by far the most complicated and expensive room in the house. Allowing a kitchen design specialist to review the layout of that one room will be worth whatever fee she may charge.
- *Invite an interior designer.* We've talked about how the furnishings, the activities, and the

shapes of the spaces that hold them have to work together. The interior designer will be thrilled to have input before the walls are in place, and getting his or her input now will save you the anguish of finding out later that your couch won't fit through the front door, or that you'll have to put great-grandfather's portrait back into the attic because there's still no wall to hang it on.

How will you pay for this meeting? All the professionals' fees will come out of your soft-costs allowance. Set aside enough money for two hours for three professionals for this design review meeting and allow for all of these fees in your soft-costs budget when you first set it up.

After the meeting is finished, pay the architect to revise both the final design development drawing and the Task Abstract List with new cost estimates on every task.

Precaution 4: Hire a good remodeling cost estimator. (Do not talk to general contractors just yet.) Your designer has given you her best cost estimate, but she is not in the market buying plumbing services or cabinets every day. A seasoned remodeling cost estimator can give you a much more accurate estimate. If the professional estimator comes to a different conclusion than the designer, the estimator is probably right. Once you see an accurate cost estimate, you may want to make another round of changes to the design development drawings before work begins on the final construction set.

To find a seasoned cost estimator, follow the protocols in Section 3.1. The right cost estimator for your project should have lots of experience pricing *residential remodels,* or he won't be worth his fee.

You may find that your best candidates are employed full-time by residential architecture and engineering firms and can't give you their undivided attention. If you choose to hire someone with a full-time job, allow him at least ten days to complete the estimate once he begins work.

Provide your estimator with a copy of the designer's final Task Abstract List, but remove her prices and have the estimator fill in the blanks with his own. Give the estimator lots (dozens) of Alternates to price for you too. The more options you are willing to consider while you're fiddling with your project costs, the better the final plan will be. The estimator will need to see the condition of your home for his prices to be accurate. Offer him a tour.

The price of a good cost estimate will depend on the extent and complexity of your work, the size and condition of your property, and the availability of your estimator. Generally a good remodeling cost estimate should cost you no more than a few hundred dollars.

The more information you can get from the cost estimator, the easier the remainder of your project will be.

If your cost estimate is more than 5 percent higher than your Initial Construction Contract Allowance, go back to your designer and make some changes. Use that long list of Alternates to help you make substitutions that you can afford.

After a few weeks of hard work, you and your architect will have developed a high-impact, cost-effective design that makes you very happy, and she'll ask you to sign off on the final revision of the design development drawings. She won't start on the detailed construction drawings until she gets your authorization to do so.

Phase 3—Construction Drawings

Your design work is now done, although your architect and her team have a great deal yet to do.

This last phase of design is really very intense, and the considerations are purely technical. Questions that will need to be answered during this phase include: How many amps will you need in your electrical panel to serve all the fixtures, outlets, and switches? How big does the air handler in your HVAC unit have to be? How will the framing for the new addition tie into the framing of the existing house? How should the carpenter finish the stair rail? What is the color number of the stain you selected for the hardwood floors? Which manufacturer will give you the best value for your money on your new windows? How will the gutters attach to the house?

It will take the architect and her team of experts several weeks to produce a set of construction drawings that tell the contractor exactly how to build your new space, and this is where you'll spend the remainder of her fee.

While this team is hard at work, you've got other things to tend to—we'll get to those in a minute.

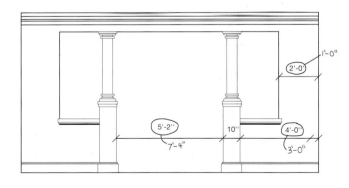

OPENING DETAIL A-A
From Kitchen

Detail of opening between kitchen and dining area with changes to architect's drawing.

The Architect's Contract

If you decide to buy your design services one step at a time, you may find that a good discussion followed by a carefully detailed reiterate-and-confirm letter (see Section 3.1) will provide you with an adequate description and an enforceable agreement.

If you want to use a formal contract, read your architect's prototype very closely. Most design contracts specifically shield the designer from responsibility for her own errors and omissions.

No matter how you structure your design contract, please ensure that the following conditions are included in your agreement:

• *Design documents must include a separate list of Alternates.* By including Alternates in your construction drawings (separated from the work you want in the contract), you can get competitive bids for items you are not committed to purchasing. This will allow you to make quick changes if you have to (for example, to swap out the expensive cabinets for the less expensive ones when the contractor discovers that half of your floor framing needs to be replaced and you need to cut back on your cabinet costs to cover the cost of this repair). Since you've had all your Alternates priced ahead of time, you will know the implications of your decision without slowing down the work. (Good idea!)

• *The designer must work within your Initial Construction Contract Allowance.* Don't sign off on any phase of the design, or pay for it, until you have a written cost estimate from your designer, that estimate is in Task Abstract List format, and the total of all estimated costs is no higher than your Initial Construction Contract Allowance.

• *The designer owes you a free redesign if your bids are all 15 percent or more higher than the designer's cost estimate*, and the revisions are to be finished within four weeks of the notification of receipt of the too-high bids.

• *If you're working on a historic property*, write two additional items of work into the design contract: first, the designer's final documents should include everything you need for your application for review— the submittal to the historic commission— and second, the commission must approve the design in order for the design package to be considered finished.

• *If more than two dwelling units or an income-producing building are on your property*, the commercial code may apply, and in that case your contract should stipulate that all documents required by the inspections department for commercial permit submittals be prepared by the designer.

3.3 THE SPEC WRITER

Using an architect to design your remodeling project is a traditional choice, and a good one.

But if you plan to spend most of your remodeling budget on repairs or replacement of existing materials and appliances, and you don't intend to change exterior walls or do anything that requires artistic sensibilities to describe the work, using a *spec writer* can be a very good and less expensive alternative.

A specification is a written document that describes the same work that the architect's drawings describe. The specs can actually be more specific if the item they're describing is a piece of machinery, but they are not very good at describing curves. If you are planning to build archways or fancy cabinetry, specifications won't work.

A GLOSSARY OF ARCHITECTURAL TERMS

DESIGN DOCUMENTS A package of drawings and/or written specifications that describes every detail of every task in your renovation plan.

ELEVATION The view you see when you look straight ahead at a vertical surface such as a wall full of cabinets.

If the architect refers to your front *elevation* drawing, she probably is referring to the drawing of the front exterior wall of your house, which would show your front door, your front porch and steps, and all of the windows and roof details.

PLAN The view you get when you look down from the sky, take the roof and ceiling off the house, and see the outline of the perimeter walls and the rooms inside the home.

Technically, the house is "cut" at about 4 feet above the floor. Items shown on a drawing in dotted lines exist above that 4-foot level. Overhead cabinets in your kitchen, for example, would be shown as dotted lines. Items shown in solid lines would be visible at or below that 4-foot level. Lower kitchen cabinets would be drawn in solid lines.

When designers refer to a floor plan, they not only refer to the layout of the rooms; they also refer to the point of view they will use to represent the layout. They will draw the layout in *plan*.

SCALE A way to draw a full-sized object in the right proportions, but in smaller (or larger) dimensions.

The scale is usually indicated in the lower right-hand corner of the drawings, along with the stamp and signature of the designer and the date that the drawings were finished or last revised.

"Eighth-inch scale" or "eighth scale" is expressed as "$\frac{1}{8}$" = 1'-0"," which means that $\frac{1}{8}$ inch of drawn detail represents 1 foot of real object.

There may also be a note on the drawing that says "NTS" which means "Not to Scale." It usually indicates that the designer has doodled something quickly and that the drawing is not meant to indicate the exact dimensions of the real object, just a general layout.

SECTION A drawing of what an item would look like if you sliced it and opened it. Sections are often used to more closely define details.

Where the architect indicates that there are built-in bookcases, for example, she has to specify the thickness of each piece of lumber, the shape of the trim pieces, the distance between shelves, whether or not the shelves will be adjustable, whether the edges of the shelves will be squared or rounded, and so on. All of this will be shown in the section or detail drawing if the architect visually "slices" the shelves open from top to bottom.

A complete set of architectural drawings will provide a section drawing for every design detail that requires more information than the plan and elevation drawings can provide.

SPECIFICATIONS The paragraphs of technical writing that describe the materials to be used and the performance standards that must be met.

The drawings may indicate that there will be an addition with a new roof. Specifications will be used to make note of the manufacturer, style, and color of shingles and the kind of manufacturer's warranty the client wants to have on those shingles. Specifications can describe all the details that you can't see in a drawing.

Plain Jane

Next door with just a little landscaping

Look at the two red brick homes in the photos above. They sit side by side on a nice street in a nice neighborhood. I call them "the siblings" because they were obviously built alike at their inception by either a common owner or a common builder or both. But they have been handled very differently through the years. The structures are still the same, but the landscaping makes them look very different.

Landscaping is so important. It can either complement or obscure the beauty of your

home. Below are a few examples of what I mean.

Take your camera for a long walk and make observations about what style of landscaping you like best. Buy one hour of time from a registered landscape architect, and spend that hour just walking around your house with him. The landscape architect will share some ideas with you, and you can decide after that conversation whether or not to hire him to do a complete landscaping plan.

Houses with landscaping

Finding the 1-Inch-Long-by-0.06-Millimeter-Thick Steel Sewing Implement in the 10-Foot-High Pile of Cut-and-Dried Wheat

Good residential remodeling spec writers are hard to find.

Some residential spec writers work full-time for architecture or engineering firms, so begin your search by calling a good residential design firm. Ask to speak to the spec writer to see if he will moonlight for you. Some spec writers prefer to work as freelance consultants for several smaller firms. Ask the smaller firms for referrals to these folks.

You might try talking to other professionals who use spec writers on a regular basis. Talk to project managers at nonprofit agencies who are responsible for repairing and remodeling affordable housing. They won't be interested in expensive or artsy details, and they may be working with federal grant money, which doesn't allow much for professional fees. You might try asking for referrals from owners of rental properties, or property managers who purchase and renovate low- and moderately priced housing units. Try calling your local housing department or the local public housing authority, and ask for the person who runs the housing rehabilitation program. Find out who writes the specs for those projects. Follow the search and interview tips from Section 3.1 to find and engage the best possible candidate.

Be sure to find a spec writer with *years* of experience writing *residential remodeling* specifications for projects like yours, or you won't get good value for your money.

When you review samples of the spec writer's work, look for lots of quality-control statements, for instance, "materials installation should be done in accordance with the manufacturer's recommendations," or "all wood siding should be caulked and primed prior to painting," or "new paint should achieve full coverage," or "fixtures with major components made of plastic are not acceptable." You get the idea.

Starting in the Middle

You thought the spec writer would be a good designer for you because you are planning a simple project: no fancy woodwork, not much in the way of changing the floor plan. Since spec writers are more likely to be better technicians than they are artists, you won't be spending much time on concept design here; you'll probably jump right into design development and start selecting replacement materials and finishes.

If this is your first contact with a design professional, begin by sharing your preliminary plan and a little bit about how you chose some of the materials you like. Share with the spec writer how you expect your lifestyle to change over the next five to ten years or so, and how you want to alter your house to accommodate those changes.

When he asks for your budget, give him your Initial Construction Contract Allowance.

You've chosen to work with a technical designer rather than an artistic one, so your Master Plan (in Task Abstract List format) will be very useful.

Listen to how he would incorporate your needs into a comprehensive remodeling plan, and if you like what you hear, ask him to give you a proposal to do three things:

1. Prepare a ⅛-inch scale, dimensioned, *existing* floor plan of your home (unless you've already gotten this drawing from another designer).

2. Prepare a ⅛-inch scale, dimensioned *proposed* floor plan, based on the scope of work you've outlined. (If your floor plan will not change, you won't need a proposed floor plan.)
3. Prepare a one-page preliminary cost estimate using the Task Abstract List format with prices for every major task required to complete your design scheme. This will be a revised and more detailed Task Abstract List than the Master Plan list you created, and it will include cost estimates for each task.

The Spec Writer's Contract

If you hire a spec writer, be sure that the following work activities are included in your professional services contract:

- The spec writer should *prepare two (identical) sets* of complete and detailed specifications. One set of specs should include cost estimates for every task. This set is for your files. The other set should have a blank line next to each work item. You'll use this set for bidding (more about this soon).
- The spec writer should provide you with scaled, dimensioned existing and proposed floor plans, with all stairwells, decks, rooms, and major services or hookups drawn and labeled. Exterior elevations are generally not required.
- If you plan to remodel a *multifamily property,* the spec writer should provide you with one set of specs for each building exterior, and one set of specs for each apartment interior. If you have four apartments in one building, you should get five sets of specifications.
- Your spec writer should allow for one round of *edits* in his or her price—two rounds if your property is in a historic district.

Refer to Section 3.2 for additional suggestions, made in reference to the architect's contract. They would apply here too.

Rehabilitating a Dilapidated Downtown Duplex

About ten years ago I worked with a team of investors who had purchased a dilapidated duplex in the downtown area of a small city. The town planners had designated the six-block area surrounding this building as a community revitalization area, which meant that they were making very-low-interest loans available to owners who wanted to make improvements. The unimproved properties would probably be condemned, demolished, and replaced with newly constructed infill housing. My enterprising investors wanted to do a remodel that would bring in better tenants and higher rents so that they could reap the benefits of the improving neighborhood real estate values as the revitalization plan took effect.

The short version of the home inspection report was that everything needed to be repaired or replaced. The structure needed all new windows, the kitchens and bathrooms needed major makeovers, and the units needed both electrical and plumbing repairs.

There had been a kitchen fire in the left-side apartment that scorched the cabinets and drywall. Until this wall was opened up, it was anybody's guess what damage had been done to the framing and the roof.

The existing room layout (opposite) didn't meet the current minimum housing code because the occupants would have to walk through bedrooms (private spaces) to get from the living room (a public space) to the kitchen (another public space). This was no longer allowed.

This was going to be a substantial remodeling project, even without any fancy, artistic design elements. The investors hired a spec writer with years of experience working on HUD-funded housing—the perfect candidate—to create their construction documents.

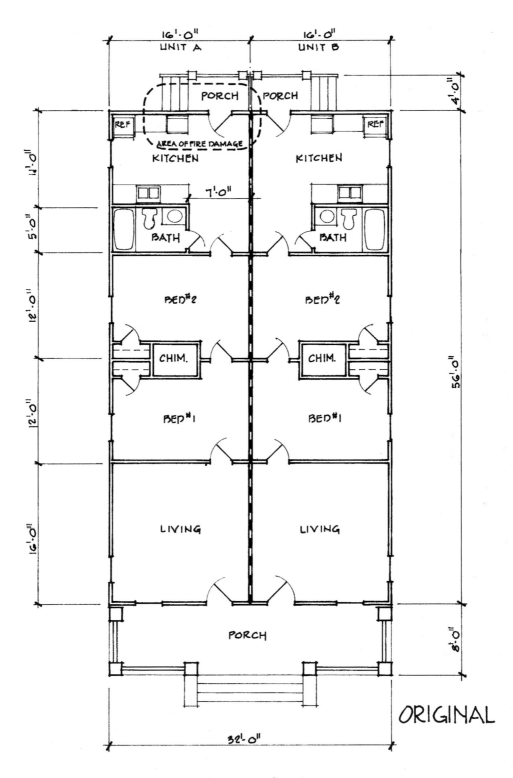

16'-0"
UNIT A

16'-0"
UNIT B

4'-0"

PORCH   PORCH

REF   REF

AREA OF FIRE DAMAGE

KITCHEN   KITCHEN

11'-0"

7'-0"

BATH   BATH

5'-0"

BED #2   BED #2

12'-0"

CHIM.   CHIM.

56'-0"

BED #1   BED #1

12'-0"

LIVING   LIVING

16'-0"

PORCH

8'-0"

32'-0"

ORIGINAL

Duplex—existing floor plan

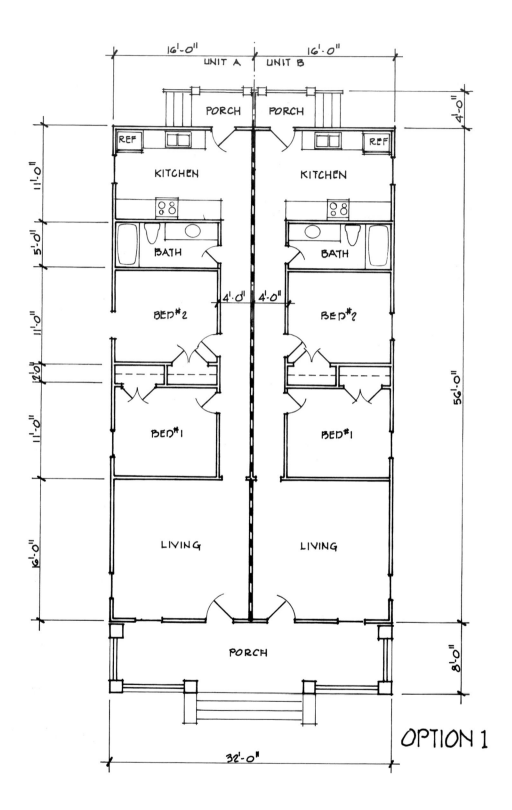

16'-0"   16'-0"

UNIT A   UNIT B

4'-0"

PORCH   PORCH

REF   REF

KITCHEN   KITCHEN

11'-0"

BATH   BATH

5'-0"

4'-0" 4'-0"

BED #2   BED #2

11'-0"

56'-0"

2'-0"

BED #1   BED #1

11'-0"

LIVING   LIVING

16'-0"

PORCH

8'-0"

OPTION 1

32'-0"

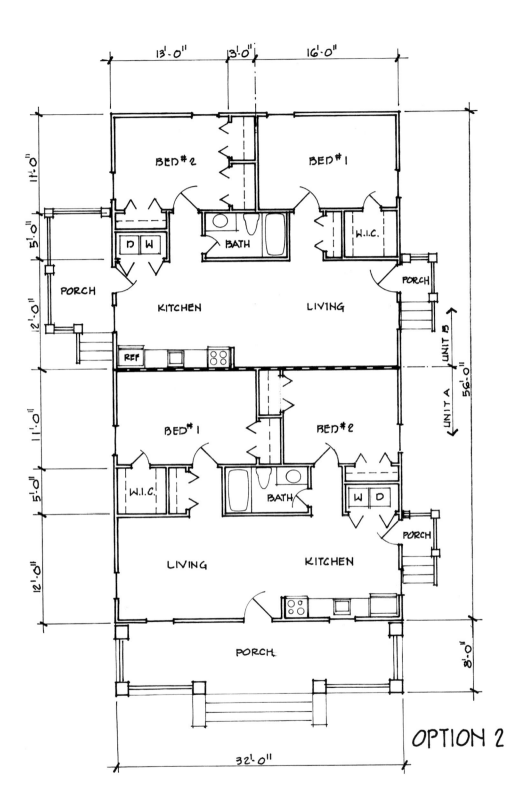

13'-0" 3'-0" 16'-0"

11'-0"

BED #2   BED #1

5'-0"

D W   BATH   W.I.C.

PORCH   KITCHEN   LIVING   PORCH

2'-0"

REF   UNIT A   UNIT B

11'-0"   BED #1   BED #2   56'-0"

5'-0"   W.I.C.   BATH   W D

LIVING   KITCHEN   PORCH

12'-0"

PORCH   8'-0"

OPTION 2

32'-0"

Since the investors wanted to upgrade the apartments, the spec writer prepared a dimensioned existing floor plan and two different proposed floor plans for the owners' review. Have a look at pages 66 and 67. The dotted line in the center of the structure represents the party wall—the wall that separates the two apartments. In option 1, the apartment layout hasn't changed much, but in option 2, the apartments are arranged one in front of the other, and the room layout works very differently.

Choosing a Design

If you were a prospective tenant, which design would you rather live in, option 1 or option 2?

If you were a banker, which would you consider the better investment?

If you were the neighbor who had just put $70,000 into a sweet little bungalow next door, which design would you encourage the investors to build?

The property was built in the 1940s. Calculate the cost of work on each of the proposed designs using the Preliminary Cost-Estimating Chart in Section 2.3, and make note of these costs; they represent the different Initial Construction Contract Allowances that would apply to the two designs. Divide these numbers by 0.72 to add back the allowances for soft costs and surprises to find the Total Project Budget for each design. How much of a difference will there be between the two project budgets?

If you were the investors, which design would you choose to build?

If you were the investors, which plan would you expect to pay you back faster? You could charge higher rents for the apartments in option 2, but you would spend less to build option 1.

Excerpts from this set of specifications are included on pages 70 and 71 for your review. The complete set of specs was more than twenty pages long.

In real life, the duplex sits in a historic district, and preservation guidelines applied. The letters *HP* after a task number in the specifications indicate that the work is governed by the historic preservation guidelines. The letters *LBP* after a task number indicate that lead-based paint regulations and work guidelines must be followed. The contractors needed to know this.

Look at these specifications and see how well they define the work. The Task Abstract List for this project would come directly from the task numbers in the specifications; the spec writer used the standard construction divisions. You wouldn't have to carry around all twenty pages of specifications in order to do a site inspection—all you would need would be the one-page Task Abstract List.

Finished duplex

DUPLEX REHAB
Developing a Task Abstract List from the Specifications

SEC	Item #	Partial Task Abstract List—from Specifications
100		**Demolition and Site Work**
	101	Landscape after removal of hazardous materials
200		**Foundation and Structure**
	201	Add foundation supports
	202	Remove and replace damaged front porch rails and pickets
300		**Exterior Envelope**
	301	Install two mailboxes
	302	Remove and replace flat roof systems
	308	Replace damaged siding
		etc.

PRELIMINARY COST ESTIMATES—OPTION 1 vs. OPTION 2

Option 1—Preliminary Cost Estimate
Total square feet of heated space = 32 x 56 = 1792 s.f.
Level of work: 5 Minimum Rehab, Poor Condition = $60/s.f.
Est. construction cost: 1792 s.f. x $60/s.f. = $107,520
Est. Total Project Budget = $107,520 / 0.72 = **$150,000**

Option 2—Preliminary Cost Estimate
Total square feet of heated space = 32 x 56 = 1792 s.f.
Level of work: 5 Moderate Rehab, Poor Condition = $80/s.f.
Est. construction cost: 1792 s.f. x $80/s.f. = $143,360
Est. Total Project Budget = $143,360 / 0.72 = **$200,000**

EXCERPTS FROM THE DUPLEX SPECIFICATIONS

GENERAL NOTES AND SPECIAL CONDITIONS STATEMENT

1. For the sake of brevity, descriptions of work in this write-up are in outline form. It shall be assumed by all parties that work described in this write-up will be finished completely and in every respect in accordance with the highest construction standards in the area, and ready for use by owner and tenants.

2. The units are identical. The scope of work shall be the same for both units. What is specified for one unit shall apply to the other equally, unless otherwise noted.

3. This property is in a local historic district. The General Guidelines for Working in Historic Districts, attached, shall apply. Questions regarding special requirements for historic preservation work may be directed to the Historic Districts Commission [telephone number here].

4. There is lead-based paint on many surfaces of this building. Contractor shall use Safe Work Practices in all areas where paint is being disturbed. Questions regarding special requirements for work on hazardous materials may be directed to OSHA [telephone number here]. The contractor must pass a clearance test that verifies that the property is free of all lead-based paint hazards before work will be considered complete. The owner will pay for the first clearance test. If the work fails, all rooms of the residence shall be recleaned, and both the cost of cleaning and the cost of the second clearance test shall be deducted from the contractor's final check.

5. Contractor shall stipulate allowances for materials costs wherever they are required by the specifications. If the owner selects an item with a higher cost than the contractor's allowance, the additional costs will be borne by the owner.

6. Time is of the essence. The schedule for completion of this project is critical. It is the contractor's responsibility to meet this completion date without additional charge to the owner. Late penalties shall apply in accordance with contract terms and conditions if the schedule is not met, and, in addition, contractor shall reimburse owner for any rents lost due to delay of completion of the work.

7. Work shall not be considered complete until the contractor cleans all new plumbing fixtures and rods out plumbing lines, and all surfaces are free of paint drips and overspray, including paint that was present before the contractor's work began.

100 Demolition and Site Work

101LBP: Landscape around foundation in the following manner, after all other work is completed.

Remove all visible paint chips from soil to approximately 6 feet from the foundation wall surrounding the house.

Prepare foundation beds by digging a trench 6 inches deep by 3 feet wide measuring from the foundation wall, entry stoop, or steps, all around the dwelling unit.

Fill beds with sifted topsoil to 6 inches higher than surrounding yard level. Grade this new soil to slope away from the home for positive drainage.

Plant sixteen 5-gallon flowering bushes in locations designated on the proposed floor plan attached.

Mulch the surface, and water the newly landscaped area every other day for three weeks immediately following the completion of the grading work.

200 Foundations and Structure

201: Stabilize and add foundation supports to meet current structural code requirements. Work shall include, but not be limited to, the following:

Repoint all existing brick piers.

Remove all rotten or charred wood (girders, joists, subflooring, and underlayment) in the damaged kitchen areas and replace with new.

New work must be reviewed and approved in writing by a licensed structural engineer of the owner's choosing.

202HP: Remove all damaged and severely deteriorated front porch railings and pickets. Install new railings and pickets where old ones were removed and at both sides of all entry steps and stoops, to match original materials and design.

300 Exterior Envelope

301: Supply and install two new metal mailboxes for the house. Installation shall meet current postal service requirements. Mailbox shall match Old House Hardware SKU#196-984 or approved equal.

302HP: Remove existing roof systems for all the flat and nearly flat areas of the roof over the existing kitchens at the rear of the house.

Install a new membrane roofing system, which shall be single-ply EPDM. Include installing all membrane flashing, underlayment, and decking in accordance with manufacturer's specifications. Also include removal and replacement of all deteriorated or charred sheathing, wood rafters, fascia board, boxing, and moldings. New materials shall match existing (original) work. Where no sheathing exists or where existing sheathing does not meet current building code or is rotten, install new H-inch exterior-grade plywood.

NOTE: The actual amount of sheathing replacement required may differ from the assumption above. The value of this work will be adjusted to reflect the actual approved quantities required. Provide unit prices here for additional work: Replace additional sheathing: $_____ per square foot.

Submit references for owner's approval, prior to beginning work, certifying that roofer is qualified to install this system.

308HP: Replace deteriorated and fire-damaged wood siding with new siding to match original. Contractor shall include an allowance for a total of 800 linear feet of new wood siding. Repair all other areas of wood siding with epoxy consolidant. All new wood must be rot resistant. New exterior wood must be back-primed, including end grains, prior to installation.

NOTE: The actual amount of siding replacement required may differ from the assumption above. The contract value of this work will be adjusted to reflect the actual approved quantity required. Provide unit prices here for additional work: Replace additional siding: $_____ per linear foot.

NOTE: Contractor and owner shall review all areas of the exterior before removing any siding. Any siding removed without approval of the owner shall be replaced in kind (to match original materials) at the contractor's expense.

FOUR

Pre-Construction

4.1 INSURANCE

If you have meticulously checked your contractor's references and you know that you will be dealing with someone with integrity, you already have the best insurance you can get. But in case something goes wrong and the remedy requires more than you or your contractor can afford, you may want to consider some extra protection.

Requirements

Your state laws set the minimum amount of general liability insurance that any general contractor has to have, but you can set any number you like as long as it is higher than that minimum, and you can ask your contractor to carry more than just general liability insurance. Talk to your insurance agent about what your options are, but here are the four standard forms of coverage for construction projects.

Cash Retainage

International construction standards allow the owner to withhold 10 percent of what the contractor has earned out of every payment except the final check. This 10 percent, called "retainage," insures the owner against the premium price a second contractor would charge to finish the job if for any reason the first contractor could not. Assuming the original contractor finishes the job, when everything is completed to the owner's satisfaction, the contractor is paid in full.

General Liability Insurance

Combined general liability insurance includes coverage for property damage and personal injury.

The amount and type of general liability coverage you require and the form that the insurance coverage takes, beyond what your state laws require, is up to you. The contractor will carry the insurance you ask for if he wants to do the job, and he will no doubt pass the cost back to you by burying it in his bid as a part of his overhead markup. The cost of insurance is a legitimate project-related expense.

Require that your contractor have coverage worth at least twice the after-remodel value of your home. Increasing coverage limits on an existing policy is not very expensive.

Require that your contractor's combined general liability insurance be underwritten on the *occurrence* basis so that you can still be compensated for a legitimate claim if you discover problems after the job is over and his policy has expired. If you accept a policy written on the *claims-made* basis, your claim won't be honored unless it's made during the time the policy is in force.

Require that the *certificate* of insurance you get from the contractor lists you in two places:

1. As "certificate holder"—your name and home address if you're a property owner, or your company name and address if you are acting on behalf of a company or a non-profit or government agency, and
2. As "additional insured"—in the box on the certificate that's called "Description of Operations." In this box the contractor's insurance agent should list the address of the project property and say that (the owner's name) "is additional insured as their interests may apply." This phrase is straight out of the statutes and means that as long as you have an ownership interest in the property the contractor is working on, you have access to the coverage under this policy to the extent that there is coverage available.

Write to the contractor's insurance agent, who will be listed on the certificate, and ask that you be notified in writing if the policy lapses, expires, or is terminated for any reason before the date that your contractor's warranty obligations have all been fulfilled.

Workers' Compensation Insurance

State laws differ, but each state sets a trigger that requires a contractor to carry workers' compensation insurance. In North Carolina, if the contractor regularly employs three or more workers (not including the owners) he has to carry workers' comp.

The North Carolina statutes also say that the *property owner* is responsible for checking to see if the contractor should have this coverage, and then, if he should, that he does have it. If a worker is injured and the property owner neglected to check the contractor's status and get a certificate of coverage if it's required (or a disclosure, signed by the contractor, if it's not), the property owner is held doubly liable for

damages (pays twice the amount of the award) and can be charged with a misdemeanor for that negligence as well. I bet you never would have thought of that one.

Check the laws for your state to see what will be required of you and your contractor. The state department of insurance, the contractors' licensing board, or the local chapter of the homebuilders' association should be able to give you this information.

Bonds

Bonds are three-party contracts that involve you, your contractor, and the bonding agent. The agent puts his own money on the line to provide you with a guarantee that your contractor will fulfill the conditions of the construction contract. You are specifically included in the policy coverage.

There are three kinds of bonds that ensure the performance of a construction contract:
1. A *bid bond* guarantees that the contractor will hold his bid price for a certain period of time (set by you) and will pay a penalty if he withdraws.
2. A *payment bond* ensures that the contractor pays his vendors and subcontractors in a timely manner.
3. A *performance bond* ensures that the contractor performs his duties in accordance with the construction contract terms and conditions.

As a general rule, payment and performance bonds are used only if the project budget exceeds $100,000. Bid bonds are used only if the bid amount exceeds $250,000. Bid bonds are used only on very large and complicated jobs where if a low bidder were to withdraw his bid, the owner's funding might be in jeopardy.

Contractor's Disclosure Form for
Workers' Compensation Insurance Coverage

The undersigned contractor hereby attests to the following:

1. I am a professional construction contractor.

2. Under the laws of the State of _____, I am required to carry

   Workers' Compensation Insurance if

   _____

   _____

   _____

3. Select ONE of the following:

   ☐ I am NOT required to carry this insurance.

   (OR)

   ☐ I AM required to carry this insurance. Documentation of coverage shall be provided to
   property owner prior to the signing of a construction contract.

Contractor agrees to initiate the completion of a new disclosure form if or when the contractor's
status under the law changes, and a new disclosure form for each policy year that the contract is
in effect, including during the warranty period as stipulated in the contract.

Signed _____

Company Owner's Signature _____

Print Owner's Name _____ Date _____

Print Company Name and Complete Address _____

_____

Tax ID# _____

Before you ask your contractor to secure bonds, you must weigh the value of the protection a bond would give you against the cost of securing such protection. The cost of the bond and the fees to prepare a bond application will be passed along to you in the contractor's bid price, as they are both legitimate costs of fulfilling the contract conditions.

To secure a bond, the contractor will have to hold aside cash in an escrow account and will have to prepare documents and pay for certified financial statements as well. He will be required to invest quite a bit of time preparing the application.

Smaller contractors sometimes cannot get bonds because they can't show the agent the kind of financial balance sheet that is required. That doesn't mean they are bad contractors; it only means they don't have a hefty bank account.

Included on pages 76-77 is a sample Combined Performance and Payment Bond Form for you to review.

Assignment of Liability

Liability is assigned by law in different ways for different business structures. It may be important for you to know the business structure of the firm you intend to hire.

- In a sole proprietorship, the risks of the owner and the risks of the business are inseparable.
- In a partnership, each partner is fully responsible for the business acts and debts of all the other partners.
- In a corporation, the law separates the personal activities and obligations of the owners from those of the business.

This is not a book about insurance, so I won't go into any more detail here. If I have succeeded in convincing you that setting out your insurance requirements is not a simple task and should not be taken lightly, then I'm happy and you'll be safe.

Be sure to consult your attorney and a good insurance agent before you write insurance requirements into your contract or decide what supplemental coverage to purchase for yourself.

4.2 WHEN IN ROME...

Nasty disputes often result from simple misunderstandings. Mastering the politics of the job site is just another form of insurance.

How you communicate will be as important as *what* you communicate. Here are some tips that may help you understand how to work with and talk to your contractor in a way he will understand.

While your architect is finishing those complicated construction drawings, you can be making some decisions about how you'll run your project.

Hunker Down or Move Out?

In case you have any doubt about whether or not you should stay in the house during the construction period, let me give you some helpful hints:

- When you have a contractor working in your home, it's not yours anymore; it's his. It's very important that you understand this and that you are prepared for it.
- If you leave personal property in the way of the contractor's workers, it's almost inevitable that something will be damaged.
- If you're in the house while it's under construction, you'll have to deal with safety hazards, a lack of privacy, security risks, and lots of inconvenience that you may prefer to avoid.

Combined Performance and Payment Bond Form

Date _____

_____
(Contractor's firm name, address/zip, phone number)

_____
(Surety's firm name, address/zip, phone number)

_____
(Property Owner's name and mailing address)

KNOW ALL MEN BY THESE PRESENTS, that we, the Principal and the Surety, are held and firmly bound unto the Property Owner, hereinafter called the Contracting Body, for the payment of which sum well and truly to be made, we bind ourselves, our heirs, executors, administrators and successors, jointly and severally, firmly by these presents, in the penal sum of the total contract amount which is:

_____
(Write out contract value in words here)

$ _____
(Use numbers here)

THE CONDITION OF THIS OBLIGATION IS SUCH, that whereas the Principal entered into a certain contract with the Contracting Body, as (Contract Description)

_____

and the contract is hereto attached,

NOW, THEREFORE, if the Principal shall well and truly perform and fulfill all the undertakings, covenants, terms, conditions, and agreements of said contract during the original term of said contract and any extensions thereof that may be granted by the Contracting Body, with or without notice to the Surety, and during the life of any guaranty required under the contract, and shall also well and truly perform and fulfill all the undertakings, covenants, terms, conditions, and agreements of any and all duly authorized modifications of said contract that may hereafter be made, notice of which modifications to the Surety being hereby waived, then, this obligation is to be void; otherwise to remain in full force and virtue.

AND, THEREFORE, if the Principal shall promptly make payment to all persons supplying labor and material in the prosecution of the work provided for in said contract, and any and all duly

Combined Performance and Payment Bond Form

authorized modifications of said contract that may hereafter be made, notice of which modifications to the Surety being hereby waived, then this obligation is to be void; otherwise to remain in full force and virtue.

IN WITNESS WHEREOF, the above-bounden parties have executed this instrument under their several seals on the date indicated above, the name and corporate seal of each corporate party being hereto affixed, and these presents duly signed by its undersigned representative, pursuant to authority of its governing body.

SIGNATURES:

Contractor Signature _____

Print Contractor Name _____ Date _____

Contracting Firm Name _____

Complete Address _____

Tax ID# _____

Bonding Agent Signature _____

Print Agent's Name _____ Date _____

Bonding Company Name _____

Complete Address _____

Tax ID# _____

NOTARY:

STATE OF _____ COUNTY OF _____

I do hereby certify that (Contractor Name) _____, and (Agent

name)_____ personally appeared before me this day and

executed this document. Witness my hand and notary seal, this ____ day of _____, 20____.

Notary Signature _____ My commission expires _____

(Notary Seal Here)

GLOSSARY OF INSURANCE TERMS

If you are ever in the position of having to make an insurance claim, it will help you to talk to the agent in her own language. I am not an insurance expert. The definitions below are taken in part from a textbook called *Principles of Insurance* by R. I. Mehr and E. Cammack. Please consult a qualified insurance professional if you have questions.

ABSOLUTE LIABILITY, also known as liability without fault, occurs when public policy demands that a person be held liable for injury to others although the injury may be neither intentionally nor negligently inflicted. This one is tricky.

A **BOND** is a three-party contract that protects the property owner by holding the bonding agent responsible for the contractor's performance of the construction contract. A bond involves three parties: a principal (the contractor) who promises performance; a surety (the bonding agent) who guarantees fulfillment; and a third party called the obligee (the property owner) to whom these promises are made. If the principal (the contractor) does not achieve what was promised (the contract), the surety (the bonding agent) must indemnify (compensate and hold harmless) the obligee (the property owner). The surety is called upon only if the principal fails to live up to the agreement.

BREACH OF CONTRACT involving skilled tradespersons is the violation of an implied warranty to render the service for which the professionals have been hired.

COMBINED GENERAL LIABILITY COVERAGE includes both property damage and personal injury insurance. There are two ways that liability coverage can be underwritten:

- Under an *occurrence-basis* policy: if the insured event happens during the policy period, but is not discovered until after that policy has expired, the insurer is still obligated to defend and pay for any claims.
- Under a *claims-made-basis* policy: the insurer is obligated only for the defense and payment of those claims made against the insured while the policy is in force.

CONTRIBUTORY NEGLIGENCE occurs when the plaintiff's conduct (the person complaining of the injury) failed to meet the standard required for his or her own protection and safety, and that failure contributed to the cause of the loss. (If you intend to occupy your property during the construction period, read this paragraph again!)

A **HAZARD** is the cause of the peril that was the cause of the loss. For example, the fact that your house burned down is the loss; the fire that burned it is the peril; but that old electric space heater was the cause of the fire, and so the space heater was the hazard.

INSURANCE is a system for reducing risk by combining a sufficient number of policyholders to make their individual losses collectively predictable. All policyholders in the pool share the cost of a predictable loss proportionately, which lowers the individual's cost of protection.

An **INSURANCE CERTIFICATE** summarizes the characteristics of the policy or contract. A certificate is not a contract, although it does describe the contract.

An **INSURANCE CONTRACT** is an agreement for the insurance underwriter to provide indemnity, or compensation for loss or injury, to the insured. This contract is also called the *insurance policy*.

LIABILITY ASSUMED UNDER CONTRACT transfers one party's liabilities to another. The contractor who buys insurance transfers his liabilities to the insurance underwriter.

LIABILITY INSURANCE POLICIES are two-party contracts under which the contract between the insurer and the insured benefits a third party; the insurer agrees to indemnify the injured third party under circumstances that are carefully defined by the terms of the policy.

LOSS is the unintentional decline in or disappearance of value, arising from a contingency (an unexpected event). A good example of a loss might be that your house burned down. You have "lost" your home. A loss must be unintentional, must be definable, must have a calculable value, and must be confirmable in order for a claim to result in compensation.

NEGLIGENCE is when a person fails to use ordinary care or prudence in conducting his or her affairs and as a result causes others to suffer bodily injury or property damage.

OWNERS' AND CONTRACTORS' PROTECTIVE LIABILITY INSURANCE protects the insured against liability for actions of independent contractors, including liability due to the insured's failure in supervising independent contractors' work. Some obligations, such as the owner's

obligation to protect the public, cannot be transferred or delegated to the contractor. The owner may be sued even though the contractor uses great care—as well as when the contractor fails to provide appropriate safety measures. Protection of this sort is sometimes called *builders' risk insurance*.

PERIL is the cause of a loss. An example of a peril would be a fire. Specific perils might be covered in an insurance policy only if they were capable of producing a loss so large that the insured could not bear such loss without economic distress. Buying insurance that would protect you from the peril of a broken shoelace, for example, would not make sense.

RISK is uncertainty concerning loss. Insurance underwriters can calculate, based on experience, a probability of certain risks being present under certain circumstances.

STRICT LIABILITY is most commonly applied to products, when manufacturers and vendors of goods are held liable for injuries caused by defective products sold by them, regardless of the manufacturers' fault or negligence. To prove strict liability, the claimant must prove that the product was both defective and unreasonably dangerous.

WORKERS' COMPENSATION is insurance that allows employers to compensate workers injured on the job or workers who develop work-related diseases.

- Construction work will stir up dust, mildew, and other irritants that could cause severe health problems.
- You may have a hard time maneuvering safely around extension cords, scattered debris, and building materials.
- Your presence will be a distraction to the workers.
- A contractor can work faster in an empty space than in an occupied one, and when he saves time, you save money, so the most *cost-effective* decision you can make is to move yourself and all your personal effects *out*.

If you are considering trying to occupy the space during the work period, test your decision by preparing a plan for minimum occupancy that would give the contractor maximum free space. Could you live in only your master bedroom and bath for three to six months? How would you prepare your meals? What would you do about securing your valuables?

The Deposit Dilemma

If you can arrange it, do not give your contractor a deposit; pay him only for work that is completed, that complies with the construction drawings and specifications, and that meets your quality standards. However, there are times when paying a deposit is appropriate:

- If you are using a very small contractor. One-man businesses and handyman services, for example, struggle with cash flow as a matter of course.
- If you are ordering expensive items that have to be prefabricated by a third party way ahead of installation. For example, if you have selected kitchen cabinets made of some exotic and rare wood, the fabricator would not be willing to invest her money on your

behalf without getting a partial payment from you first. Your general contractor would be the one you give the check to because the work is in the contract you signed with him.
- If you want to hire a big shot who is in such great demand that he has lots of other lucrative alternatives. If you won't give him his deposit, someone else will.

In the first two examples, the contractor should be asking for just enough of a deposit so that he can get his crew started. In the third case, the contractor will ask for as much as he can get.

If you pay a deposit, be sure you know what it's for, record it, and get a signed receipt from the general contractor.

Find an Attorney

Things can go wrong despite your careful planning, and if they do, you'll want to have established a relationship with an attorney with a specialty in construction law. These attorneys get repeat business and referrals from *contractors*; you're just a one-job wonder. You have to be proactive and make this contact before you even begin work.

Sources for reliable referrals include your local and state bar associations, the clerk of the court in your county courthouse, other lawyers, local homeowners' associations, property managers and developers, the local chapter of the National Association of Home Builders, Realtors, nonprofit agencies that build affordable housing, and your local government's housing department. Once you have a few good lists of names, follow up with calls and interviews, and make your decision. Follow the protocols in Chapter 3, now as always, with two minor changes.

When you've found a candidate you like who is willing to work with you, schedule a short meeting and use your first meeting wisely. If you're dealing with a firm (as opposed to a sole practitioner), ask which attorney would represent you. Meet that person, include her in this first meeting if possible, and learn something about her background such as how long she has been practicing construction law and what kinds of disputes she has helped to settle.

Immediately after the interview, send a reiterate-and-confirm letter that recounts what you told the attorney about your project (in one sentence), what services she has agreed to provide, and what fee she has quoted you (usually an hourly rate). This will accomplish a few things for you:

- The attorney will develop some respect for your good sense because you wrote a letter like this.
- She will have to create a file with your name on it to put this letter into.
- There is a record of what you discussed, what she advised you to do, and a fee quote.
- If you don't call her again for six months, she'll have something to remind her of your project and her commitment.

Set the Terms of Your Construction Contract

Administrative issues, such as when and how the contractor will be paid, are not addressed in the construction drawings and specifications, but they must be addressed in the construction contract somewhere.

Every contract is made up of two parts: the "What Are We Going to Do?" part, and the "How Are We Going to Do It?" part. The construction drawings and specifications are the "What" part, and the Terms and Conditions Statement (also called General and Special Conditions) is the "How" part. A complete construction contract would include both the construction drawings (which your architect is working on right now) and the Terms and Conditions Statement.

You'll find a copy of a battle-tested Terms and Conditions Statement in the appendix. It will protect you, in plain English, from every problem I've ever encountered on a remodeling project; it has never failed. You are welcome to use it. That's why it's there.

There are other Terms and Conditions Statements available, of course. You may want to have a look at the American Institute of Architects (AIA) standard contract between owner and contractor, or you may want to call your local chapter of the National Association of Home Builders to see what the contractors like to use. You'll find that the appendix contains everything that these other contracts do, and more. I'm on your side; the other documents are designed to protect the people who paid for them to be written.

Project Files

Good project files keep your documents available, organized, secure, and mobile. A simple accordion file, a banker's box with twelve hanging folders, or a 3-inch ring binder with twelve tab dividers will do. Create the following file categories using abbreviations that you'll recognize three years from now.

1. Real Estate Documents and Valuations
2. Planning, Master Plan, and Project Budget
3. Home Inspection Contract and Report
4. Architect's Contract and Design Documents
5. Consulting Agreements and Soft-Costs Accounting
6. Hazard Treatment Assessment & Remediation Documents
7. Contractor Interview Logs, Bid Packages, and Negotiations

8. Construction Contract and Change Orders
9. Progress Evaluations, Copies of Contractor Checks, and Construction Accounting
10. Periodic/Informal Site Reports and Photos
11. Correspondence
12. Punch List and Warranty Claims

The only important document that won't fit in a box or your binder will be the complete original set of your construction contract documents. Construction drawings are usually created on sheets of paper that are at least 24 by 32 inches, often larger. Purchase a cardboard tube from an art or architectural supplies store; roll up this pristine, original set; place it carefully in the tube; and store that tube somewhere there is no chance it will get damaged or be exposed to high temperatures or humidity.

Keep a copy of just the Terms and Conditions Statement (with the signatures and the work schedule) in your file.

You will also have a *copy* set of the complete package, including the drawings. Keep this set handy, maybe in the trunk of your car. You will be referring to it every week.

Remodeling Is a Team Sport
Since you and the general contractor are going to be the only parties who sign the contract, you are, by definition, the only decision makers, and you are the only parties who ought to be talking to each other.

You have your team—your spouse or partner and your friends, a designer, perhaps an engineer, and maybe a remodeling coach like me. Add your behind-the-scenes advisers—your nosy neighbor, your nephew who is in his sophomore year of architecture school, and your best shopping buddy—and

you can imagine how important controlling who talks to whom can become. We may all offer helpful advice, but we're not going to pay for the results—you are.

Your general contractor has his team too—the plumber, the electrician, other subcontractors, perhaps a superintendent—all of whom have a particular job to do, but none of whom have the legal or financial responsibility for the project as a whole like the general contractor does.

The rule is: Team captain talks to team captain. If either captain allows any of the players to cross the line, the captain will be liable for any expense incurred. It behooves you both to enforce the boundaries.

Choosing Who Will Be the Contractor's Boss
You always get to be the boss when it's your house and your money, but if you have a legal partner, the two of you must decide which one will be the contractor's only contact—who will answer questions and communicate your (joint) decisions. You and your partner can have disagreements and discussions in private, but never in front of the contractor; not if you want the job to go smoothly.

If you need to designate someone who is not one of the property owners to be your decision maker, you must execute a *limited power of attorney* so that the individual you have designated has the right to act on your behalf. Once you have done this—once you are no longer the decision maker—you must live with whatever your agent decides, and you must pay for it as well. On pages 84 and 85 is a sample limited power of attorney for your review.

Incidentally, although there is no law against changing your mind, if you rescind the power of attorney, or refuse to honor it once work has started, you will scare everybody, and the work will slow down or may come to an abrupt halt. You don't want that to happen.

The Contractor Is Not Your Guest

Contractors need to get in and get out and to stay focused on the quality of their work while they're there. That's how they make their money and build their business, and that's their goal. During the project work schedule, your home becomes their place of business.

Forget what your mother told you about treating people in your home as guests. Just stay out of the contractor's way. The more clear space you can give him, the faster he will work, the less he will have to pay his laborers, the less likely he will be to look for shortcuts, the more motivated he'll be to keep his crew on the job, and the happier you'll be with the end product.

Don't go get a pizza for the guys' lunch. Don't have a fresh pot of coffee brewed when they all arrive in the morning. Don't bring treats. Expect their respect, but don't demand their attention unless it's necessary.

Subcontractor Complaints

If a subcontractor complains to you about not being paid, advise him to take this matter up with the general contractor directly. Stay out of it! There may be a very good reason why the general contractor is withholding a payment, or he may not be withholding it at all. If more than one subcontractor complains of late payments, this may be a sign of a pretty big problem. We'll talk more about this in Chapter 5 in the first section, 5.1, about disputes.

Side Deals

If a *sub*contractor comes to you with a special deal, thank him, but discuss it with the general contractor. The subcontractor may have a great idea, but the general is the one responsible to the city inspectors, and the only one who can tell you what your options are.

Emergency Communications

The only time you should discuss anything at all with a subcontractor is in an emergency, when neither the general nor his superintendent is on site. Leaky pipes and sparking electrical lines would qualify as emergencies. As soon as the situation is under control, place an urgent call to your general contractor and let him know what has happened. Ask him to come within twenty-four hours to meet with you and the subcontractor who helped you, to determine the cause and to fix the problem before the work goes any further.

The Importance of Timely Complaints

If you've asked the contractor to paint the bathroom orange and you notice that his subcontractor is painting it purple, *say something!* Contact the general contractor right away and discuss the problem only with him. He will redirect the painter.

If you express your concerns while the tradesman is still on-site with his tools and materials, the general will appreciate it because it won't cost anything to get the sub to correct the work. If you wait until the tradesman has finished and the general has to call him back, the general will have to pay the sub to return.

Your architect just called; your drawings are ready for bid. Are you ready to start talking to contractors?

Limited Power of Attorney for Property Owner's Agent Form

(PAGE 1 OF 2)

Project Property Address _____

Property Owner:

Name _____

Mailing Address _____

Home Phone _____ Business Phone _____

Fax _____ Mobile Phone _____

Owner's Agent:

Name _____

Mailing Address _____

Home Phone _____ Business Phone _____

Fax _____ Mobile Phone _____

Property Owner hereby designates and appoints the person listed above as his/her legal Agent, to act in their name and stead, in the following ways:

- To make decisions about the extent and type of renovation work to be done on the project property listed above

- To select bidders, review bids, and offer a contract

- To sign the construction contract and commit the Property Owner's funds to renovation work under the contract

- To identify, negotiate, and execute any change orders required during the construction period

- To approve or reject the contractor's work

- To approve and release, or withhold for a specific cause, payments to the contractor

Limited Power of Attorney for Property Owner's Agent Form

This instrument is drawn and executed with the express intention that all powers and duties here-under conferred upon the agent shall be in compliance with and shall continue in effect pursuant to the provisions of State of _____ general statute #_____ unless or until this instrument is specifically withdrawn or nullified in writing and signed by the Property Owner, or until the renovation work at the project property is complete and the contractor has been paid in full, whichever comes first. Property Owner hereby ratifies and confirms that all things done by this Agent, within the scope of authority spelled out above, shall be done in the Property Owner's name and with his/her full approval and support.

Property Owner _____ Date _____

Agent _____ Date _____

NOTARY:

STATE OF _____ COUNTY OF _____

I do hereby certify that (Owner Name) _____, and (Agent

name) _____ personally appeared before me this day and

executed this Limited Power of Attorney. Witness my hand and notary seal, this _____ day of

_____, 20_____.

Notary Signature _____ My commission expires _____

(Notary Seal Here)

4.3 THE GENERAL CONTRACTOR

The perfect contractor has integrity, excellent references, years of experience, the ability to communicate complicated information clearly, a pleasant temperament, and fair prices. Wherever will you find such a paragon?

Can You Act As Your Own General Contractor?

All the property owners I have ever worked with have considered acting as their own general contractors—doing some of the work themselves, and hiring the subs directly—despite the fact that they had no experience managing a construction crew and were not prepared to take on all of the risks and obligations that traditionally fall on the general contractor's shoulders. I suspect they thought they would have more control, which helped them feel less anxious, and that they would save money by cutting out the middle man.

It's been my observation that owners who act as their own general contractors will pay much more for the job before it's over, and will take much longer to finish than those who have the good sense to leave this complicated task to an experienced practitioner.

Here are a few reasons why being your own general contractor won't work the way you think it will, and definitely won't save you money:
- You'll have a hard time getting subcontractors to come when you call. They will finish jobs for their regular customers (established general contractors) first, then come to work on your job when they have nothing else to do. This will stretch out your construction schedule by quite a bit. If you told me you had an electrician who was sitting by the phone waiting for your call, I'd have to wonder why he had no other work.
- You'll soon grow tired of working every weekend, and your resentment will show. Any problems you and your mate had before you started will be magnified when you are tired, unavailable, frustrated, and impatient.
- The more experienced the construction *team* is, the more efficiently they can work and the more quickly they can finish (which saves you money). You will not have the benefit of long relationships with your subs, and your team members may not even know one another.
- You won't know how to coordinate the work on the site. In anticipation of foul-ups and wasted time, the subs will *raise* their prices, and they won't miss a chance to stay ahead of their costs by charging you aggravation tax as well as real costs for mistakes. They have to protect themselves.
- You will not want to be in a position of insuring your subcontractors' work when they don't have adequate (or any) insurance.
- You won't have any negotiating leverage. Not only are you inexperienced, but you have nothing to barter with—you don't have any future work to offer. And if you think withholding a check will motivate a sub to work harder for you, you are sadly mistaken. The sub will walk.

Your best option is to engage a general contractor with integrity, glowing references, and years and years of experience doing projects *just like yours*. It will actually save you money and speed up the process considerably, and all of the financial risk will be on his shoulders—where it should be. Your job is to be the boss. Honest.

How Do You Find a Good General Contractor?

Select your contractor carefully. He's going to bring muddy strangers with saws and hammers and drills into your home when you're not there. This relationship is at high risk for frayed nerves and quick-tempered misunderstandings . . . compelling reasons to put some serious time and energy into your search for the perfect contractor.

Good referrals might come from many resources, including (but promise me, not exclusively) from your next-door neighbor. Try calling home equity lenders first. They inspect the work they're funding before they release checks, and they've seen lots of job sites. Try calling a good residential architect or two, the local chapters of both the National Association of Home Builders and the American Institute of Architects, property insurance agents, Realtors, and anyone else you can think of who might use, or monitor the work of, good contractors on a regular basis.

Interviewing Contractors and Their References

Your best protection against disputes is to *check references*. Find out everything you can about your candidates. Find out where their mother-in-law goes to church and what color socks they wear on Wednesdays. Dig, dig, dig!

Good recruiters use interview strategies that draw out both the facts and the candidate's real feelings about the subjects they are discussing. We can learn a lot from the masters, and by using their techniques we can get to the essence of who our candidates really are and what they really have to offer.

Here are a few good interviewing tips:

- Humility helps. In this instance, the candidate usually knows more about the subject than the interviewer; motivate the contractors to share their expertise with you. It may not be a bad idea to frame some questions as if you were asking for advice. That may loosen your candidate's tongue, and it will certainly tell you how good they are at solving problems, a skill you're going to have to rely on once work begins.

- If you think they're not being candid with you, ask a question in three different ways at three different times during the interview; the third answer will usually be the truth.

- Ask questions that must be answered in paragraphs; avoid questions that can be answered in one word.

- Listen hard. Definitely listen more than you talk. We all have thousands of words in our vocabularies. At some level we are choosing the words we use. They mean something and they give away lots of secrets. You have heard of Dr. Freud?

- If you can get your candidate to talk about a past problem, notice if he takes responsibility for his own actions.

- Listen for references to a long history of happy clients and a "family" of subcontractors who have worked with him for years and without conflict.

Before you are done checking on him, find out if he has ever been in serious trouble by contacting the contractors state license board, the Better Business Bureau, the state attorney general's office, and the state department of insurance.

At the end of this section there are interview logs that suggest questions you may want to ask each contractor and each of their references, and room for you to make notes on their answers. If you are serious about doing a thorough background check—and I hope you are—you're going to do at least ten interviews to check out each candidate—one with the general contractor, five with clients, three with subs and vendors, and at least one with a consumer protection agency. By the time you're done, if you haven't kept notes, you'll forget who said what about whom. The interview logs will help you keep everything straight, and they'll also remind you to ask all of the interviewees the same questions, giving them all an opportunity to address the same issues. That way you can compare their statements and look for inconsistencies.

Will Any Good Contractor Do?

Typically, the good *new-construction* contractor is a production builder and a good businessman. When you build a house from the ground up, you have no existing conditions to work around, so work can move along at a predictable pace. When the schedule is predictable, the contractor's risk of losing money is minimized.

A new-construction contractor who is asked to do a remodel will want to create the open work areas he is used to by removing your drywall or plaster. The alternative is that he'll try to use remodeling work techniques without having the proper experience. Either of these alternatives will add considerably to your costs without bringing you any benefit.

The good *remodeling* contractor is an artisan, a craftsman. Remodeling contractors have to solve problems as they arise and work around obstacles they can't see, which makes the work schedule unpredictable. Under these conditions,

the risk of losing money on the job is pretty high. Experience is the key. The more often your remodeling contractor has worked on projects just like yours, the more apt he is to be able to control his work schedule, and the less apt you are to argue over unanticipated costs.

What Is the Difference Between the General Contractor and a Subcontractor?

The general contractor (also called "GC" or "the general") has a basic understanding of the work in every trade, knows which subs have the right skills for your project, hires the best subs he (you) can afford, insures them, warrants their work, sets and monitors the schedule, and pays everybody from the checks you give him. He shoulders all the risk, and he reports to you.

The subcontractors report to the general contractor. They do only the work in their trade, their insurance has to meet only the requirements that the general contractor sets, and they must follow his orders—not yours—to get paid. If you try to direct or redirect the work of a subcontractor, you'll be showing your inexperience and confusing the whole lot of them.

Contractors' Licensing Requirements

There are state laws that govern the licensing of persons who represent themselves as general contractors.

Ask your state department of insurance, the local chapter of the National Association of Home Builders, or the contractors state license board about contractor licensing requirements in your state. The contractors state license board keeps files on license holders. Ask how long your candidates have been licensed. Ask how you would know if a license were to lapse or be revoked during the work period, and how that might affect your rights under the licensing laws. Also ask if any of your candidates have been involved in complaint proceedings or lawsuits, or have had their licenses pulled or allowed them to lapse within the last five years or so. A lapsed or revoked license is usually a sign of legal or financial trouble.

There are different levels of contractor licenses that set different upper limits on the value of the contracts the contractor can sign. Ask the licensing board if the contractors you're talking to have the appropriate licenses to do work up to the amount of your Total Construction Budget (including your allowance for surprise costs).

What, exactly, does the fact that the contractor has a license mean to you? To earn his license, the contractor must pass an exam about the building code and must set aside an escrow fund of several thousand dollars as evidence of his financial solvency. This means that he knows what the code requires and that he will probably be able to keep his subs paid and working pretty steadily. That's good. But I must tell you that I once had a secretary who was a licensed general contractor. She'd never seen a job site and didn't know which end of the screwdriver was supposed to hit the nail, but she passed the test and had the cash to show the state.

In some states, using a licensed contractor means that the state provides you with protection, a sort of general warranty fund, that you wouldn't have access to if you used an unlicensed contractor. It has been my experience that you can consider this additional protection as useful to you as a contractor's general liability insurance policy. That is, you may be able to make a claim to either insurance if the contractor leaves behind significant structural problems, but short of that it will be difficult to get support.

Bidding the Work

Detailed, competitive bids will tell you the actual market value of every task in your project, and, if you read between the lines, they'll tell you whether your drawings are clear and complete. You may invite as many contractors to bid as you wish, but my experience has taught me that if your contractors feel there is too much competition, which would lower their odds of winning the job, it will be the *better* contractors, the ones who have other lucrative options, who will walk away. Three really good bids ought to give you all the information and options you need.

Contractors who prefer not to be open about where their costs are, those who won't compete or who won't provide a price for each task on your final Task Abstract List, may propose an alternative. Other pricing schemes go by lots of different names, but in the end you'll either pay a lump sum or pay for time and materials.

- A *lump sum* pricing scheme sets one fixed price for everything—all of the work plus the general's markup. Changes will be extra. How will you know how much he should credit you when you delete work, and how will you know what to pay him for the work he has partially completed if you don't know the value of each completed task? Do you trust him to tell you what you're supposed to pay him? We'll talk more about calculating fair payments in a minute.
- *Time and materials* ("T&M") and *cost-plus* pricing systems allow the contractor to bill you for time (labor—based on some unverifiable time-tracking system) and materials (based on receipts from his vendors) with a fixed

(negotiated) percentage of each bill as a markup for his overhead and profit margin. Whatever the final cost of the job is, you will have paid for every bit of it. The contractor is refusing to take any responsibility. Changes are incorporated in the invoices as the job progresses at whatever they cost the contractor, even if the changes are required because he made a mistake.

Materials invoices represent deals made between the contractor and his vendor. How will you know what he actually paid for anything? And it will be difficult to monitor the number of hours an electrician spends on the site, even if you install a punch-clock. When a contractor offers you a T&M or a cost-plus contract, it is most often because he wants to protect himself from all risk.

In my opinion, these pricing alternatives are not conducive to developing or maintaining trust between you and the contractor. If you sign a contract under any pricing system other than a detailed cost breakdown, your contractor will have control of your costs. Do you want that?

4.4 THE BID CYCLE

So you're going to competitively bid your job. I'm happy to hear it. Competitive bids help you keep your costs down, you'll finally know what the market value of your job is, and the bids will tell you—before you begin work— whether or not your drawings are clear and complete.

When you have selected three great contractors, mail each of them an Invitation to Bid (see page 97). They should receive it about ten days prior to the walk-through date. They're busy and need time to clear their schedules.

Preparing a Bid Package

You are going to invite all three contractors to meet at your home at the same time. Yes, you are. It's the only way to ensure that they all hear exactly the same information and make the same assumptions while they're preparing the bids. As a bonus, this will minimize misunderstandings and disputes once work begins. Reminding them that they are competing for the job won't hurt either, and nobody will have the opportunity to settle in at the kitchen table and talk your ears off either. There are lots of good reasons to manage the bid this way.

Prepare for the bid meeting by assembling a package that includes all of the forms listed below. Samples of all the forms are included in this book, most of them in this chapter.

- *A neighborhood map* indicating the location of the project property;
- *Another neighborhood map* indicating where the contractors should submit their bids, if that address is different from the project address;
- *A site survey* of your property if you have one, especially if you plan to build an addition or add a new deck;
- *Instructions to Bidders*, which explain very briefly how the bids must be prepared and how the project will be conducted;
- *A copy of the Contract Terms and Conditions Statement* (see the appendix for a sample, or use another general conditions statement of your choice) so the bidders know the terms of the contract they'll be signing if they win;
- *A Bid Summary Form*, which asks your bidder to tell you which licensed subs he plans to use, when he can start, and how long he thinks the job will take; attests that he has seen the site (so he can't charge extra for conditions he was made aware of at the walk-through); and ensures that he's read the contract (so that he knows what he'll be responsible for).

General Contractor Interview Log

Firm Owner's Name _____ Date _____

Company Name _____

Company Address _____

Tax ID _____ Mobile _____ Office _____

Introduction: I'm a homeowner who intends to do a substantial remodel on a [size and style of home, e.g., 2,300-square-foot 1950s Tudor] in [area or neighborhood designation, e.g., in a suburb north of Atlanta]. I've spoken to [professional(s) that gave you his name, e.g., Jane Doe at the ABC Homeowner's Association] and they suggested that you might be the best contractor for me. Do you have a few minutes to answer some questions? [Do not make a face-to-face appointment at this point.]

How did you get into this business?

Describe the last three jobs you completed.

What sorts of surprises do you expect we'll find in my home, based on your experience with similar structures?

Why do so many contractors seem uncomfortable about submitting a detailed bid?

As I understand it, state law determines when a contractor has to carry workers' comp insurance. What is the trigger? Do you have this insurance?

What do you think I should do to beef up my own insurance?

How do you handle hidden problems? I have a stain on one wall of my dining room but can't see behind it to figure out what's going on.

What strategies do you use to keep the work moving quickly?

What sorts of things can I do to help you do your best work for me?

General Contractor Interview Log

If we were to strongly disagree about something, what do you think would be the best way for us to come to consensus? Is there anything I'm not asking that I should be asking?

Would you provide me with a few references, please?

Notes _____

_____

_____

_____

_____

_____

_____

_____

List of client references with similar projects completed in the last two years

	Owner Name	Project Address	Daytime Phone
1)			
2)			
3)			
4)			
5)			
6)			
7)			
8)			

General Contractor Interview Log

List of subcontractor references

1) _____   _____
   Contact Name   Trade

   _____   _____
   Company Name   Office Phone

2) _____   _____
   Contact Name   Trade

   _____   _____
   Company Name   Office Phone

3) _____   _____
   Contact Name   Trade

   _____   _____
   Company Name   Office Phone

List of vendor references

1) _____   _____
   Contact Name   Trade

   _____   _____
   Company Name   Office Phone

2) _____   _____
   Contact Name   Trade

   _____   _____
   Company Name   Office Phone

3) _____   _____
   Contact Name   Trade

   _____   _____
   Company Name   Office Phone

Past Client Interview Log

General Contractor Name _____ Date _____

Client Name _____ Project Address _____

Introduction: I understand that you had some work done by [name of general contractor]. He suggested that I call you; that you might be willing to provide him with a reference. Would you be willing to spend a few minutes talking to me?

What is the age and architectural style of your home? When did you do your remodel?

Who was your designer? What were some of your design challenges?

How did you find this contractor? What convinced you that he'd be a good candidate?

What sort of work was included in your project?

How many other general contractors did you get prices from before you signed your contract with him? Was he the low bidder?

Remodeling can be a little scary. What was your biggest concern, and how did his behavior help set your mind at ease?

How many changes did you make once work started? How did he handle changes? Who determined what the cost of the change would be?

How did he maintain the work momentum on the site?

How did you monitor his work?

How did you determine when he should get paid? Who initiated the payment process?

What would you say were his strongest and weakest skills as a contractor?

What kind of problems have you called him about since the job ended?

Was there ever a time when you needed to reach the general contractor but couldn't? What was going on at that time? How did you resolve the problem?

Is there anything you'd like to tell me that I'm not asking about?

Subcontractor Interview Log

General Contractor Name _____ Date _____

Subcontractor Company Name _____ Contact _____

Tax ID# _____ Office Phone _____

Introduction: [Name of general contractor] gave me your name and suggested that you might be able to provide a reference for him. Can you spare a minute or two to answer a few questions?

How long have you known this general contractor?

How frequently do you work for him?

How many (other) general contractors do you work for on a regular basis?

Do you trust this contractor to set your price, or does he consult you before he submits a bid?

Do you work on a handshake or do you have written contracts?

How does this contractor determine when you get paid?

How does he maintain the work momentum on the site?

Was there ever a time when you needed to reach the general contractor but couldn't? What was going on at that time? How did you resolve the problem?

What would you say were his strongest and weakest skills as a general contractor?

What age and style of home do you most often work on?

Have you ever done [briefly describe your project] with this general contractor? [Ask about the other project and find out when the work was completed. Is that project on the list of references?]

If you were to discover a problem while you were working in my house, how would you handle it?

If you had a good idea—one that might save me some money—what would you do about it?

Vendor Interview Log

General Contractor Name _____ Date _____

Vendor Name _____ Contact _____

Tax ID# _____ Office Phone _____

Introduction: [Name of general contractor] gave me your name as a reference. Would you take two or three minutes to answer some questions for me?

How long have you known this general contractor?

What kind of materials do you most often sell him?

How frequently is he in your shop?

Do you extend him a credit line, or would you do so if he asked for one?

Do you deliver to the site, or does he send someone to pick up the materials?

Have you ever done custom fabricating or made special orders for him? If so, did you require a deposit beforehand?

Does he consult you before he submits a bid so that he has exact prices, or does he pretty much know what you're going to charge him? If your costs have gone up and he hasn't allowed enough in the bid to pay you properly, how do you resolve this?

How does this contractor ensure that your products will be available when he needs them?

Have your product prices fluctuated a lot lately? Do you hold your price once you've quoted a job, or do you raise your price whenever you have to cover new costs?

If the contractor discovered a defect in any of your materials, how would you address that?

How does this contractor determine when you get paid?

Was there ever a time when you needed to reach the general contractor but couldn't? What was going on at that time? How did you resolve the problem?

Invitation to Bid Form

Project Property Address _____

Pre-Bid Walk-through Date/Time _____

Bid Due Date/Time _____

You are invited to submit a bid for the renovation of the property listed above.

You must attend the scheduled pre-bid walk-through in order for your bid to be accepted.

You will receive instructions and bid forms at the pre-bid walk-through, and may inspect the property and all areas of work at that time.

If you wish, you may pick up the bid package prior to that walk-through by calling the name and number listed below. However, no questions will be answered and access to the site is denied prior to the formal walk-through.

Submit bids by hand or by mail to:

Name _____

Address _____

City/State/Zip _____

in a sealed envelope that says "BID" no later than the date and time specified above.

Bid prices must be guaranteed for sixty days from the bid submittal date.

If you have any questions, please call.

Name _____   Phone _____

Thank you.

Instructions to Bidders Form

(PAGE 1 OF 2)

Project Property Address _____

You are invited to submit a bid for the renovation of the property listed above.

SUBMITTING A BID

Bidding contractors must be able to commit a construction crew exclusively to this project within sixty days of the submittal of this bid. Contractors who are not prepared to do this are asked not to submit bids.

The enclosed bid forms must be used to submit a bid on this project. Any changes to these forms, missing information, or any other irregularities in the bid package may be cause for rejection of the bid and disqualification of the bidding contractor.

Bidders must submit the following to the owner at the time and place indicated below:
• the INSTRUCTIONS TO BIDDERS form, signed and dated, and
• the BID SUMMARY FORM, completed and signed, and
• the BID BREAKDOWN FORM with individual task item pricing, and
• a WORKERS' COMPENSATION DISCLOSURE form, and
• a copy of your state GENERAL CONTRACTOR'S LICENSE if your bid will exceed licensing limits set by state law.

SEALED BIDS are due at: _____

on (date): _____, no later than (time): _____.

ABOUT THE DESIGN DOCUMENTS

The project property will be made available at a scheduled pre-bid walk-through meeting so that the contractor may inspect all existing conditions that will be disturbed or otherwise affected by the proposed work. Contractors are encouraged to ask questions of the property owner or the owner's agent or technical adviser at that meeting, in order to be sure they understand the intent of the design documents.

All work indicated on any document in the bid package is included in the scope of work, and it is conclusively presumed that the contractor has accounted for the cost of all such items in his bid price.

Details of all site conditions, installation instructions, and work methods are not spelled out in these documents. Plans are diagrammatic and not intended to indicate all details. The general contractor is responsible for confirming all dimensions and conditions on-site, and for executing the work in conformance with all regulations, ordinances, and codes, and in accordance with the highest prevailing standards of craftsmanship.

Instructions to Bidders Form

Overhead and profit margins are to be included with every line-item price, not separated from the work costs.

ABOUT DOING THE WORK AND GETTING PAID

Work may not begin until the contractor executes a contract with the property owner, they agree on a start date, and the contractor secures and provides to the owner all required insurance, bonds, permits, licenses, and so forth, as required in the contract terms and conditions statement included in this bid package.

Payments are tied to work momentum; contractor must complete set percentages of work in order to be eligible for a payment. Payments will be issued about once a month, and within three to five business days after the value of work complete is agreed upon and the percent-complete target has been met.

There is a penalty for missing the completion date.

SELECTING THE WINNING BIDDER

In making a final selection for the award of the general construction contract, consideration will be given to the proposed work schedule, and to the proposed subcontractors, as well as to the contractor's references and prices. The owner reserves the right to reject any and all bids or to waive any formalities in the bid process, except those bound by law.

ATTEST

Contractor attests that he/she has understood and agrees to comply with the instructions listed above:

Company Name _____

Owner's Signature _____

Print Owner's Name _____ Date _____

Office Phone _____

Mobile Phone _____

Beeper _____

Bid Summary Form

Project Property Address _____

Walk-through Date _____

Sealed bid is due at: _____

Before: _____ p.m. on: _____

1. I have inspected the project property. I have familiarized myself with the plans and specifications dated _____, given to me as design documents for this project, and understand the character and extent of the work as described.

2. I have read and I agree to abide by the Terms and Conditions of the contract. I understand the construction standards and my other contractual responsibilities.

3. I propose to furnish all labor, materials, equipment, permits, and insurance necessary to perform the work according to highest prevailing professional standards, for the lump sum of $ _____, excluding all Alternates.

The proposed price is based on the attached Bid Breakdown Form. If the total of all individual prices on the Bid Breakdown Form do not add up to the same number as the lump sum bid above, the lower number shall stand as my bid price.

4. If I am offered a contract for this project, I am available to begin work on _____, and I believe I can complete the project in _____ weeks.

5. I propose to use the following subcontractors on this project:

Electrical _____ License # _____

Plumbing _____ License # _____

Mechanical _____ License # _____

6. This bid will be good for sixty days. If a contract is not executed before that time expires, I may decline the contract or propose a renegotiation of the contract price.

7. I testify that I have not colluded with any other person or firm with regard to the submission of this bid.

BIDDER: (General Contractor)

Company Name _____

Owner's Signature _____ Date _____

Print Owner's Name _____

Office Phone _____ Mobile Phone _____ Beeper _____

- *A Bid Breakdown* form, which is your final scope of work in a Task Abstract List format, with the costs column left blank so the contractors can fill in their bid prices for each and every task on the list;
- A complete set of drawings and specifications;
- *A Contractor's Disclosure Form for Workers' Compensation Insurance Coverage* (see Section 4.1); and
- *A Performance and Payment Bond* form if bonding will be required (see Section 4.1).

Make ten copies of this entire package so that each bidder gets two sets, and you and your designer (who will be there to answer any technical questions) each have a set. You'll have to find a local blue-printer in order to make copies of the construction drawings. Ask your designer for a resource.

Keep the *original* package in your bid file. Bring the rest of the packages to the walk-through.

Do not allow any bidder to visit the site or to ask you questions *before* the formal walk-through.

The Pre-Bid Meeting

When you look at the blueprints, you see a lot of lines and notes. When your contractor looks at them, he sees the finished space and all the work that it will take to turn what you have into what you want.

Don't feel that you have to escort experienced contractors on a tour of your home and explain your wish list. Give them the drawings and turn them loose. Here are the rules for the pre-bid walk-through:

- Allow all bidders free access to every part of the property that will be affected by the work in the project. They may take an hour or so to look at everything in the drawings. You

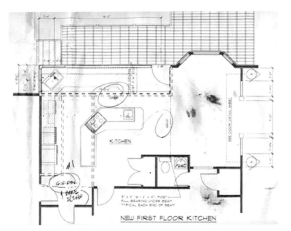

Your drawings

What the contractor envisions when he sees your drawings

The finished project

and your designer should stand quietly in the front yard, or sit quietly at the kitchen table. Be accessible, but don't be distracting.

- Do not talk to any of the bidders one-on-one. That action would imply favoritism, and the others will wonder if it means that guy's already got the job. They may drop out. You don't want that to happen.
- If one of the bidders asks a question, call all bidders together and repeat the question. When you answer it, all bidders will hear and everyone will think the same way about that issue when they are preparing their prices.
- If one of your bidders doesn't understand a vague statement in the documents, clarify, but don't change, the scope of work. You want to keep confusion and bidding errors to a minimum—you can negotiate small changes later.
- If you have a drop-dead date for completion, let the contractors know this at the walk-through, and be clear with them that there will be a penalty for missing that date.
- If you plan to vacate the space during the work period, be sure to emphasize that too, so the bidders know they can count on saving some time. Saving them time should save you money.

Make notes of all questions and of all the information that was given in response. Immediately after the walk-through, issue the same letter to each bidder summarizing all of the questions and answers that were exchanged at the site. If you use the opening and closing paragraphs in the reiterate-and-confirm letter from Chapter 3, they will be obligated to include the work in their bids and in their contract work.

Be sure to file your copy of the letter in your Contract file as a reminder that you'll

need to review these issues during the final contract negotiation.

Requests for a Second Look

Sometimes there is a particularly difficult bit of work in your project and the bidders will want to come a second time with the appropriate subcontractor and take a closer look before they price it. This is a legitimate request. Invite all bidders to this second walk-through and be sure that your designer is there as well. The questions that will be raised at this second visit will probably be more complicated and technical than those asked at the first.

If any one of the bidders tells you that he can't make the second viewing, reschedule so that all three will be able to come.

Confirm your invitation to the second meeting in writing.

If the one that made the original request is the only one that shows up at the second walk-through, that's okay. They all had the opportunity. Your invitation should clearly state that there won't be another chance.

Setting the Bid Due Date

I always ask the contractors how much time they think they'll need to complete the bid. For a contractor, a day or two more or less can be the difference between guessing and getting real prices. Sometimes it's in your best interests to let them set the bid submittal date. In most cases you ought to be able to get bids within ten days of the walk-through.

Receiving and Analyzing the Bids

Each of your three bidders has now returned a bid package to you. First check to see that each package is complete, that all bidders have returned every form they were required to return, and that all signatures are in place. If there is a form or two missing, call and get them delivered to you within twenty-four hours or that contractor's bid will be turned down. Treat documents that were not properly signed the same way. The contractors have spent a lot of time on these bids; you'll get the forms.

The documents that must be submitted with a bid are described in the Instructions to Bidders form. The contractor won't have to secure the insurance certificate or bond unless he wins the project.

The Bid Comparison Spreadsheet

One bid won't have any meaning to you, but three bids will. What you need now is a tool that will help you compare the three bids with one another and to your professional cost estimator's numbers—both line by line and bottom line to bottom line—to see if your bidders all understood the job the same way. Your Bid Form, which was derived from your final cost estimate, will be the starting point for the development of a Bid Comparison Spreadsheet. We're just going to add a few columns.

On page 104 is a Bid Comparison Spreadsheet for your review. To compare the three bids, copy all of your contractors' bid prices onto this spreadsheet. Be sure to proofread for accuracy; you'd hate to lose a great contractor because you transposed a few numbers.

Before you read any further, study my Bid Comparison Spreadsheet and circle the numbers that just don't seem right to you.

Irregularities in the Bids

Keep a copy of the Bid Comparison Spreadsheet with the original bid numbers on it in your bid file; create a duplicate on which you will integrate some adjustments, and let's see what happens. If you're using a computer spreadsheet, copy the first spreadsheet onto a blank form before you begin editing it. Never overwrite an original worksheet.

Review the editable spreadsheet to see which prices are off the mark.

If you have bids all over the map on most of the task lines, your drawings stink. There's no other explanation. But I don't expect that to happen to you because you chose an experienced and well-regarded architect, and she created a great set of drawings for you.

Here's an example of what I would do with the odd numbers:

- Line 001: Testing for hazardous materials makes Bidder #2 uncomfortable. Ask him to find an appropriate subcontractor and send you a bid number.
- Line 201 is a problem nobody can see. They clearly don't know how to estimate the repair cost. Move this work out of your contract and down to the top of your Alternates list. You'll be able to define and price a repair once demolition is completed and the damages are exposed.
- Line 202: Ask Bidder #1 to review his price and get back to you with a written confirmation or a new number.
- Line 301 is not a bid error. Bidder #1 just thinks it will take a little more work than the others do.
- Line 501 is a clerical error by Bidder #2. Don't think you'll get this work for one-tenth of what the others have bid. Ask him to review this number and confirm or revise it for you.
- Lines 502 and 601: Your cost estimate was wrong.
- Line 602 requires review and clarification by your designer. Redefine the cabinets and the door style more carefully for all three bidders and invite them all to confirm or revise their bids on this item, in writing.

Bid Comparison Spreadsheet: Small Kitchen Remodel

Sec	Item	Task List	Final Cost Est.	Bidder #1	Bidder #2	Bidder #3
000		**Treatment of Household Hazards**				
	001	Test for hazards and provide lab report	$ 600	$ 600	by others	$ 600
100		**Demolition and Site Work**				
	101	Remove and discard all existing cabs & ctrtps	$ 1,000	$ 1,000	$ 1,000	$ 1,000
	102	Remove sheet vinyl flooring and subfloor	$ 2,000	$ 2,000	$ 2,000	$ 2,000
200		**Foundation and Structure**				
	201	Repair floor framing under sink cabinet	$ 600	$ 800	$ 1,600	$ 200
	202	Install subfloor: match adjacent rms	$ 1,600	$ 1,900	$ 1,600	$ 1,600
300		**Exterior Envelope**				
	301	Repair siding at kitchen entry door	$ 400	$ 500	$ 400	$ 400
400		**Doors and Hardware**				
	401	Install louvered bifold doors at laundry	$ 600	$ 600	$ 600	$ 600
	402	Replace pantry door and hardware	$ 400	$ 400	$ 400	$ 400
	403	Replace kit. entry door w/ 1/2-glass door	$ 600	$ 600	$ 600	$ 600
500		**Windows**				
	501	Replace 1 window over sink with 2 windows	$ 2,200	$ 2,200	$ 220	$ 2,200
	502	Install new skylight over breakfast nook	$ 2,600	$ 3,000	$ 3,000	$ 3,000
600		**Interior Finishes**				
	601	Install new tile flooring	$ 3,000	$ 3,600	$ 3,600	$ 3,600
	602	Install new ABC cabinets w/door style #1	$ 24,000	$ 24,000	$ 30,000	$ 27,000
	603	Install new man-made countertops	$ 4,000	$ 4,000	$ 4,000	$ 4,000
	604	F&I refrig, D/W, Wash/Dry, and disposal	$ 4,000	$ 4,000	$ 4,000	$ 4,000
700		**Paint Prep and Painting - Int. & Ext.**				
	701	Patch drywall walls & ceiling	$ 600	$ 600	$ 600	$ 600
	702	Prime and paint interior - 3 colors	$ 2,000	$ 2,800	$ 2,200	$ 2,200
	702	Prime and paint repaired siding & kit. entry	$ 500	$ 500	$ 500	$ 500
	703	Paint new int. doors and windows over sink	$ 600	$ 600	$ 600	$ 600
800		**Plumbing**				
	801	Install new double-bowl, st.st. sink & faucet	$ 1,000	$ 1,200	$ 1,200	$ 1,200
	802	Replace plbg under sink; add shut-of valve	$ 1,500	$ 1,600	$ 1,500	
	803	Replace water heater in pantry	$ 1,000	$ 1,000	$ 1,000	$ 1,000
900		**HVAC**				
	901	Install new range hood with exhaust to ext.	$ 800	$ 800	$ 800	$ 800
1000		**Electrical**				
	1001	Install 4 new outlets over ctrtop	$ 800	$ 800	$ 800	$ 800
	1002	Upgrade circuits to appliances	$ 1,600	$ 1,600	$ 160	$ 1,600
		Total Cost	$ 58,000	$ 60,700	$ 62,380	$ 60,500
		Budget & Bid Variance	$ 56,000	108%	111%	108%
1100		**Alternates**				
	A1	Repair existing window over sink	$ 300	$ 300	$ 300	$ 300
	A2	F&I Tiffany-style chandelier in bkfst nook	$ 800	$ 800	$ 800	$ 800
	A3	Upgrade cabinet door to style #3 (net add)	$ 2,200	$ 2,200	$ 2,200	$ 2,200
	A4	Install (less expensive) XYZ Cabs (net deduct)	$ (3,000)	$ (3,000)	$ (3,000)	$ (3,000)
	A5	Install new stone countertop (net add)	$ 4,500	$ 4,500	$ 4,500	$ 4,500
	A6	Relocate new water heater into attic (net add)	$ 2,400	$ 2,400	$ 2,400	$ 2,400
	A7	F&I unvented range hood w/light (net deduct)	$ (400)	$ (400)	$ (400)	$ (400)
	A8	Install lighting under all wall-hung cabinets	$ 2,200	$ 2,200	$ 2,200	$ 2,200
	A9	Replace two existing ceiling fixtures	$ 250	$ 250	$ 250	$ 250

- Line 702: Ask Bidder #1 to review and confirm or revise his number.
- Line 802: Ask Bidder #3 to send you a price.
- Line 1002: Ask Bidder #2 to review and confirm or revise his number.

You can send one letter to each bidder that includes all of the requests that apply to that contractor. Do *not* tell them why you are asking about each of the numbers—whether their original number is high or low. Do tell them that you need written responses within five business days, that *no* response will be considered a confirmation of the original bid, and that they may only respond to your questions—they may not call to talk about the project, and they may not change any numbers you haven't asked about.

Which bidder made the most mistakes? What would you read into that? Will you even know this answer until all of the responses come back?

The sample spreadsheet is not realistic; you'll never see exactly the same price from all bidders across any one line, but if the difference between the bid and the cost estimate is greater than 10 percent, you may want to find out why.

When you get your responses, copy and adjust your spreadsheet and file the query letters with their responses in your Contract file. No matter which contractor you bring to the table, you'll have a list of items you must cover before you can close the deal.

On page 106 is the Adjusted Bid Comparison Spreadsheet.

How have the adjustments changed the order of lowest to highest bidder?

The differences between your adjusted bids and the cost estimate, and the variations among the bids themselves, have been diminished by

offering the bidders a chance to double-check their numbers. If all three bids are within 5 percent of your Initial Construction Contract target number, you are in a good position to negotiate your contract.

There is no law that says you must hire the low bidder, although nobody wants to pay any more than needed. Which contractor would you choose to negotiate with? If you need to cut costs, how would you expect to do that?

Copy the Adjusted Bid Comparison Spreadsheet onto a new worksheet, and file a hard copy of the original form in the bid file. If you are ready to begin your negotiation, select a candidate, copy this spreadsheet but delete the columns of bids from the two you chose *not* to talk to, and bring only two sets of numbers to the table: your final cost estimate and your winner's bid numbers.

Make Good Use of Bad Bids

If all of the bids are still more than 5 percent from your Initial Construction Contract Allowance, you can invite each bidder to a short, private meeting to discuss cost-saving ideas. Adjust each bid by incorporating that bidder's cost-saving ideas, but do not apply one bidder's ideas to any other bid. Once all three bids have been adjusted, you will probably have at least one bid that is affordable.

If that doesn't work, and if all of the original bids were 15 percent or more above your cost estimate, take this long list of cost-saving ideas to your designer and ask for that free redesign. Have her incorporate the suggestions she thinks will lower your costs without compromising the integrity of the design—then rebid the revised drawings.

If the original bids are more than 5 percent but not more than 15 percent above your cost estimate, you're skunked. You'll have to

Adjusted Bid Comparison Spreadsheet: Small Kitchen Remodel

Sec	Item	Task List	Final Cost Est.	Bidder #1	Bidder #2	Bidder #3
000		**Treatment of Household Hazards**				
	001	Test for hazards and provide lab report	$600	$600	$600	$600
100		**Demolition and Site Work**				
	101	Remove and discard all existing cabs & ctrtps	$1,000	$1,000	$1,000	$1,000
	102	Remove sheet vinyl flooring and subfloor	$2,000	$2,000	$2,000	$2,000
200		**Foundation and Structure**				
	202	Install subfloor: match adjacent rms	$1,600	$1,900	$1,600	$1,600
300		**Exterior Envelope**				
	301	Repair siding at kitchen entry door	$400	$500	$400	$400
400		**Doors and Hardware**				
	401	Install louvered bifold doors at laundry	$600	$600	$600	$600
	402	Replace pantry door and hardware	$400	$400	$400	$400
	403	Replace kit. entry door w/ 1/2-glass door	$600	$600	$600	$600
500		**Windows**				
	501	Replace 1 window over sink with 2 windows	$2,200	$2,200	$2,200	$2,200
	502	Install new skylight over breakfast nook	$2,600	$3,000	$3,000	$3,000
600		**Interior Finishes**				
	601	Install new tile flooring	$3,000	$3,600	$3,600	$3,600
	602	Install new ABC cabinets w/door style #1	$24,000	$24,000	$24,000	$24,000
	603	Install new man-made countertops	$4,000	$4,000	$4,000	$4,000
	604	F&I refrig, D/W, Wash/Dry, and disposal	$4,000	$4,000	$4,000	$4,000
700		**Paint Prep and Painting - Int. & Ext.**				
	701	Patch drywall walls & ceiling	$600	$600	$600	$600
	702	Prime and paint interior - 3 colors	$2,000	$2,800	$2,200	$2,200
	702	Prime and paint repaired siding & kit. entry	$500	$500	$500	$500
	703	Paint new int. doors and windows over sink	$600	$600	$600	$600
800		**Plumbing**				
	801	Install new double-bowl, st.st. sink & faucet	$1,000	$1,200	$1,200	$1,200
	802	Replace plbg under sink; add shut-of valve	$1,500	$1,600	$1,500	$1,600
	803	Replace water heater in pantry	$1,000	$1,000	$1,000	$1,000
900		**HVAC**				
	901	Install new range hood with exhaust to ext.	$800	$800	$800	$800
1000		**Electrical**				
	1001	Install 4 new outlets over ctrtop	$800	$800	$800	$800
	1002	Upgrade circuits to appliances	$1,600	$1,600	$1,600	$1,600
		Total Cost	**$57,400**	**$59,900**	**$58,800**	**$58,900**
		Budget & Bid Variance	**$56,000**	107%	105%	105%
1100		**Alternates**				
	201	Repair floor framing under sink cabinet	$600	$800	$1,600	$200
	A1	Repair existing window over sink	$300	$300	$300	$300
	A2	F&I Tiffany-style chandelier in bkfst nook	$800	$800	$800	$800
	A3	Upgrade cabinet door to style #3 (net add)	$2,200	$2,200	$2,200	$2,200
	A4	Install (less expensive) XYZ Cabs (net deduct)	$(3,000)	$(3,000)	$(3,000)	$(3,000)
	A5	Install new stone countertop (net add)	$4,500	$4,500	$4,500	$4,500
	A6	Relocate new water heater into attic (net add)	$2,400	$2,400	$2,400	$2,400
	A7	F&I unvented range hood w/light (net deduct)	$(400)	$(400)	$(400)	$(400)
	A8	Install lighting under all wall-hung cabinets	$2,200	$2,200	$2,200	$2,200
	A9	Replace two existing ceiling fixtures	$250	$250	$250	$250

pay for the cost-saving revisions to the construction drawings, but not revising the drawings will mean the project will stall.

The same bidders probably won't bid a second time, and it will be a lot of work to select three more. See if you can pull the first round out of the fire without getting burned.

4.5 NEGOTIATING

In order to win in any negotiation you must bring three things to the table: an understanding of what the other guy really wants (not just what he says he wants); the willingness to work hard to get a deal that benefits both parties; and the intestinal fortitude to walk away if despite your best efforts you haven't gotten most of what *you* want.

What the General Contractor *Really* Wants

Seventy-five percent of your contractor's direct job-related costs will pay for labor, and twenty-five percent will pay for materials.

Remodeling, by definition, is full of surprises, so his labor costs are often unpredictable—when he bids, he's gambling with the largest part (75 percent) of his price.

Since his labor costs are by far his largest expense, and are definitely his most costly risk, your contractor *really* wants complete control over his work schedule.

The Negotiation

If all your bids are close to your budget, invite the contractor you liked the best—not necessarily the lowest bidder—to a negotiation. Invite your designer as well in case you need help with technical questions or design revisions. Try to complete the negotiation in one meeting; it will be another signal to the contractor that you understand the process and

that you are committed to getting this job done both right and fast.

Create another Adjusted Bid Comparison Spreadsheet with two columns of numbers (the cost estimate and the winning bidder's adjusted bid numbers) and a third, blank column for the final, revised prices, and bring this form to the negotiation. Remove the columns that show the other two bids. This will be your Contract Negotiation Spreadsheet. A sample of a Contract Negotiation Spreadsheet is included on page 108 for you.

Getting the Price Down

If three very good contractors have agreed to competitively bid, they've already carved all of the fat out of the project, which has raised their level of risk as high as they are willing to go.

If you press one of your bidders to simply lower his price to meet your budget, he may just walk away.

If you are dealing with a not-so-perfect contractor, and he *agrees* to lower his price without taking work out of the contract, he will have to cut his *costs* by using cheaper labor or materials in order to get back the money he just gave away. This would be the source of lots of headaches for you.

The best way to lower your bidder's price is to revise the design to lower his costs. That means you have to begin to make good use of your long list of Alternates and begin to omit the more expensive choices and substitute the less expensive ones . . . again. You ought to be able to do this pretty quickly by now.

I hope a little light just went on in your head. The way you develop your list of Alternates is very important to the success of your contract negotiation, and they will come in handy during the construction period as well, as you will see shortly.

Contract Negotiations: Small Kitchen Remodel

Sec	Item	Task List	Final Cost Est.	Bidder #3	Negotiated Final Bid
000		**Treatment of Household Hazards**			
	001	Test for hazards and provide lab report	$600	$600	$600
100		**Demolition and Site Work**			
	101	Remove and discard all existing cabinets and countertops	$1,000	$1,000	$1,000
	102	Remove sheet vinyl flooring and subfloor	$2,000	$2,000	$2,000
200		**Foundation and Structure**			
	202	Install new subfloor: match level of adjacent rooms	$1,600	$1,600	$1,600
300		**Exterior Envelope**			
	301	Repair siding at kitchen entry door	$400	$400	$400
400		**Doors and Hardware**			
	401	Install louvered bifold doors at laundry closet	$600	$600	$600
	402	Replace pantry door and hardware	$400	$400	$400
	403	Replace kitchen entry door with 1/2-glass door	$600	$600	$600
500		**Windows**			
	501	Replace single window over sink with two windows	$2,200	$2,200	$2,200
	502	Install new skylight over breakfast nook	$2,600	$3,000	$3,000
600		**Interior Finishes**			
	601	Install new tile flooring	$3,000	$3,600	$3,600
	602	Install new ABC cabinets w/door style #1 **(clarified)**	$24,000	$24,000	$24,000
	A4	**Install (less expensive) XYZ cabs (net deduct)**			($3,000.00)
	603	Install new man-made countertops	$4,000	$4,000	$4,000
	604	Furnish & install new refrig, D/W, Wash/Dry, and disposal	$4,000	$4,000	$4,000
700		**Paint Prep and Painting - Int. & Ext.**			
	701	Patch drywall walls & ceiling	$600	$600	$600
	702	Prime and paint walls, ceiling and trim - 3 colors	$2,000	$2,200	$2,200
	702	Prime and paint repaired siding and kitchen entry door	$500	$500	$500
	703	Paint new interior doors and windows over sink	$600	$600	$600
800		**Plumbing**			
	801	Install new double-bowl, stainless steel sink & faucet	$1,000	$1,200	$1,200
	802	Replace all plumbing under sink; add shut-of valve	$1,500	$1,600	$1,600
	803	Replace water heater in pantry	$1,000	$1,000	$1,000
900		**HVAC (Heating, Ventilation & Air-Conditioning)**			
	901	Install new range hood with exhaust to exterior	$800	$800	$800
1000		**Electrical**			
	1001	Install 4 new outlets over countertop backsplash	$800	$800	$800
	1002	Upgrade circuits to kitchen appliances to carry new load	$1,600	$1,600	$1,600
		Total Cost	$57,400	$58,900	($55,900.00)
		Budget & Price Variance	$56,000	105%	100%

Signatures: D.Contractor   D.Homeowner

Sec	Item	Task List	Final Cost Est.	Bidder #3	Negotiated Final Bid
1100		**Alternates**			
	201	Repair floor framing under sink cabinet	$600	$200	$200
	A1	Repair existing window over sink	$300	$300	$300
	A2	Furnish & install Tiffany-style chandelier in breakfast nook	$800	$800	$800
	A3	Upgrade cabinet door to style #3 (net add)	$2,200	$2,200	$2,200
	A5	Install new stone countertop (net add)	$4,500	$4,500	$4,500
	A6	Relocate new water heater into attic (net add)	$2,400	$2,400	$2,400
	A7	Install unvented range hood with light (net deduct)	($400)	($400)	($400)
	A8	Install lighting under all wall-hung cabinets	$2,200	$2,200	$2,200
	A9	Replace two existing ceiling fixtures	$250	$250	$250

Ask the designer and the contractor for help making these final revisions. Sometimes, for example, it's actually less expensive to replace old windows than to repair them—which might feel counterintuitive to you.

The contractor may point out that the new HVAC unit or the proposed electrical panel has more capacity than you actually need. Discuss his suggestion. If you all agree, change the design and substitute a smaller unit. (You may want to consult an engineer before you do this.)

If you change any of the design details during the negotiations, have your architect edit the documents in red marker. Each red mark should be bold and clear, and initialed and dated by every party at the table. If you want an agreement to be enforceable, you have to have it in writing. Remember to update your Task Abstract List and the bid prices on that spreadsheet, and to have all parties initial that too.

Sweat Equity

The term "sweat equity" refers to the way that your free labor can increase the value of your home without adding to the costs. If you choose to try this, I offer two words of caution:

- *Amateur workmanship can actually lower the value of your home* which, by definition, is not cost-effective. Don't take on more than you can reasonably expect to do well, and
- The general contractor has to be able to meet his deadline. Don't plan to do any work that would slow him down by interrupting the work of his subs.

The best tasks for the homeowner to do are those that do not require more skill than they have, and that can be done either before the contractor begins work (for example, cleaning out the basement or the attic or doing some demolition) or after the job is signed off and the contractor has his final payment (for example, painting or purchasing and installing new appliances).

If you plan to reduce the scope of work in his contract by doing sweat-equity work during the contract period—while he's working on the site—the two of you must sign a Sweat-Equity Agreement. Included on page 110 is a copy of that form.

If your work will not affect his schedule—you'll be working before he gets there or after he's done—all you have to do is omit the work you choose to do from his contract.

Closing the Deal

Change the task descriptions on your worksheet as you negotiate changes, and put the contractor's final prices next to each edited task description. When you've finished your negotiation, add up the new prices and write the total cost of all final contract items at the bottom of the tally sheet.

You and your contractor will both sign this sheet. This is your Final Contract Price Agreement. When you go home, you'll create another copy, without all of the scribbles and arrows and notes, attach the clean copy to the signed, annotated copy, and send a copy set to him. Included on page 111 is a Final Contract Prices Spreadsheet.

Ask your designer to take a copy of the negotiation notes and to mark all the drawings in bold red marker in preparation for the signing of the final contract.

Not Closing the Deal

I'd be surprised to hear that you were unsuccessful at this negotiation, because you have been very careful about tracking costs from the outset, but I suppose it can happen.

SWEAT-EQUITY AGREEMENT

Date: [The day you sign the contract]

Project	(address)
Owner	D.Homeowner
GC	D.Contractor

This Agreement is hereby incorporated into the Contract by reference and shall be subject to all stipulations and covenants of that Contract, once it is fully executed.

Section	List of Changes	Cost
SwEq	Owner to install-only plywood in attic	$ (1,000)
SwEq	Owner to demo deck; contractor to haul	$ (1,000)
	Total Net Change	**$ (2,000)**

The homeowner agrees to hold the contractor harmless from any damages that may occur as a result of his presence on the site, including any property damage, personal injuries, medical costs, or legal fees.

Current Contract Value	$ 259,500
Plus/Minus This Change Order	**$ (2,000)**
Equals New Contract Value	**$ 257,500**

Total Calendar Days in Current Schedule	168
Time Added by This Change Order	**0**
New Total Calendar Days in Schedule	**168**
New Number of Four-Week Pay Periods (Total Days / 28 Days)	**6**
New Percent-Complete Required for Each Check Release (100% / # Payments)	
	16.7%

Signatures	Date
D.Contractor	d
D.Homeowner	d

Final Contract Price: Small Kitchen Remodel

Sec	Item	Task List	Initial Contract
000		**Treatment of Household Hazards**	
	001	Test for hazards and provide lab report	$ 600
100		**Demolition and Site Work**	
	101	Remove and discard all existing cabinets and countertops	$ 1,000
	102	Remove sheet vinyl flooring and subfloor	$ 2,000
200		**Foundation and Structure**	
	202	Install new subfloor: match level of adjacent rooms	$ 1,600
300		**Exterior Envelope**	
	301	Repair siding at kitchen entry door	$ 400
400		**Doors and Hardware**	
	401	Install louvered bifold doors at laundry closet	$ 600
	402	Replace pantry door and hardware	$ 400
	403	Replace kitchen entry door with 1/2-glass door	$ 600
500		**Windows**	
	501	Replace single window over sink with two windows	$ 2,200
	502	Install new skylight over breakfast nook	$ 3,000
600		**Interior Finishes**	
	601	Install new tile flooring	$ 3,600
	A4	**Install XYZ Cabs**	**$ 21,000**
	603	Install new man-made countertops	$ 4,000
	604	Furnish & install new refrig, D/W, Wash/Dry, and disposal	$ 4,000
700		**Paint Prep and Painting - Int. & Ext.**	
	701	Patch drywall walls & ceiling	$ 600
	702	Prime and paint walls, ceiling and trim - 3 colors	$ 2,200
	702	Prime and paint repaired siding and kitchen entry door	$ 500
	703	Paint new interior doors and windows over sink	$ 600
800		**Plumbing**	
	801	Install new double-bowl, stainless steel sink & faucet	$ 1,200
	802	Replace all plumbing under sink; add shut-of valve	$ 1,600
	803	Replace water heater in pantry	$ 1,000
900		**HVAC (Heating, Ventilation & Air-Conditioning)**	
	901	Install new range hood with exhaust to exterior	$ 800
1000		**Electrical**	
	1001	Install 4 new outlets over countertop backsplash	$ 800
	1002	Upgrade circuits to kitchen appliances to carry new load	$ 1,600
		CONTRACT PRICE	**$ 55,900**

If you are unsuccessful in your negotiations with this contractor, you can begin negotiating with another contractor, but you already know what the market price of your job is, and if you begin to work with someone who submits an extra-low bid, you will almost certainly be sorry later.

You could choose to put some of your personal savings into the Initial Construction Contract Allowance, but you may *not* steal from the set-asides for surprises and soft costs.

If you just can't seem to get to a price you can afford without giving up your reason for doing the project in the first place, you can still sell this house and buy another. You've spent a few months and a couple of thousand dollars coming to this conclusion, but you have not yet committed to the cost of the construction work, which is 90 percent of the cost of doing a project, so maybe it was worth the effort to know for sure that you had to move.

The Final Details

The Bid Summary form that the contractor signed and returned to you in his bid submittal asks him to tell you how long he thinks it will take him to finish the job. Refer to that sheet and use that length of time as your contract work schedule. I would be a little concerned if he objected to that.

Set the Start-Work Date

The Bid Summary also asked the contractor when he thought he could start. See if that date is still good. He may have signed another contract since he submitted your bid.

No contractor should have more jobs than he has crews. The work will go more smoothly and the crew will finish faster when they're focused on your project. Even if you have to wait a few weeks (or months) for him

to start, he'll finish faster if you have his undivided attention.

Your start date will be the day his work crew is next available, which could be sixty to ninety days from the date you sign the contract. You may not even be able to set the start date until the contractor can predict when the crew will be finished with their current job. That's okay. Set a deadline for *establishing* this start date. And don't pay any deposits until the contract is fully executed.

Setting the Payment Schedule
Hot Tip
If you expect your contractor to be 100 percent finished when the schedule is 100 percent lapsed, then he had better be 20 percent finished when the schedule is 20 percent lapsed. Read that three times. It's important.

How will this logic affect the way you set his payment schedule?

One payment a month is the construction industry norm, so on a job that he anticipates will take *four* months to complete, you should offer him *four* payments, but (here's the part where you take control) require that he complete *one-fourth* of the job before he gets each check. Tie the release of checks to his momentum, not to the calendar.

The wise contractor will see the opportunity to keep more profit in his pocket if he can finish *earlier* than he planned to; he can get his check faster if he finishes one-quarter of the job *before* the schedule is one-quarter lapsed.

When you've set your start date, know how long the job will take, and have established what his momentum ought to be, fill in the blanks on your Terms and Conditions Statement. If you use my contract form (in the appendix), you'll find the work and payment schedules at the end, just above the signatures.

Assembling the Contract Package

Every contract has to address two basic questions: (1) What are we going to do? and (2) How are we going to do it? The "What" is defined by the drawings and specifications; the "How" is spelled out in the General Conditions statement (see the appendix). These documents, combined, make up your construction contract.

Before you sign this contract, you ought to have in hand all of the following documents:

- A signed copy of the negotiated bid prices, called the Contract Price Agreement;
- A copy of the contractor's license (if required by your state's laws);
- Original copies of the contractor's general liability insurance certificate, and his signed Workers' Compensation Disclosure form with evidence of coverage if he is required to carry workers' comp;
- The bid documents, including the signed Instructions to Bidders, the signed Bid Summary form (revise the final price on the Bid Summary in red, and have the contractor initial it); and
- Other agreements such as the clarification letter you sent after the bid walk-through, and the query letter and his response that were filed prior to the bid negotiation.

Original copies of everything on the list above ought to be in your Contract file.

When you have everything he owes you, make ten copies of the final, edited contract documents (just the drawings and the general conditions statement), and schedule a pre-construction walk-through meeting for three weeks prior to the start of work.

This is not as redundant as it may sound. When a contractor wins a job, he often puts your file and your drawings in a pile of others like them, writes your name on the start date on his wall calendar, and forgets about the job until it's about three weeks away. Between your negotiation and the first day of work, while your project will be the *only* thing on your mind, it will be the farthest thing from his. He's busy with somebody else.

Reviewing your project before he begins work is a very good idea. It will begin to shift his focus back to you.

4.6 PRE-CONSTRUCTION ACTIVITIES

There are a number of things you can do while you're waiting for the contractor's crew to be available that will prepare both you and your property for the mess and stress of the construction work period. Here are some suggestions.

The Pre-Construction Meeting

About three weeks prior to the official start-work date, your project team will get together, on the job site, for that pre-construction meeting. During the negotiation, you were all thinking on your feet. In the time between the negotiation and the start date, which can be several months, you may have forgotten the details, someone may have had a good idea that you'll want to explore, or it will occur to one of you that an idea you considered before is not such a good one. In addition, your contractor has probably discussed the job with his key subcontractors by now, and they may have observed something that needs to be clarified or changed.

You have ten copies of the contract documents. Give the contractor *five* sets—two to submit to the inspections department when he requests his building permit (one of which will be stamped and returned to him, and left on the site for the building inspectors), one to leave on the site for the workers to refer to and to mark up, one to carry around in his truck, and one he'll keep clean and safe in his files.

Keep a set for yourself or your agent, and if you are using a remodeling coach like me, give a set to the coach.

If there is a bonding agent, she may want a set, and if you borrowed money from a bank to finance the project, the banker will want a set too, although these folks don't need to be at the pre-construction meeting.

If you have spare sets, keep them somewhere handy. If you need to consult an attorney, an engineer, a hazard remediation contractor, a historic preservationist, or anyone else not familiar with the daily progress of the job, you'll have a clean set of drawings and contract terms to share with them.

Hold your pre-construction conference on the project site. If you're remodeling your home, your kitchen may be the perfect conference room. Walk around and review every work task. If any changes are made to the final documents at this meeting, mark *every set,* including the spare sets, in bold, red notes and have *every* meeting participant initial and date *all* the edit marks on all ten sets.

When the meeting is over, if you haven't done so already, you and the contractor will sign *all* copies of the contract Terms and Conditions Statement, and shake hands all around.

You've got yourself a project! . . . *Start packing!*

Expect Stress

Once the work starts, your contractor must take charge of the work site, but you must stay in charge of the *project.* Let's take just a minute and see what sort of damage control you can do to prepare yourself for the work ahead.

It's been my experience that stress is directly related to expectations. If you envision a neat and clean little job site, you will find the reality extremely stressful.

Last Chance: Stay Put or Move Out

When you initially thought about whether you'd move out or stay—when you were making your administrative decisions back in Section 4.2—you may have decided to stay in order to avoid having to move into Aunt Ruth's guest room, to avoid the cost of storing your stuff and renting an apartment, or because you thought staying would allow you to keep a closer eye on things. But now that you understand just what kind of commotion there will be once construction starts, you may want to change your mind.

Important Note: The Wild-Guess Soft-Costs Estimate Chart on page 41 (Section 2.4) does not have a line item for the cost of storage or temporary housing. There are so many options, there was no way to estimate this cost. It may have to come out of your pocket if you don't have any money left in the soft-costs allowance once you're paid all your professional consultants, or you may want to reduce your Initial Construction Contract Allowance and move a little extra up into the soft-costs budget. Do not change the amount you've set aside for surprises.

If you have chosen to move, I hope you have secured a space in which you can live *comfortably* for the duration. You don't want to have to sell this glorious, finished house as a condition of a divorce settlement.

Preparing the Site

Your contractor will be responsible for protecting any fixed objects such as swing sets or finished hardwood floors that will remain in place and the grand piano, which simply can't be moved, but if you use the contract form in the appendix, *you* are responsible for packing up anything you can pick up. If you leave prescription medications, sharp objects, food, pets or pet paraphernalia, sensitive electronic equipment, photographs, bicycles, jewelry, or other personal belongings where they can be damaged or borrowed, they probably will be.

You can help your contractor and ensure the safety of your home and your belongings by doing some extra protection work yourself. Your contractor is responsible for all protection work under the Terms and Conditions Statement in the appendix, and you must be careful not to relieve him of this duty. The following suggestions represent safety measures that go a little beyond what the average contractor would do.

- If you have in-ground lighting around the driveway or the garden, remove it. Put your family toys and tools, and any yard or deck furniture, in a locked storage space, perhaps your garage.
- Wrap cardboard around the door jambs in the work area and secure the edges with painter's tape to avoid damage to the decorative moldings. Don't use duct tape; it will damage the wall surfaces. The contractor will remove the protection when he's ready to paint.
- You can lay a wide, heavy-duty runner, not a slippery plastic tarp, between the work area and the entry door the workers will use. You can lay two layers of heavy construction paper over any hardwood floors you want to protect.
- Wrap the grand piano in a movers' quilt and cover that with a sheet of heavy plastic that you seal closed with duct tape. You can put temporary casters or a dolly under any heavy piece of furniture that cannot be moved out of the house so that the floors won't be damaged when the contractor has to move it out of the way of his work.

- If there are rooms in your house that will get nothing but a paint job, you may wish to provide a barrier of some kind between the work area and those rooms. Three sheets of 6-millimeter-thick plastic sheeting, stapled and then sealed with painter's tape to all adjoining surfaces, will probably hold up through the worst of the mess. Nothing short of a framed and drywalled temporary wall will completely protect everything.
- You can control where the workers are allowed to go. You can give instructions to the general contractor about which entry door his crew can use and which bathroom, if you're not renting a temporary, outdoor potty. Post those instructions in writing—in at least two languages—in several locations, and hope that they are honored.
- You can even hire a mover to put all your things into one of his trailers, lock it up, leave it in your driveway, and give you the only key. When the job is done, he can simply unpack the trailer and put your stuff back. You'll pay a monthly fee for the trailer rental, and the labor cost of the move, but you'll know your stuff is safe and off the ground, and you can get at it if you need to.

Think, think, think. What do you want to protect against damage and how will you do it?

Anticipating Collateral Damage

At any given time there could be six different trades working in your house. This means there will be six trucks, six kinds of materials that must be transported into your home and set somewhere, and twelve or more workers trotting back and forth. Don't expect to save your lawn. Although according to the general conditions of your contract (see the appendix) the general is responsible for regrading and seeding any areas he has damaged, you probably ought to consider a landscaping project when the job is done.

If you have the typical paved residential driveway, it was designed to hold the weight of a car or two, but not a bulldozer or a big, yellow tree-trimming truck. You may not be able to save your driveway either.

You can build—or have your contractor build—a protective fence around any landscaping elements you don't want damaged, but there is no guarantee that barrier will be respected.

Your neighbors will be affected by your work too. A tree limb may fall onto their property, materials may mysteriously drift over the lot line, all that noise and additional traffic could be a problem, or they may feel their security is at risk. Notify them that you are about to remodel and what the work schedule will be. Introduce them to the general contractor, and encourage them to notify both of you if they observe an accident or any suspicious activity when you're not around.

Permits and Inspections

Your contractor, not you, should apply for and pay for the construction permit. The person who signs for the permit will be responsible for scheduling and passing a number of inspections and for completing the project in accordance with the building code. Those are not your responsibilities; they're his.

You would think that passing a municipal inspection would provide you with some assurance that the work is okay, but you should be aware that federal law excuses municipal employees, including building inspectors, from responsibility for their actions (a dusty relic

that came over from England with the first settlers; something about immunity for the king's minions). They cannot be held liable for any problems they do not catch, and they cannot fail a contractor for poor-quality work, only for doing work that does not meet the technical requirements of the building code.

Easy-as-Pie Project Accounting System

If you want to stick to your budget, you have to ensure that the sum of your commitments never exceeds what you had planned to spend. That sounds simple, but you've got three distinct pots of money; how will you track it all? All you'll need is two pieces of paper. Sheet 1 is for your soft costs.

Your soft-costs allowance is capped at 10 percent of your Total Project Budget and most of this money will be spent before you go out to bid. Let's look at that one first. You have already established budget numbers and line-item allowances for your soft costs, so set up this form and fill in what you know. There are sample forms on pages 117–120 to help you. If you know how to use a computer spreadsheet program, this will be a breeze.

Sheet 2, the Construction Accounting Sheet, is just a little more complicated.

Your two construction funds—the money committed to the construction contract and the set-aside for surprises—are like locks in the Erie Canal—as one (the contingency fund) empties, the other (the contract amount) fills up, but the combined, *total* amount of water (money) in the two locks doesn't change.

In order to keep track of these fluid funds, the Construction Accounting Sheet is broken down into *three* parts:

SAMPLE SOFT-COSTS ACCOUNTING SHEET SETUP

				PAYMENT LOG		
Total Construction Budget	100%	$100,000				
Soft-Costs Allowance	10%	$10,000				
		Allowances		Amount	Ck.Dt.	Ck.No.
Planning:						
Home Inspection		$ 300				
Wine-and-Design Party		$ 100				
Additional Insurance		$ 125				
Design:						
Concept Design		$ 600				
Design Development		$ 1,800				
Construction Documents		$ 1,500				
Post-Bid Final Payment		$ 700				
Architect at Meetings @ $150/hr	2 hrs	$ 300				
Structural Engineer @ $100/hr	1 hr	$ 100				
Kitchen Designer @ $65/hr	1 hr	$ 65				
Interior Designer @ $65/hr	1 hr	$ 65				
Professional Cost Estimate		$ 300				
Pre-Consruction:						
Environmental Consult		$ 300				
Loan Closing Costs		$ 350				
Construction:						
Attorney - Document Review @ $150/hr		$ 150				
Attorney - Disputes @ $150/hr						
Remodeling Coach @$50/hr						
Planning Phase		$ 100				
Design Review		$ 100				
Construction Phase		$ 500				
Total Anticipated Soft Costs =		$ 7,455				
Total Construction Budget =	90%	$ 90,000				
Construction Contract Amount =	72%	$ 72,000				
Construction Contingency Allowance =	18%	$ 18,000				

1. The contingency fund—the money that is uncommitted when you begin construction but is available for surprises and other changes;
2. Progress evaluations, which we will address in Chapter 5 when we discuss monitoring the contractor's work; and
3. Contractor payment calculations.

When you're ready to start your own project, you can use the blank Construction Accounting Sheet as your model and set up a spreadsheet for your project; fill in the information about the budget, and you'll be ready to roll. You will have plenty of opportunity to use these accounting forms when you work on Our Project in Part Two.

SAMPLE SOFT-COSTS ACCOUNTING SHEET: CONSTRUCTION WEEK 6

		Allowances		Amount		Ck.Dt.	Ck.No.
Total Construction Budget	100%	$100,000					
Soft-Costs Allowance	10%	$10,000			**PAYMENT LOG**		
Planning:							
Home Inspection		$	300	$	300	c	d
Wine-and-Design Party		$	100	$	100	c	d
Additional Insurance		$	125	$	125	c	d
Design:							
Concept Design		$	600	$	600	c	d
Design Development		$	1,800	$	1,800	c	d
Construction Documents		$	1,500	$	1,500	c	d
Post-Bid Final Payment		$	700	$	700	c	d
Architect at Meetings @ $150/hr	2 hrs	$	300				
Structural Engineer @ $100/hr	1 hr	$	100	$	100	c	d
Kitchen Designer @ $65/hr	1 hr	$	65	$	65	c	d
Interior Designer @ $65/hr	1 hr	$	65	$	65	c	d
Professional Cost Estimate		$	300	$	300	c	d
Pre-Consruction:							
Environmental Consult		$	300	$	300	c	d
Loan Closing Costs		$	350	$	350	c	d
Construction:							
Attorney - Document Review @ $150/hr		$	150	$	150	c	d
Attorney - Disputes @ $150/hr							
Remodeling Coach @$50/hr							
Planning Phase		$	100	$	100	c	d
Design Review		$	100	$	100	c	d
Construction Phase		$	500	$	100	c	d
Total Anticipated Soft Costs =		$	7,455	$	6,755		
Total Construction Budget =	90%	$ 90,000					
Construction Contract Amount =	72%	$ 72,000					
Construction Contingency Allowance =	18%	$ 18,000					

SAMPLE CONSTRUCTION ACCOUNTING SHEET SETUP

Total Construction Budget: $100,000
Initial Contract Amount: $72,000
Initial Contingency: $18,000

CHANGE ORDER LOG

CO#	Change Date	A Contract Amount	B Net Change	C=A+B Revised Contract	D=LastBal - CO Remaining Conting.	E Current Sched	F Days Added	G=E+F Revised Schedule
1								
2								
3								

PROGRESS EVALUTIONS

Wk#	Eval. Date	A # Days in Sched.	B # Days Lapsed	C=B/A %-Sched Lapsed	D Contract Amount	E T.Amt. Earned	F=E/D %-Contr Earned	Target: $6,000 per week for check
2			14					
4			28					
6			42					
8			56					
10			84					
12			112					
14			140					
etc.								

CONTRACTOR PAYMENTS

	A T.Earned to Date	B Minus 10% Retain.	C=A-B Balance #1	D Minus All Prev.Pay'ts	E=C-D Balance #2	F Minus Late Fees	G=E-F AMOUNT PAID	Check Date & Number
DEP								
Ck 1								
Ck 2								
Ck 3								
Ck 4								

SAMPLE CONSTRUCTION ACCOUNTING SHEET: CONSTRUCTION WEEK 6

Total Construction Budget:	$100,000
Initial Contract Amount:	$72,000
Initial Contingency:	$18,000

CHANGE ORDER LOG

CO#	Change Date	A Contract Amount	B Net Change	C=A+B Revised Contract	D=LastBal - CO Remaining Conting.	E Current Sched	F Days Added	G=E+F Revised Schedule
1	(Day 32)	$72,000	$5,000	**$77,000**	$13,000	17 days	4	**121**
2								
3								

PROGRESS EVALUATIONS

Wk#	Eval. Date	A # Days in Sched.	B # Days Lapsed	C=B/A %-Sched Lapsed	D Contract Amount	E T.Amt. Earned	F=E/D %-Contr. Earned	Target: $6,000 per week for check
2	(Day 14)	117	14	12%	$72,000	$10,000	14%	$24,000
4	(Day 28)	117	28	**24%**	$72,000	**$24,500**	**34%**	**$24,000**
6	(Day 42)	**121**	42	35%	**$77,00**	$26,727.27	35%	$48,000
8			56					**$48,000**
10			84					
12			112					
14			140					
etc.								

CONTRACTOR PAYMENTS

	A T.Earned to Date	B Minus 10% Retain.	C=A-B Balance #1	D Minus All Prev.Pay'ts	E=C-D Balance #2	F Minus Late Fees	G=E-F AMOUNT PAID	Check Date & Number
DEP							$15,000	(Day 0) #
Ck 1	**$24,500**	$2,450	$22,050	$15,000	$7,050	—	**$7,050**	(Day 28) #
Ck 2								
Ck 3								
Ck 4								

FIVE

Construction

5.1 DISPUTES

Everything you've done so far has been designed to protect you from disputes. Before we discuss strategies for monitoring the work in progress, I want you to understand why I'm going to suggest the monitoring system I have developed—that golden, unbroken paper trail that starts with your first Task Abstract List and ends when you have issued the final payment to your contractor.

Neither you nor your contractor would gain anything by sabotaging the project. You're in this together. But stress can drive any otherwise sane person to do things she never dreamed she would, and spending lots and lots of money when you're not quite sure of what you're doing and don't quite feel like you're in control can make you pretty tense.

Most disputes start with simple misunderstandings. You need to know the early signs of trouble, how to resolve a problem before it escalates, and what to do if you can't stop the whole thing from tumbling down around your ears. Forewarned is forearmed.

I am not an attorney. None of what follows here is legal advice. It is, however, all based on years of experience.

The Very Worst Thing That Can Happen

If the contractor loses momentum and begins to see that he'll need more time to complete the job than the contract will allow, and that the extra costs will have to come out of his own pocket, it's likely that he will take action to protect his profit margin.

He can't cut his losses and walk off, leaving you with an unfinished project—that would ruin his reputation.

He can't add men to the job to catch up because he can't charge you for the extra labor.

He has only two options left: he can take the good (expensive) workers off the job and replace them with workers who can't command as high a wage because they are not as skilled or experienced, or he can begin cutting corners on his work methods and materials.

The root of all of the horror stories you've heard about overcharging, shoddy work, and unethical behavior is that the contractor saw that the job was not going to run smoothly and he feared losing money, so he took the only path that was available to him. I'm not suggesting that you excuse him; I'm only hoping that you will understand that when a contractor faces financial loss and begins cutting corners, there may be something *you* can do to get him back on track.

When the Delay Is Not His Fault

Two kinds of problems that can cause a work slowdown have easy remedies.

1. If the delay was event driven (the cabinet delivery was two weeks late) and beyond the

contractor's control, then it wasn't his fault and he shouldn't be punished for it.

2. If the contractor has had men working hard on your site every day and he's still running behind, it may be that the construction schedule was overly optimistic.

In both of these instances, you and your contractor ought to be able to find a way to not punish him for something that was not his fault. Note that simply adding time to his schedule will not help him, since he still would have to pay for the labor on the site during that extended period. You might excuse late fees or add a payment to help him with cash flow (not add money to the contract, but pay more frequently . . . we'll talk more about that).

If neither of these examples is applicable, then he's not manning the job properly, and that is a serious problem. He's lost his focus. You have to motivate him to recommit to your deadline.

Time Out! You Decide to Stop the Work

If you begin to notice shoddy workmanship, it may be a sign that the contractor is cutting corners.

While stopping work *temporarily* implies that you believe there may be a solution that will lead to an acceptable outcome, it also means that your contractor's crew will not be working or getting paid for the duration of the dead time. Waste no time in finding a resolution. They have bills to pay.

Document your stop-work order in writing, with photos of the problem work. Copy your contractor and your attorney. If the contractor's work is generally acceptable, and there is work that he can be doing on other areas of the site, stop work only in the problem area; keep the rest of the job moving if you can.

If shoddy work is not your problem, if you have a problem that is complicated and needs some time to figure out—if you uncover a serious structural problem and need the help of a structural engineer, for example—and if there is no other work that the contractor can be doing while you're researching solutions, stop all work for a *specific time period*, roll up your sleeves, and figure out how to get the work going again.

As soon as you have decided on a solution to the problem, and *before* the end of the specific stop-work period, call a meeting at the site, provide the contractor with a repair plan, and release the contractor to continue working.

If the problem was not the result of negligence or intentional bad faith on the part of your contractor, extend the work schedule, or forgive late fees. This will take the edge off and keep him from considering more drastic measures to ensure his profit margin.

The go-back-to-work letter should be dated *no later than* the official end of the stop-work period if you plan to nurture the tattered remains of the goodwill of your contractor and his subs.

The Bond

If you got performance and payment bonds from your contractor at the outset, and he's not keeping up with his schedule, your first call ought to be to the bonding agent. The agent has guaranteed that the contractor will complete his contract on time, and he's put up his own money to insure this. He'll act quickly to correct the problem.

Incidentally, if you ask the bonding agent to help, he will send you a few forms to fill out. The deadlines for submittal of each form will be clearly marked. If you ignore these deadlines, your claim will be dismissed and you will have relieved the agent of his responsibilities.

Mechanics' Liens

When a general contractor gets into financial trouble, he will keep the money you give him and stop paying his subcontractors. The subs know that you are the source of all payments, so they will try to get you to pay them directly. To do this they will file a lien on your property.

Here's how mechanics' liens work. Once the suit, or lien, is filed in court, the plaintiff—the person who is filing the complaint—has ninety days to "perfect" the lien; that is, he has to submit documents to the court that will convince a judge that he has good reason and legal grounds to encumber your property—that you really do owe him some money.

Then *you* will be asked to provide the court with some documentation that shows that you do *not* owe him money. Provide your attorney with a copy of the court's request for documentation along with copies of all relevant paperwork so that he can advise you what to send back.

In my experience, documents have been sent to court by mail, so there were no court costs, just a small attorney's fee.

When you pay the general contractor, you pay for certain work that has been completed by his subs. If you can show the court exactly what you paid for in each check and a few pictures of the condition of the site when you released each check, you can prove that the money the subcontractor is seeking has already been given to the general. (I'm going to show you exactly how to keep records so that this

response will take you exactly five minutes to pull together. Never fear.)

If the judge decides that the plaintiff has no case against you, the lien will not be "perfected," and the case will be dismissed. The subcontractor will be told that the general has his money, and he'll begin chasing the general.

You're going to be fine.

Call the Attorney

When the delays start stretching out and you see that the contractor is beginning to cut corners, it's time to get your attorney involved.

Time is not on your side. Try to solve your problem with a single meeting. Invite whomever the attorney suggests, and get a solution on paper and signed before you leave her office.

If you and your contractor are too tense, have your attorney and his attorney talk to each other without either of you in the room. They'll be cool and objective. They have to discuss any solutions with you before an agreement is finalized. There will be time for negotiation, and by then you'll be ready.

Mediation

If you two and your attorneys can't come to a comfortable agreement and get the work going again, ask the contractor if he will agree to share the cost of hiring an impartial, professional mediator. This option is cheaper for both of you than a lawsuit, and there's still a chance you can get your job finished.

The results of a mediation hearing are not binding. The mediator will follow an agenda that your attorney will be familiar with, and will suggest a resolution when the hearing is completed. Your attorney should construct a formal agreement and secure signatures from both you and your contractor so that the results stick.

Arbitration

The result of an arbitration hearing *is* legally binding. If your positions are irreconcilable, try asking the contractor to share the cost of engaging an arbitrator. This is your last chance to avoid the courtroom. Work closely with your attorney to select the documents you'll introduce as evidence, and to determine how to present them. Choose your words carefully. Arbitrators will give you only a few minutes to present your case. If the arbitrator doesn't ask for information, don't volunteer it.

For more information about arbitration procedures, you can contact the American Arbitration Association at 1-800-778-7879 or on the Internet at www.adr.org.

Going to Court

Judges are called judges because they use their own judgment when they decide a case. They don't always follow the letter of the law; they rely a lot on precedents—decisions that other judges have made in similar cases. You never know what you'll get, and a court case can get very, very expensive. If you have any other alternatives, try them first.

Contract Termination

When you have reached the point of no return—when there is nothing you can do to make this partnership work and you don't want the contractor on the site anymore, it's time for a contract termination.

Consult an attorney about the laws that govern the cancelation of a contract, and follow her advice. Act quickly and change the locks.

Abandonment

When there are no tradesmen on the site for days at a time at regular intervals, or for one extended period of time, and you have tried to contact your contractor but he has not responded, the contractor may be deemed to have "abandoned" the site.

There are state laws that govern abandonment settlements. Consult your attorney for advice as soon as you can identify the problem, and allow the attorney to advise you about paying—or not paying—the contractor. You must work quickly. The contractor is a man in trouble; he may have your house keys, and he may act irresponsibly.

Recovery (Hooray!!!)

If you have legally removed the contractor from your site, regroup!

Rehire your designer to describe the scope of work that remains, including highlighting the work that is in place but has to be corrected by the new contractor.

Then look for a contractor who is willing to pick up a half-finished, messed-up job for an angry and paranoid owner, and is fool enough to warrant *all* of the work.

In my experience, the only contractors who are willing to do this are either not very good and have no other work; are not very smart and don't understand the risk of warranting another man's bad work; or are financially unstable themselves and are grasping at straws. No decent contractor would put off a perfectly good job with a nice client to pick up a half-finished project for a client with legal and financial problems, without charging a high premium for doing so. Covering his risk is a legitimate cost of doing business in this case. Please check references very carefully on your next contractor.

Plan on a delay of 60 to 120 days before you can begin work again; then find a new contractor, or, if you're lucky, find new bidders, and follow the yellow brick road.

Progress evaluation—breezeway 1

Progress evaluation—breezeway 2

Charles Schulz, creator of the *Peanuts* cartoons, once said, "Don't worry about the world coming to an end today. It's already tomorrow in Australia." Remember that and keep a level head.

Now that you know what can go wrong and what that can cost you, I'm going to show you how to keep your job on track and stay in charge and out of trouble.

5.2 PROGRESS EVALUATIONS

Because you have been so diligent during the planning and design phases, all you have to do during the construction period is to monitor the contractor's momentum, keep good records, and issue fair and timely payments. This turns out to be the easy part.

Informal Site Reports and Photos

Take your camera onto the work site whenever you're there. You can keep track of the work progress by dating each photo. You will also want to mark each photo with the location of the shot and what it is meant to display.

In addition to photographs of the work in progress, you should keep *site notes*. Every visit should generate a quick report that indicates the date of the visit and the time of day, the weather conditions (light snow/freezing cold; warm and mild; hurricane winds with torrential rains; etc.); the number and kinds of tradesmen working on the site (four electricians, two plumbers, two carpenters); and the items that are being worked on (wiring bonus-room ceiling, moving kitchen plumbing, framing new walls for mudroom). Keep all original progress photos and site reports in the file called Informal Site Reports and Photos.

Formal Progress Evaluations

You and your general contractor will meet every two weeks on the same day of the week and at the same time of day to review and record his progress and determine if he has earned a payment. He has to earn a predetermined percentage of his contract in each four-week pay period in order to get a check, remember? If you want him to be 100 percent done when the schedule is 100 percent lapsed, then he'd better be 20 percent done when the schedule is 20 percent lapsed. Here is how you will track that.

You have the Contract Price Agreement, which contains the final negotiated list of tasks and prices. Find that form and copy it onto a blank sheet. It ought to look something like the form shown on page 126.

		CONTRACT PRICE AGREEMENT	A
Sec	**Item**	**Task List**	**Contract Prices**
000		**Household Hazards**	
	001	Test/report hazards	$ 600
100		**Demolition and Site Work**	
	101	Demo cabs & ctrtps	$ 1,000
	102	Demo floor to framing	$ 2,000
200		**Foundation and Structure**	
	202	New subflr to match adjacent	$ 1,600
300		**Exterior Envelope**	
	301	Repair siding @ kit.door	$ 400

Now you will need a tool to help you establish the value of the work that has been completed since he began work or since the last evaluation. We're going to put our old friend the Task Abstract List to work in yet another way. We'll have to make a few small changes so we can continue to keep the entire list on one sheet of paper.

- Compress the work descriptions into the fewest words possible. For example, instead of saying "Furnish and install new refrigerator, washer and dryer, range and dishwasher," try compressing this description into something like this: "F&I appl: refr, W/D, range, d/w" or better yet, "F&I ref.W/D.range.d/w." Would you remember what that meant in two weeks?
- Combine related tasks to shorten the list. You will keep the original, complete spreadsheet in the file in case you need to refer back to it. For example, if your contract calls for the repair of exterior window moldings, the trim around the roof, and the porch rail, combine these three tasks into one line that might say, "Repair ext. trim."

- Now add four blank columns after the one with the initial contract prices in it.
- The first column with the final negotiated prices becomes the *Initial Contract* column.
- The second column heading should say *Changes*.
- The third should say *Revised Contract*.
- The fourth should say *Percent Complete*.
- The fifth and last column should say *Amount Earned*.

You're going to complete one of these Progress Evaluation Spreadsheets every two weeks. As you complete each evaluation, save the completed form and copy it onto a new spreadsheet for the next evaluation. Never discard or write over a completed form or spreadsheet. Each one should be preserved so that you will ultimately have that unbroken paper trail. If you are ever tangled in a dispute, this continuity will be invaluable.

Included on page 127 is a sample of what the first few lines of your Progress Evaluation Spreadsheet should look like.

PROGRESS EVALUATION SPREADSHEET - SETUP

Sec	Item	Task List	A Initial Contract	B Changes	C = A + B Revised Contract	D %-Compl.	E = C x D Amount Earned
000		**Household Hazards**					
	001	Test/report hazards	$600		$600		
100		**Demolition and Site Work**					
	101	Demo cabs & ctrtps	$1,000	none	$1,000		
	102	Demo floor to framing	$2,000	so far	$2,000		
200		**Foundation and Structure**					
	202	New subflr to match adjacent	$1,600		$1,600		
300		**Exterior Envelope**					
	301	Repair siding @ kit.door	$400		$400		

Making Fair Assessments

Your goal is to agree with your contractor on what *percentage* of each task he and his crew have completed.

The two of you will walk around the entire project and assess his progress on every item on your Progress Evaluation Spreadsheet — every task in the project. Discuss any differences of opinion. Ask him what is involved in replacing a window, for example, before you decide how much of that task he has completed. You ought to be able to agree on a percent complete that will seem fair to both of you.

Don't count work-in-place that you find unacceptable.

That's easy to say, but what exactly is the definition of acceptable? "Acceptable" materials have no defects except the defects in the original materials that are being left in place or reused, or defects that are natural and expectable in the new materials. For example, if you're installing a granite countertop in your kitchen and the color of your slab is not exactly the same color as the sample your designer provided you, that's not the contractor's fault. It's inherent in the natural stone that no two pieces will look exactly the same.

"Acceptable" *workmanship* is a little more difficult to define. If you've used the contract form in the appendix it states that you expect the work to meet the highest standards of construction craftsmanship in your area. If you haven't used the form in the appendix, there should be some other reference to a measurable standard. If you can't agree about whether the molding is installed correctly, ask your designer to make a judgment call or visit a project site where one of your local big-shot contractors is working.

If the contractor has done what is indicated in the designer's drawings and specifications, if the new materials are without unnatural flaws, if he is working within his schedule, and if the workmanship is good or better, the work-in-place ought to be considered "acceptable."

Measuring the Work Progress

Assessing work progress must be a collaborative effort or you will be leaving yourself open for a dispute.

As you and your contractor discuss and agree on how much work he has completed, put a number in the percent-complete column—like this:

Once you've finished assessing his progress on every task in the contract, both of you should sign *your* copy of the Progress Evaluation Spreadsheet.

Take this form home and calculate the total value of acceptable work in place by multiplying the percent complete on each task by the price of that task, and adding up these

ESTABLISHING THE %-COMPLETE at the WALK-THROUGH

Sec	Item	Task List	A Initial Contract	B Changes	C=A+B Revised Contract	D %-Compl.	E=CxD Amount Earned
000		**Household Hazards**		none			
	001	Test/report hazards	$ 600	so far	$ 600	100%	
100		**Demolition and Site Work**					
	101	Demo cabs & ctrtps	$ 1,000		$ 1,000	100%	
	102	Demo floor to framing	$ 2,000		$ 2,000	80%	
200		**Foundation and Structure**					
	202	New subflr to match adjacent	$ 1,600		$ 1,600	0%	
300		**Exterior Envelope**					
	301	Repair siding @ kit.door	$ 400		$ 400	40%	

CALCULATING THE AMOUNT EARNED TO DATE

Sec	Item	Task List	A Initial Contract	B Changes	C= A+B Revised Contract	D %-Compl.	E=CxD Amount Earned
000		**Household Hazards**					
	001	Test/report hazards	$ 600		$ 600	100%	$ 600
100		**Demolition and Site Work**		none			
	101	Demo cabs & ctrtps	$ 1,000	so far	$ 1,000	100%	$ 1,000
	102	Demo floor to framing	$ 2,000		$ 2,000	80%	$ 1,600
200		**Foundation and Structure**					
	202	New subflr to match adjacent	$ 1,600		$ 1,600	0%	$ -
300		**Exterior Envelope**					
	301	Repair siding @ kit.door	$ 400		$ 400	40%	$ 160

subtotal amounts. This will tell you how much the contractor has earned so far.

Tracking the Contractor's Momentum

Let's use the example of that small kitchen remodel—a four-month (sixteen-week) project that has a contract value of $55,900. A four-month project will have four, four-week pay periods or 112 calendar days in the work schedule. To stay on schedule and earn a check each month, the contractor must earn one-quarter of the contract amount every time one-quarter of the contract schedule (four weeks) has elapsed. Here is how you would check the contractor's *momentum*.

1. Find out what percentage of the schedule has elapsed by determining how many calendar days have elapsed since the contract start date, and divide that number by the total number of calendar days in the contract work schedule. If this was your second two-week walk-through, twenty-eight days would have passed since the start date of the contract:

   Example: Total number of calendar days that have passed (28) divided by total number of days in schedule (112) = 0.25, or 25%.

2. Now find out what percentage of the total contract he has earned so far by dividing the total amount he has earned to date by the total value of the contract.

   Example: Total earned to date per your calculations ($14,000) divided by total value of the contract ($55,900) = 0.25, or 25%.

3. Now compare the two percentages. In this example, 25 percent of the schedule has elapsed and the contractor has earned

25 percent of the value of his total contract, so he's on schedule and he's eligible for a check.

He has hit his mark at the end of the first month. That's great.

In Section 5.4, we'll talk about the difference between the total amount he has earned and the amount you will actually pay him.

Red Flags

If your contractor is behind schedule—if 25 percent of the schedule has elapsed, but he's completed only 22 percent of the work—you've got a problem.

You will be doing him a favor if you write him a letter notifying him that his momentum is starting to slip. Attach a copy of the most recent, signed, Progress Evaluation Spreadsheet with all of your calculations on it.

Your letter will get his attention, and it will show that you notified him in time to get caught up. Keep a copy of this letter attached to that evaluation in your files.

Quietly begin doing your friendly and informal site inspections more frequently. Record how many workmen are on the site and what they're working on when you're there. Take lots of pictures. Start preparing for the worst. It may never come, but you want to be ready if it does.

If this were the case—25 percent of the schedule had passed but he'd earned only 22 percent of his contract—would you pay him? We'll talk a little more about that. It's an important question.

5.3 CHANGES

You have minimized the probability of unanticipated costs by having a thorough home inspection and by using a top-notch and highly experienced residential architect. You've set aside a contingency fund for surprises and prepared a list of Alternates that you're ready to put into the contract if you have to make a quick change.

Let's look at how and why you would make a change after the work has begun.

The Gottas Versus the Wannas

There are only two kinds of changes you might make once the job is under way:

1. *Obligatory*: You discover a problem that you didn't know was there, and this condition requires a repair. You have no choice. You must do this.
2. *Discretionary*: You choose to make a change. You don't need to, but you want to.

You have no control over the former, but you have complete control over the latter. If you worked hard on your Master Plan and reviewed your designer's work carefully, the number of discretionary changes ought to fall somewhere between none and very, very few— except if you have money left in the surprises budget and you choose to make a few last-minute upgrades.

Hidden Problems and Obligatory Repairs

We've talked about the challenge of pricing a repair when only the symptoms are visible.

Remember the example we considered a few chapters ago? The floor framing needed repair, but nobody could actually see what the extent of the repair was going to be, and the bid prices for the mystery repair were clearly wild guesses. If you cannot see the deficiency, you can't write a precise description for its repair, and you can't price an undefined repair.

You could include an ambiguous statement in your design documents such as "repair as needed," but that would be risky for both you and your contractor; you could open up the floor before your architect even finished the drawings so that the work would be in the contract, but that would leave you with a big open hole for many weeks, which you wouldn't want; or you could try a third alternative— the one I recommend.

After you've negotiated and signed your construction contract, and when the work is about to begin, ask the contractor to expose all of the problem areas before he does any other work. If you choose not to deal with the mess you uncover, you can always cancel the construction contract, pay the contractor to patch up what he took apart, and put the house on the market. The contractor understands this and will give you a reasonable price for doing a major repair if the remainder of the job hangs in the balance.

If you anticipated the problem and bid your best-guess repair as an Alternate, and you guessed *correctly*, execute a change order that incorporates that repair Alternate into your contract.

If you anticipated the problem and bid a best-guess repair as an Alternate, but you guessed *incorrectly*, redefine the repair, renegotiate the cost, and execute a change order. The price the contractor put on work in the Alternate list will help you by setting a starting point for your negotiations. For example, if he bid $2,000 to replace four floor joists, and now you know he needs to replace five of them, you'll have a pretty good idea of what his price should be for the revised scope of work.

In either of these cases, the cost of the change will come out of your contingency fund.

If you uncover a structural problem, find a structural engineer to help you define the repair and negotiate the price of the work. Have that same engineer inspect the work in progress. There may be additional deterioration beyond what you have already discovered, and you may have to execute a second change order to complete the repair properly.

Your engineer's fee will come out of your soft-costs allowance, and the cost of the repair will come out of your contingency for unanticipated costs.

You will probably spend most of your contingency money, that 18 percent of your Total Project Budget you set aside for surprises, in the first phase of your project, immediately after demolition. That's when everything will be opened up. You are already prepared for any surprise costs. You're cool!

Discretionary Changes

When your contract is about 40 percent complete, after the demolition is done and the structural framing has been completed, it would be safe to assume that you won't find any more surprises. You will know what the balance in your contingency fund is, and that remainder can be used for last-minute upgrades.

Actually, to pinpoint the time for this change, you need to make your discretionary changes *after* the framing is up but *before* the drywall is nailed to it so that the contractor can make alterations to the framing or install special supports, wiring, or plumbing behind the drywall if he needs to.

In addition, this will be as long as the contractor can wait to submit his orders for long-lead items such as cabinets and countertops, custom floor coverings or fancy moldings, or hard-to-find appliances and fixtures. If you miss this window of opportunity, you may have to pay a penalty to stop an order for something you no longer want, or you may not receive your new items on time, which would delay your contractor's work and lead to the types of

larger problems that we have already discussed.

Ask your contractor to tell you when he wants your discretionary changes, and respect that deadline.

Completing a Change Order Form

Verbal agreements are not enforceable. Changes to the construction contract must be written down and signed by both you and your contractor. The form that is used to institute a change is called a *change order*.

Every change order must address the three big issues: scope of work, schedule, and cost. Included on page 124 is a blank form for your review.

Let's continue to use the examples we've been discussing.

If you recall, during the contract negotiations we took the floor-framing repair out of the contract because the bid numbers indicated that the contractors were afraid of pricing something they couldn't see. Your contractor agreed to open up the kitchen floor before he did any other work, to let a structural engineer help you define the repair.

Imagine that the work started last week. The contractor opened up the floor on Day 1. Your structural engineer was on call, and he showed up later that day. Within seventy-two hours, you received copies of the engineer's drawing that clearly described what the contractor had to do, and the contractor priced the repair at $3,200, which your engineer thought was a fair price. The whole negotiation took about five days to complete. Let's execute a change order.

• Fill in the top of the form. In this case, we'll assume that this is your first amendment to the contract, so this will be Change Order #1. The project address is probably your home address.

CHANGE ORDER # _____
Date: _____

Project   (address)
Owner   D.Homeowner
GC   D.Contractor

This Change Order is hereby incorporated into the Contract by reference and shall be subject to all stipulations and covenants of that Contract, once it is fully executed.

Section	List of Changes	Cost

Net Change to Contract Value

Current Contract Value
Plus/Minus This Change Order
Equals New Contract Value

Total Calendar Days in Schedule
Time Added by This Change Order
Revised Total Calendar Days in Schedule
Number of Four-Week Pay Periods in Revised Schedule

Signatures   **Date**

- In the body of the form in the center of the page, assign a section number from the Task Abstract List to this work. In this case the section number would be 200 because this is a structural framing repair.
- Next to that number, describe the new work. You might say: "Repair floor framing per engineer drawing" (or "Repair flr fram'g— eng.dwg."), and record the price as "+$3,200."
- If you are making more than one change on Change Order #1, you'll list each one in a similar fashion and carry only the amount of the *total net change* down into the calculations below the list.
- Your contractor may ask for those five days back. That's fair; indicate that you're adding five days to his schedule, as well as $3,200 to his contract amount.

When the change order is signed by both of you, the copy with the original signatures should go into your Contract and Change Orders file along with photos of the area affected by the change. A photocopy of the change order should be given to the contractor. This document is now a binding agreement and an integral part of your construction contract. He is obligated to do the work, and you are obligated to pay him for it.

The change order must be signed by both you and your contractor before he begins the work it describes. If he starts work before the form is fully executed, he works at his own risk. You may choose not to make the change after all, and the contractor will be obligated to undo what he's done, at his own expense.

There Is No Other Money, Honey

When you record a change order on your project accounting spreadsheet, you'll be moving the amount of the change order out of your contingency fund and into your contract amount. Note that the total amount of money in your budget hasn't changed, but that the money has come out of the set-aside and is now in the contract—like the water in the canal locks.

As the project progresses, you may find more problems and need to spend more of your contingency on change orders—which will move more of the set-aside into the contract amount.

When you show a $0.00 balance in your set-aside fund, you have no more money left in your budget. If you have another unanticipated expense at that point, you must do one of two things: either omit some work (and money) from the construction contract and put that money toward the surprise repair, or contribute some of your personal savings to pay for the added expense. We've done everything in our power to prevent this from happening, but there are no guarantees.

5.4 PAYMENTS

Your contract payment schedule is set up so that the contractor can expect to take home a check every four weeks if he does his part and works diligently. If he really lights a fire under his subs, he can collect his checks more often than once a month—he can have a check each time he hits a percent-complete benchmark you've set in your contract pay schedule. Under normal circumstances, your second two-week progress evaluation ought to generate his first check.

CHANGE ORDER #1

Date: _____

Project	(address)	
Owner	D.Homeowner	
GC	D.Contractor	

This Change Order is hereby incorporated into the Contract by reference and shall be subject to all stipulations and covenants of that Contract, once it is fully executed.

Section	List of Changes	Cost
200	Repair floor framing in accordance with engineer's drawing, attached.	$ 3,200
	Net Change to Contract Value	**$ 3,200**

Current Contract Value	$ 55,900
Plus/Minus This Change Order	$ 3,200
Equals New Contract Value	**$ 59,100**

Total Calendar Days in Schedule	112
Time Added by This Change Order	5 days
Revised Total Calendar Days in Schedule	**117**
Number of Four-Week Pay Periods in Revised Schedule	4

Signatures	Date
D. Contractor	d
D. Homeowner	

Before you do your second formal progress evaluation, copy the completed spreadsheet from your first evaluation onto a clean form and file the first evaluation without changing it.

Erase the amounts earned in the fifth column from this new evaluation form, but leave the percents-complete so you don't make the mistake of backtracking. Add any change orders that you may have executed during the last two weeks so that the form is up-to-date. Take two copies of this new Progress Evaluation Spreadsheet to the site for the second walk-through and give a copy to your contractor.

While you are on the site with the contractor, overwrite the percentages from the last evaluation on every line item with new values. When all of the tasks have been evaluated, both of you must sign your spreadsheet; then you take it home and do the math to find out how much the contractor has earned to date, and what percentage of the total contract amount that represents.

If he is working to his schedule, and he has earned enough to be eligible for a check, then cut him a check right away. There's no excuse for a delay. If he has not earned enough yet, you both have a problem.

Deductions

Assuming he's earned a check, what the contractor has earned and what you will pay him will not be the same number.

It is a universal practice to withhold 10 percent of the total amount the contractor has earned until he's absolutely and completely finished and you sign off on the job. The reason you hold that 10 percent is so that if for any reason he can't finish the job, and you have to hire another contractor to pick up where he left off, you'll have enough money left to pay the second contractor the premium price the second contractor is going to charge you. We talked a bit about that in Section 5.1, on disputes.

You will also deduct the total value of all prior payments, including any deposits, from the amount of his check, because you have already paid him this money.

Releasing a Check

Let's go back to the small kitchen project and see how this works. The contract schedule has four four-week pay periods. You have just completed your second two-week progress evaluation, so his first four weeks have passed and he's eligible for his first check—he's earned 25 percent of the contract that, including the first change order, is now worth $59,100, not $55,900. In addition, before work started you gave him a $5,000 deposit so that he could order the special cabinets you wanted. This is how you will calculate the check you owe him.

Total Amount Earned to Date	$14,775
Minus 10% Retainage	$1,478
Equals Balance #1	$13,297
Minus All Previous Payments:	
Deposit for Cabinets	$5,000
Equals Balance #2	$8,297
Minus Late Fees (not an issue until the last check)	0
Equals Amount Due	$8,297

Write the check for $8,297, and call him when it's ready. If the bank that made your loan is going to release the checks, give your loan officer a copy of your Progress Evaluation

Spreadsheet with the check calculation attached, and ask that the check be processed within seventy-two hours.

When the contractor picks up his check, have him sign and date a *photocopy* of the check, and have a witness, an upstanding citizen but *not* a spouse or family member, sign and date the photocopy as affirmation that he got this check. The signed, dated, and witnessed photocopy of the check has been acceptable evidence of payment in mediation hearings for me in the past.

If you wish to have more formal documentation, have the contractor sign a lien waiver form (see pages 141–142 in Section 5.5) and have it notarized. I use the lien waiver only for the final payment, but your banker or the bonding agent may require the lien waiver with every payment.

Attach the contractor's check to a *copy* of the signed Progress Evaluation Spreadsheet so that you and the contractor both know exactly what you're paying for. Attach your witnessed *photocopy* of the check, or the more formal lien waiver, to the *original* copy of the Progress Evaluation Spreadsheet and put them in your Progress Evaluations and Contractor Checks file.

Not Releasing a Check

There are two things that might make you want to withhold his check: insufficient progress and unacceptable work. Since you have stipulated his momentum as the trigger for payment in your contract, instead of just the passage of time, both of these problems ought to take care of themselves.

The contract stipulates the percentage of the total contract value the contractor has to have completed, and its relationship to the percentage of time that has elapsed, in order for your contractor to qualify for a check. There should be no dispute about his work momentum if you agreed on and both signed the Progress Evaluation Spreadsheet after you'd agreed on the percent-complete for every task. When you do the math, either he's done enough to meet your standard or he hasn't.

Withholding a check because you don't like the quality of his work is a different story.

Do not include unsatisfactory work in the assessment of how much work he's finished— "satisfactory" should be defined by your contract. If you don't count the problematic work and he still hits his percent-complete, pay him, but attach a letter to the check stating that the unsatisfactory work must be corrected before the next payment will be issued, and be very specific about what you don't like and what he has to do to correct it—don't tell him how to do his work, but do tell him what you expect the finished product to look like. You don't need to withhold the check and punish the whole crew if there is only one guy who is not performing to your standards.

If the entire crew seems to be doing bad work, when you discount the bad work and calculate the percent-complete, the absence of the greater amount of unsatisfactory work ought to keep him from meeting his percent-complete benchmark, and so it ought to keep him from getting a check, but that doesn't really solve your problem.

The Question of Quality

"Quality" is a very subjective matter. If the two of you disagree about the quality of his work, take pictures, and call a meeting that includes both the contractor and the designer.

If the designer agrees with you, ask her to help you and your contractor set a clear standard for corrective work that you all agree is fair. Within twenty-four hours of that meeting, write a reiterate-and-confirm letter that restates the standards the contractor has to meet to be paid both now and in the future. See if he can both correct the work and get back on schedule by the time your next two-week progress evaluation rolls around.

If your designer agrees with your contractor, and thinks the work is okay and he should be paid, ask the designer to explain her thinking to you. It's possible that the task you're concerned about is just not completed yet, that at this stage this is what it *should* look like, and that once he's done it will be fine. Her explanation will help you in the future. Nobody's perfect; learn something.

If you have lots of unsatisfactory work on the job, you may want to consider consulting your attorney and cutting your losses before you get in any deeper. Reread the section on disputes so you know what your options are.

Remember, though, this shouldn't happen to you, because you took my advice and checked at least ten references on every one of the contractors you put on your bidders list, and every one of them was a stellar human being . . . a paragon.

5.5 FINISHING UP

When the work is nearly done it's time to begin tying up loose ends.

Don't lose your focus now. What you do with this last one percent of the job will get you through the warranty period without problems, or will be the inspiration for another country-and-western song about how he done left you for another (job) and won't come back no more.

Contractors hate to fuss with the last few tasks; there's nothing satisfying or heroic about

tightening hinges or hanging closet shelves. You are going to keep him focused by doing two things:

- Carefully inspect the work when it's *just about* complete, and provide him with a list of all the little things you think still need his attention. This will help him finish quickly.
- Write that fat final check that includes all of the retainage you've been withholding, and show it to him—then place it carefully in your wallet and put your wallet away. He'll get the message that the minute he's satisfied you on all counts, he'll get paid. That will really keep him focused. It's downright diabolical, but it's effective!

Be tough—be sure he gets every detail finished to your satisfaction—but keep in mind that the final payment does not constitute the end of your relationship. You will need his goodwill during the warranty period too.

Substantial Completion

When the contractor says the job's *substantially* complete, he means that he is 99 percent or more finished with the work and has only a few tasks left, but it's not *absolutely* complete.

In preparation for the substantial completion inspection, you should remind yourself of all of the conditions he has to meet in order to have absolutely and completely finished the job, including submitting his paperwork, for example, before you sign off.

Double-check all change orders and be sure that all changes have been correctly incorporated into the final Progress Evaluation Spreadsheet.

Bring copies of all documents to the final walk-through, in case there are questions. Bring the whole file if you can. Neither of you wants to drag out the "amen."

Spend a few hours walking around the site. Closely inspect every single detail of the work. It might be worth a small fee to bring along someone with a keen eye for detail to review the work with you. How you choose this bird of prey will depend on the kinds of problems you've had along the way—good candidates might include the architect, the structural engineer, your best friend, or your mother-in-law. It's up to you, but you may not change your standards of acceptable work at this point.

The list you create will include things like tightening screws, touching up paint, spot-cleaning carpets, adjusting cabinet doors, installing a missing door bumper or two, leveling the stove, ensuring that no windows are painted shut—all the little stuff.

Make your list in duplicate. Write clearly and be very specific. Assign a best-guess cost to *each* task on your list. There usually aren't any material changes; use an hourly labor *billing* rate (not the contractor's payroll rate)—try $30 per hour—times the number of hours you think it will take the subs to finish the tasks on the list; then determine a total estimated value of *all* unfinished or corrective work.

If the total value of the work on the list is *greater* than one percent of the value of the total contract, the contractor gets a copy of the list as a reminder of what is left to do, but the project is not "substantially complete" and this list is not going to be final.

If the value of the remaining work is one percent—or less than one percent—of the value of the total contract, the contractor *is* "substantially complete" and the list should be issued as a *punch list*.

You'll need to be able to give the contractor his copy of the list at the end of walk-through and take a copy home for yourself; find a way to do this.

The Punch List

A punch list is the *last* list of unfinished work—not the next to last or the third from the last. Once the work on a punch list is completed, the contractor will expect to be paid.

If you are not thorough when you prepare this list, and you find other things later that you think ought to be done before you pay him, the contractor may have *strong* objections.

You'll be holding up everybody's money. The contractor won't be able to pay the subcontractors until you have paid him. In addition, he's probably promised his next client a start date and ordered that client's long-lead items. Now he has to postpone everything. Nobody will be happy with you.

Does he owe you that work? Yes. But you should have been more careful.

The Paperwork

It is stipulated in the contract form in the appendix, and should be in all construction contract forms, that the contractor owes you certain paperwork at the end of the job. That paperwork may include, but is not limited to, the following:

- **Written warranty statements** from subs and manufacturers such as the exterminator's one-year guarantee; the manufacturers' written warranties on roof shingles, cabinetry, floor finishes, appliances, water heaters, and the like.
- **Operating and maintenance manuals** for all new equipment, machinery, or appliances such as that new high-tech thermostat, the new microwave oven, the water filter, the furnace, the ceiling fans, the tilt-out windows, and so on.

Review the manuals with the contractor or with the appropriate subcontractor as a part of the final walk-through, and get a lesson in how to work any device or appliance you're not already familiar with. This will be a free lesson. Asking later will cost you money. Messing blindly with an unfamiliar device can cost you even more money! If you break this device, your warranty won't apply.

In every operating manual there is a page full of blank spaces where your contractor should fill in the name, address, and phone number of the manufacturer and the vendor; *and* the make, model, and serial number of the item; *and* the date that he installed it. His handwriting must be legible. If you can't tell a lowercase "L" from the number "1" from an uppercase "I," it won't be helpful. You'll need this information if you have to make a claim for repair of manufacturing defects or replacement of bad parts.

Model, make, and serial numbers are usually located on a silver tag attached to the back or the bottom of the appliance. Once the appliance, or whatever it is, is installed, you won't be able to get at it.

Let the contractor know *ahead of time* that completing this information in the user's manual is his responsibility. It should be stated clearly in your Terms and Conditions Statement, as it is in the appendix.

One of my clients neglected to get the serial number of the water heater. When the thermostat malfunctioned, she couldn't make a claim to the manufacturer without including that number. She paid a technician to disconnect the tank and tip it over to expose the information tag. This action voided the warranty.

- **A list of subcontractors** who worked on the job, their company names, a contact name, an address and telephone number, and their tax ID or social security number. Your warranty is the responsibility of the general contractor. If

he's smart, he's gotten the commitment from the subs to back him up. In any case, if he decides to change careers or retire, you'll still know whom you can call to get something fixed, whether it's a warranty call or a problem you encounter two years later.

- **The inspections data card** that has been posted on the site during the construction work period. It is the one that the municipal inspectors have been signing as the contractor passed his inspections. Give your contractor a copy.

- **An original certificate of occupancy** from your local inspections department. Without this, you cannot legally occupy the house. You should get one in the mail within a week or so after the final municipal sign-off. If you don't receive the certificate of occupancy, your contractor has to be the one to go to city hall and get it for you.

Hire an independent locksmith to change the locks. You don't know who has copies of your keys.

Calculating the Final Payment

To calculate the value of the contractor's final check, use the same Progress Evaluation Spreadsheet that you used for the interim payments. Be especially thorough when you inspect. Before you say he's 100 percent complete on any task, be sure that you've checked, and that he really is. Double-check any task listed on your punch list. If the old paint color is bleeding through the new one, then the paint job is not finished. Even if it bleeds through only in one place, the paint job may be 99.9 percent complete, but you're not obligated to pay for 99.9 percent complete.

Add up the total he's earned. If he is indeed finished, the total earned should equal the total amount of the contract, including all change orders. This time, when you calculate the value of his check, you will *not* deduct any retainage, but you *will* deduct all previous payments and any late fees. (Late fees, by the way, are sometimes referred to as "liquidated damages.")

As always, the bottom-line number will be the amount of the check.

Let's look at our sample project again—the small kitchen remodel—and see how this works. We will assume that there were no further changes after the change order we wrote together earlier in the book.

Momentum Evaluation	
Total Amount Earned to Date:	$59,100
Divided by Total Contract Value	$59,100
Equals % Complete	100%
Calendar Days Elapsed Since Work Started	121
Minus Total Calendar Days in the Work Schedule	117
Equals Number of Days Subject to Late Fees	4 (uh-oh)

Payment Calculation	
Total Value of the Contract:	$59,100
Total Earned to Date	$59,100
Minus 10% Retainage	N/A
Equals Balance 1	$59,100
Minus All Other Payments to Date:	
Deposit	$5,000
Payment 1 of 4	$8,297
Payment 2 of 4	$13,650
Payment 3 of 4	$12,953
Subtotal of All Payments to Date:	$39,900
Equals Balance 2	$19,200
Minus Penalties or Late Fees (4 days)	$_____
Equals Amount Due— Final Payment	$_____

Let's think for a minute.

If your contract says that your contractor must be 100 percent complete by day *X*, that's what you can hold him to. One hundred percent complete means he has satisfied all of the conditions in the contract and he's totally and unequivocally done: punch-list items finished, paperwork submitted, certificate of occupancy secured from the inspections department, everything done and ready for move-in.

If he had to work for four extra days beyond the contract completion date to meet this requirement, then he's finished four days late and he's triggered the penalties stipulated in your contract. The contract form in the appendix tells you what you can charge him per calendar day, not workday, for late completion. You may forgive these penalties, but if you charge him you must follow the contract agreement.

Would you deduct late fees from the contractor's last payment? You could save (what does the appendix say?) $_____ on your total job cost if you did. What do you think? It's entirely up to you.

Releasing the Final Payment

Always use a lien waiver form when you release a final check. There is a sample lien waiver form on pages 141 and 142 for your review.

He should not sign the waiver until you offer him the check, and you shouldn't let go of the check until he's signed the waiver. You'll have to have a notary on hand to attest to his signature on the lien waiver, or meet at the bank where the check is waiting and use the bank's notary.

The date of the final check is the date that your warranty period begins. Keep a photocopy of this check, signed by the contractor and a witness, attached to the lien waiver for your files.

Lien Waiver Form

(PAGE 1 OF 2)

Date of Draw Walk-through _____ Draw # _____

Project Property Address _____

Owner's Name _____

General Contractor's Company Name _____

COMPLETION STATUS REPORT:

% of contract value earned to date _____ %

% of contract schedule elapsed to date _____ %

CURRENT CONTRACT VALUE:

Original contract price $ _____

Value of all change orders $ _____

Total revised contract value $ _____

CURRENT PAYMENT CALCULATION:

Total earned to date $ _____

Less 10% retainage $ _____

Balance 1 $ _____

Less previous payments $ _____

Balance 2 $ _____

Less late fees (liquidated damages) $ _____

Total amount PAID at this time $ _____

Lien Waiver Form

(PAGE 2 OF 2)

AFFIDAVIT:

I do hereby certify:

- That I am the general contractor responsible for the work on the project property listed above, and
- That this payment is appropriate to the percentage of the contract work that was completed at the time of the progress evaluation referenced above, and
- That all entities providing any labor or materials for this project that were under my supervision, control, or subcontract will be paid in full within thirty days of my receiving this payment, in proportion to the work they had completed as of the date of the progress evaluation listed above, and
- That I will be fully and solely responsible for satisfying any claims or liens against the owner or his property originating from any of my subcontractors or suppliers or employees, to the extent of the total value of the payments I have received to date.

Signature of Owner of Contracting Firm _____

Printed Name _____ Date_____

Name of Contracting Firm _____

Address _____

Tax ID# _____

ATTEST

STATE OF _____, COUNTY OF _____

I do hereby certify that (Contractor Name) _____ personally

appeared before me, stating that he is the owner of the firm called

_____, and duly executed the foregoing instrument.

This is the _____ day of _____, 20_____.

Notary Public signature_____ My commission expires _____

(Notary Seal Here)

SIX

Warranty

The contractor is obligated to respond to legitimate claims for repairs during the warranty period. Know your options in case he does not.

What Does the Contractor Owe You?

The contractor owes you no more and no less than what was in his contract, including any amendments or change orders.

The warranty says that he will fix anything that he didn't do correctly in the first place, at no cost to you, for a certain period of time (usually one year) after the date of his final payment.

If you're using the contract in the appendix, you'll have a one-year warranty on all work except a new roof, and a three-year warranty on the roof. Leaks from pinholes in the roof coverings take time to show up. In my opinion, it's not unfair to ask for enough time for the work to prove itself.

What Constitutes a Legitimate Warranty Claim?

A written request for the repair of a deficiency in any work that was in the construction contract, that is sent during the warranty period, is a legitimate warranty claim.

The first year that your new construction materials are in place, they will go through a period of seasoning—stretching and shrinking in response to changes in temperature and humidity. Nail heads may protrude, seams in new drywall may crack, moldings may warp

just a little and pull away from the walls . . . this is normal and does not indicate that your contractor did a poor job. These kinds of problems are common warranty complaints. You both ought to expect them, and he ought to take care of them without hesitation.

In addition to the changes you observe in your finishes due to seasoning, no matter how carefully you did your final inspection, there will be one or two things you overlooked. It's not too late to make a warranty claim to get these fixed.

If you have more than one problem, send the contractor a complete list. Don't send one claim this week and one the next. Your contractor will appreciate this, and he'll probably be more responsive as well.

When you make your claim, ask for a *response* within a week and a *completed repair* within thirty days. Remember that by now he probably has somebody else's plumbing torn up. He may not be able to get his plumber to your house for a few days.

If the problem is small and simple to remedy, you might want to weigh the cost of making the repair yourself against the cost of chasing down the contractor. If a screw needs tightening, I'd just tighten it. If the problem involves electrical, plumbing, or HVAC work (the licensed trades), stand firm and get the tradesmen to make the repair. You'll lose both your contractor's warranty and your manufacturer's warranty on anything you tinker with.

Emergency Repairs—Leaks and Sparks

Leaks and sparking electrical connections require immediate attention. Shut off the appropriate valve or breaker, then call the contractor right away. Insist that he send a plumber or an electrician immediately. Follow up in writing that day, just for the record.

The Eleventh-Month Walk-through

Thirty days or so before the end of your warranty period, inspect every item in the contract. Use your final Progress Evaluation Spreadsheet so that you have a complete Task Abstract List to guide you. Invite your designer or your home inspector or a friend to help if you want to benefit from their keen observations. This is your last chance to file a warranty claim.

What the Contractor Does *Not* Owe You

Wear and tear is not his problem.

It is not his problem if you neglect to do proper maintenance, such as watering the newly seeded lawn.

It is not his problem if a storm dropped a large tree branch through your roof.

And, of course, any work that was not a part of his contract in the first place is not his problem either.

When Does the Contractor's Warranty Obligation End?

As long as you've made a legitimate, written warranty claim during the warranty period, your contractor owes you the repair, even if the official warranty period ends before he honors his obligation. But if all your claims are satisfied and he passed all his municipal inspections, your warranty ends when your contract says it does, usually one year after the date on the final check.

Warranty Disputes

If the contractor contends that he does not owe you the repair work you've asked for, you still have recourse. Warranty work is a part of his contract obligations. Handle this the same way you handled disputes during the work period.

Try a friendly discussion first. If you can come to some agreement, send a reiterate-and-confirm letter.

If the two of you can't agree, call in the designer. If you three can come to some agreement, send a reiterate-and-confirm letter.

If you can't seem to get him to respond to your friendly advances, get just a little unfriendly. Send him a second letter and write "cc: attorney" on the bottom of the letter. If you really have to, you can actually get the attorney involved, but this letter will usually get you a phone call.

Relying on His Insurance

If your contractor refuses to take care of something that is clearly in his contract and therefore his responsibility, try making a claim against his insurance policy.

If the building code or other laws govern your problem, or if your problem is substantial and if your contractor was licensed, you may try calling the contractors state license board and follow their procedure for filing a claim with the state.

Calling the Bonding Agent

If you got both payment and performance bonds from the contractor, call the bonding agent. You have a copy of the bond document in your files. Send only what they ask for and keep the cover letter brief. Expect a letter or a telephone call in response within a week, and then follow the agent's instructions to the letter.

Note: Both bonding and insurance agents will resist honoring a claim when the cost of the repair is less than the amount of money they'd spend on manpower to process the paperwork. Exaggerating the claim will only irritate them.

Bringing in the Big Guns

If the contractor just won't agree to make this repair, and you still think he owes it to you, ask your attorney to review your claim, and follow his advice.

Warranty disputes are candidates for mediation or arbitration just like any other dispute. Try the less confrontational and less expensive solutions first, but don't hesitate to call your attorney if the deficiency is serious and if that's what it takes to get the contractor to make the repair.

What Happens After the Warranty Period Expires?

At the end of the warranty period, the contractor no longer owes you anything that hasn't already been brought to his attention, or that isn't controlled by law.

If you still have outstanding warranty complaints, he still has outstanding warranty *obligations*, although no new claims will be honored.

If the outstanding deficiencies are controlled by law—if, for example, he did some work that never complied with the building code—there is no end to his obligation to make corrections, even if you failed to notify him of the problems during the warranty period.

But if you've got a leak in your new bathroom faucet and it started after the warranty period was up, or it started during the warranty period but you neglected to notify him in writing before the deadline, that leak is your problem now.

What About Manufacturers' Warranties?

You ought to have manuals for all new devices and appliances. They will tell you what the manufacturer's warranty period is. Refrigerators, for example, may come with a five- or ten-year warranty on the compressor even if the box is warrantied for only one year.

You'll need the help of the subcontractor who installed this appliance and his good relationship with the vendor or the manufacturer to make a manufacturing defect claim stick.

Copy the claim form in the owner's manual, the one the general contractor filled out for you. Complete the part about what you are asking for, add a photo or two if the defect is something you can see, and write a letter to the manufacturer requesting a response within two weeks. Copy the general contractor and the subcontractor that installed the defective device, attaching the same documents, and ask them to call the manufacturer as well.

Follow up with calls to everybody about a week after you think they've received their copies of your claim. More often than not, if you've maintained a good working relationship with your contractors, they will eventually help you get what you need from the manufacturer. It just might not be this month.

PART TWO

Our Project

ONE

Facing Facts

Introduction to Our Project

All of the information up to this point has been theoretical. In the absence of concrete examples, you may have found it challenging to understand. Now you have the opportunity to plan, design, and execute a complete, substantial (imaginary) remodeling project that will put all of these strategies into context. Ready?

Before You Begin

This project is your opportunity to practice all that you've just learned. As with everything else in life, you'll get out of it what you put into it. I want you to get on the phone and do the research. Visit real estate open houses. Photograph things, measure things, jot down your ideas, and take the time to analyze each of your options as if this were your own house and your own project. Try to imagine what this family in the story needs and how they would make decisions.

Anticipate spending a few days on some of the exercises—don't just breeze through. The harder you work on this project, the easier your own project will be. Make your mistakes here—while they're free—rather than later, when they're not.

The success of any remodeling project depends to a great degree on the nature of the relationships you have with the people you work with. You are going to choose the designer and the contractor.

I will give you my opinion from time to time, and I will have to provide you with some guidelines to keep the job moving, but otherwise you're in charge. If you get stumped, all of the problems have been addressed in the text in Part 1 of the book; you may find what you are looking for there.

I encourage you to work on this project with your mate or a good friend. It will be *much* more fun, and once you begin your real project, you'll have someone nearby who understands the remodeling process the same way you do, and that moral support will be invaluable.

The architect who created all of the floor plans and illustrations is just the sort of architect you would look for. He has lots of experience and lots of imagination, and he's very clever; look closely at the details in his illustrations before you make your decisions.

The house is real, of course, but the project is entirely make-believe. The photos of work in progress were taken on construction sites in three different zip codes, so they won't always precisely match the architect's plans. Let the drawings, not the photos, be your guide.

A Little History

Once upon a time there was a small city that seemed destined to grow and prosper. A patch of the old pine forest had been cut down in 1759 to create building materials for a carefully

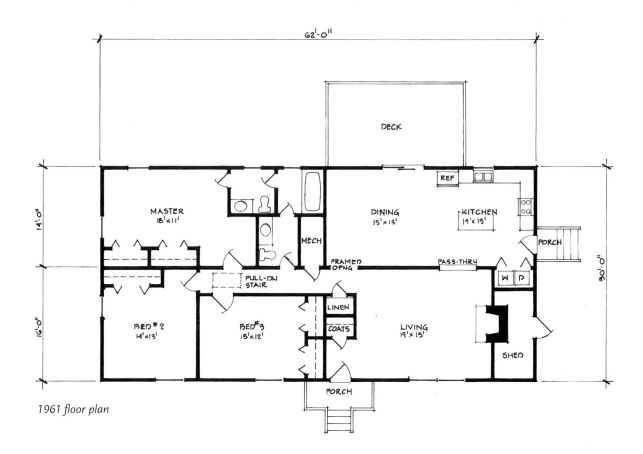

62'-0"

14'-0"

10'-0"

30'-0"

DECK

REF

MASTER
18'x11'

DINING
15'x13'

KITCHEN
14'x13'

MECH

PORCH

FRAMED
OPNG

PASS-THRU

PULL-DN
STAIR

W   D

BED #2
14'x13'

BED #3
15'x12'

LINEN

COATS

LIVING
19'x15'

SHED

PORCH

1961 floor plan

Our Project—front

Our Project—back

Our Project—living room fireplace

planned new settlement of exactly ten square blocks. By the late 1800s there were nearly 80,000 inhabitants and half a dozen small universities; the town had become a thriving market for goods and services from across the region.

By 1960 there were nearly 150,000 people living in what had become a small but unusually cosmopolitan city. There were now eight or nine colleges and universities, some of which rivaled the finest educational institutions in the country. Dozens of major corporations had built their headquarters nearby. Four large hospitals provided world-class health care, and the state was investing heavily in highways and parks. This little city was attracting the attention of businesses and families from all over the map. The climate was temperate, and the area prospered.

Our little house—Our Project—was built in 1961. It was a 30-by-62-foot box with three bedrooms and one very awkward bathroom. It had a brick front and wood siding on the other three sides, a large back deck, and a small fireplace in the living room. The previous page shows what it looked like in the sixties.

Our Neighborhood in 1985

By 1985 the population of Our City was more than 250,000. A new interstate highway formed a "beltline" around most of the suburban areas and diverted most of the rush-hour traffic away from the older, smaller, downtown streets like ours.

Our Neighborhood had improved quite a bit. Some of the original homes, built between 1940 and 1965, had been remodeled; some had been torn down and replaced with larger homes with more sophisticated design styles.

Tax photo of our project after the 1985 remodel

Our little house was, let's see, twenty-four years old at this point, and a bit of an embarrassment. It needed lots of repairs. The family that owned it in 1985 decided to remodel.

Tax records of this home contain one blurry photograph, taken after the 1985 remodel, but you can see how the new roofline, the new windows, and the recessed front entry gave the house a more contemporary look. The owners chose to demolish the original fireplace and build a new one closer to the center of the house.

Their designer did a great job of maximizing the original 1,860 square feet of space, but the twenty-four-year-old electrical and plumbing services were patched up, not replaced. Even though the remodel improved the looks and the condition of the home, it still didn't measure up to its neighbors, and the after-remodel appraised value reflected that.

During the fifteen years that followed the 1985 remodel, there were three or four different owners. Nobody seemed to stay long enough to care that the house was beginning to deteriorate, or at least they didn't care enough to do much about it.

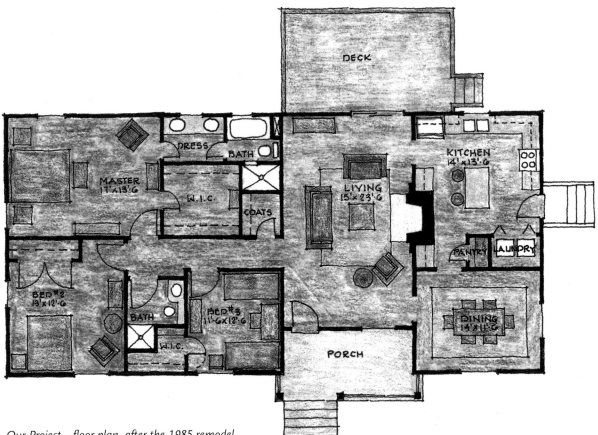

Our Project—floor plan, after the 1985 remodel

Who Are "You" and What Are You Doing Here?

"You" are the family that bought this house in 2001.

You moved here from another state when Dad was offered a nice promotion. Since you didn't know the area very well, when you were house hunting you were cautious; you followed prudent real estate investing principles and looked for the least expensive home in a really nice location.

You were lucky to find a home on Our Street! For a mere $200,000, you got a sad little house on a tiny lot . . . in an outstanding neighborhood. You paid all but $40,000 in cash from the proceeds of the sale of your last home, and the company paid for the move.

What you bought in 2001 was a 1961 house with 1961 plumbing and a 1985 floor plan. Your home inspector warned you that there was a major remodel in your future, but once you moved in, you got so busy that you put the remodel off.

In 2003 you discovered that Mom was expecting a third child. There would not be enough room in this house for a family of five. It was time to face the remodel.

TWO

Project Planning

Your house is forty-two years old. With a third baby on the way, you probably won't want to move again anytime soon, and since you anticipated remodeling when you bought the house, you will definitely choose to stay and remodel.

This is a fabulous neighborhood—homes are selling for $600,000 and up (way up!)—and you're sitting on a property you paid $200,000 for. The house needs work—lots of work!—and you're about to invest a considerable sum in this remodel. Your biggest challenge will be to plan a project with maximum impact that is also cost-effective.

No; that was not accurate. Your *biggest* challenge will be to deal with two small children, a new career, a pregnancy, and a remodel—with no old friends nearby to provide moral support. Make a note to be kind to one another. This may get stressful.

Planning will be the key to your success—the foundation for all future decisions. Spend as much time as you need to complete the planning exercises so that the remainder of the project will go smoothly.

Research

Review the research suggested in Part 1, Chapters 1 and 2, and apply what you can here.

You know that you've got a forty-two-year-old home in only fair condition with dangerously old services. If you could review

your property survey, you would see that the structure is on a triangulated lot. The front lot line is 180 feet long, but the back is only 50. If you decide to build an addition, you'll have to take that into consideration. There are no other impediments on the deed or the survey.

You found out two years ago when you bought the house that homes on this part of your street were selling for three times what you paid. You bought for $200,000, and you're holding only a $40,000 mortgage. You're in good shape financially.

The zoning and inspections administrators at city hall both seemed to think that you could count on your street to stay much the same as it is now. You're in an older area of town and it's fully built out. You're not far from a few small colleges, but nowhere near the commercial district.

What about environmental hazards? You've probably got lead-based paint, since it wasn't outlawed for use on residential buildings until 1978 and this house was built in the 60's. There may be other problems too. Better have the house tested before you start stirring things up.

What Matters Most

Go back to page 151 and have a really close look at the 1985 floor plan you are living in. Look at how far Mom has to haul sheets from the three bedrooms in order to do the laundry. Where is the linen closet? You have to use your formal dining room for all the family meals. Is that okay? Where did you put the television? Where will you work on this remodeling project? Where does Dad do his paperwork on the weekends? Where would you have a private conversation? Where do your kids play? What is the focal point of each room now, and what would you like it to be once you're done remodeling?

By the way, the front door of your home faces east. Where is the sun in the morning and where is the sun at suppertime? Where would you like to add more light and where is there already enough? How much natural light do you suppose there is in your living room?

Spend some time getting to know this house; then make your lists:
• What I like,
• What I don't like, and
• What I wish I had that I don't have now.

Sort Out Your Priorities

When your lists are complete, sort your problems into groups of related activities: (1) cooking and dining, (2) entertaining and family time, (3) beds and baths, and so on—whatever you think are the activities that are most important to your young family of four (about to be five)—and see which functions are served pretty well by the existing floor plan, and which are in dire need of help. And don't forget curb appeal; your yard could use some attention too.

When you've got all of your concerns on paper and sorted them out by activity, compare what you need the most space *for* with the amount of space allotted to that activity on the existing floor plan. Wherever you have the greatest imbalance between what you need and what you have, you have a high-priority *design challenge*. You have just identified areas where

Too-small bathroom

Too-small kitchen

redesign will have the greatest impact. You're going to put most of your time and energy into finding solutions to these design challenges.

What would you say are your three highest priorities? Write them down.

Get a Good Home Inspection

You had an inspection when you bought this old house, but if they'd told you the whole truth you probably would have run away. Let's imagine that you have found a great home inspector (refer to Part 1, Section 3.1: Hire the Best, to remember how to do that) and have gotten a thorough inspection report. Here are some of the items he would have found.

BROKEN DOWNSPOUT

All of the gutters on the house show signs of rust; some have detached from the house. Replace all gutters.

Broken downspout

TREES ALONG THE FOUNDATION WALL

Volunteer trees have taken root along the foundation wall. The roots of the largest ones have already begun breaking through the mortar joints between the bricks, below grade. Remove all vegetation that is rooted within 30 inches of the house wall.

Trees along foundation wall

PEELING PAINT

The use of lead-based paint was prohibited by federal regulations in 1978. Given the age of this house, the older paint being exposed by peeling may have sufficient amounts of lead to create a hazardous condition. Sample all painted surfaces and treat according to regulations. Call your state department of the environment and natural resources, lead hotline, for more information and a list of consultants who can help.

Peeling paint on old windows

TRIPPING HAZARD ON STEPS

An old cement repair on front steps is broken and separating from the original steps beneath it, creating a tripping hazard. The remainder of this old repair covers all three steps; all surfaces have cracked. Best solution: replace concrete steps completely. Temporary solution: repatch the repaired cracked finish.

Tripping hazard on patched front steps

LEAK ABOVE BATHROOM CEILING

The stains in the ceiling of the bathroom are caused by a leak in the roof above—there is no plumbing in the attic crawl space in this area. In addition, the water seems to be coming through the ceiling into an electrical exhaust fan, which is a fire hazard. Find the roof leak and repair it.

Leak above bathroom ceiling

DANGEROUS WATER HEATER

Replace water heater. Wires are frayed at connections to unit, insulation appears to contain colonies of mold, and the thermostat is not working properly.

Old, dangerous water heater

PITTED DRIVEWAY

This driveway was made of an inferior mixture of materials that have now disintegrated. If you apply a new layer of surface over this one, it won't last long. Remove all paving, lay new bed of gravel, and repave.

Pitted driveway

FOUNDATION ACCESS DOOR

The original wood has warped and broken and pulled away from the brick surround at the foundation access door. Reframe for a new door, and caulk the joint between the wood and the brick to seal against water penetration. Install a new door. Prime, seal, and paint the entire assembly.

Rotten foundation access door

DUCTS AND INSULATION

Original tin ductwork is now exposed by deteriorated insulation. The insulation may contain asbestos. Before you remove and replace it, call your state department of the environment and natural resources, find a qualified environmental consultant, and have it tested.

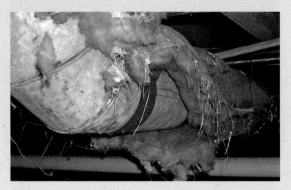

Duct insulation

WATER IN FOUNDATION CRAWL SPACE

The white line on the inside of the concrete block foundation wall is a lime deposit. Lime is the bonding agent in mortar mixtures. If the groundwater is allowed to pond against any masonry wall, the mortar will deteriorate and crumble, and the wall will become unstable. Consult a foundation repair expert for proper repair and waterproofing.

Water in foundation crawl space

KITCHEN ENTRY DOOR

Both the framing and the masonry beneath this doorsill show signs of deterioration. Repair or replace the door and frame, and pull the prefabricated concrete steps away from the house to assess any damage to the masonry work behind them.

Damage to rear kitchen entry door

WOOD ROT IN ROOF OVERHANG

Most of the roof boxing shows signs of rot. It is likely that the water damage has wicked up into the roof supports and sheathing as well; in some areas that has already happened, and the damage is visible from the attic crawl space. Have the roof inspected by a structural engineer to determine the extent of the damage, and the recommended repair.

Wood rot in overhang

KITCHEN FLOORING

Beneath the sheet vinyl floor covering in the kitchen, the ¼-inch plywood has delaminated; probably a result of termite damage; the ants are visible on the threshold. Consult an exterminator and have the entire house treated for wood-destroying insects.

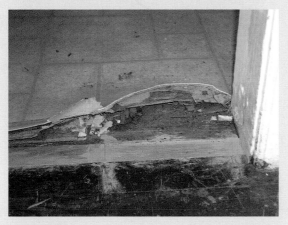

Damaged kitchen subflooring

OLD TREE STUMP

This tree stump is a working termite farm. Remove the stump, drill out the roots, and haul all debris off your property.

Termite farm in old tree stump

TERMITES IN WOOD WINDOW

Trim around this window was removed and the window was inspected for termites. A considerable amount of damage has already been done, although the exposed portions of the window, when the trim was on, did not indicate that. Treat the entire home for termites and consult a structural engineer to ensure that the framing is stable.

Termites in wood window

100-AMP ELECTRICAL PANEL

Owner complains of an intermittent problem of power shortages and tripped breakers. In my opinion, as it was designed, there is not enough power in this panel to serve the household. Consult a licensed electrician to confirm this opinion.

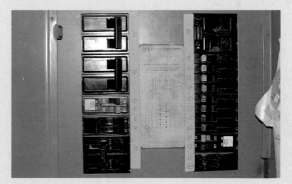

Electrical panel not code compliant

KITCHEN CABINETRY

The last owner of this house installed new stone countertops but did not replace the 1960s kitchen cabinets. The plumbing P-trap under the sink has been replaced, and water damage is evident on the floor of the cabinet. Adjacent cabinet floors are also damaged. Door hardware should be replaced as well; it's rusted and the screws are no longer holding; the original particleboard construction is beginning to lose its integrity.

Kitchen cabinet rotten floor

HEAT PUMP

The heat pump in the backyard has been knocked off the concrete pad it was designed to sit on. The case around the machinery is badly damaged. Consult an HVAC technician for an assessment of the condition of the motor, coils, and fans inside the case. The unit is ten years old and has a life expectancy of about three more years. It may be time to replace it.

Damaged heat pump

DAMAGED HARDWOOD FLOOR

This 1960s pine floor has taken a beating. Where the surface finish has been removed in the center of the floor, there is a light dusting of mold. Have your environmental consultant test this mold and treat it if it's toxic. If the mold is deeply embedded in the wood, you may have to replace the affected section to salvage the flooring. If the mold can be treated, sand and refinish the floor.

Refer to the chart in Part 1, Chapter 2, called "How Long Do Things Last?" and make a list of all the other items would that have been included in the full report.

Damaged hardwood floor

Consider Every Possible Solution

You've identified your high-priority design and repair challenges. You have all the pieces of the puzzle. Now go hunting for solutions. Remember that at this point money is no object; it's more important that you consider all possible solutions than that you worry about the fact that the cabinets you love might cost too much. Try this:

- Take your camera for a walk around your town. Visit neighborhoods you admire and see what the best local architects have designed. What do you see that both appeals to you and would address one of the priority problems in this exercise? Take pictures and put them aside.

- If there is a home and garden show nearby, attend it and ask the vendors about the latest trends in colors, technology, materials, and appliances. Find out if there is a less expensive substitute for a hardwood floor that would be just as durable and look exactly like the real thing.

- Visit new housing developments and tour the model homes and measure rooms that appeal to you. Attend Realtors' open houses too. You may discover that rooms with certain dimensions or proportions make you feel good. Make notes of these dimensions.

- Visit furniture showrooms. Find furniture *arrangements* that you like—don't worry about the furniture itself. Measure the distance *between* pieces that are arranged in a way you like. You may be surprised to find how much empty space is required to make a space work. For instance, did you realize that a 6-foot-long couch really "uses" a space that is about 11 feet wide by 8 or more feet deep? You must allow for end tables, a coffee table, and room for movement around the furniture. Consider this when you're designing a

new floor plan. Measure how much space you need behind a dining room chair in order to get into and out of it without having to twist and squirm. You may find you want a *minimum* of 48 inches between the edge of the table and the wall behind the chair. You may want more. Make notes of what you like.

- Observe the amount of natural light in rooms you like. Your house faces *east*. (Mark the floor plan so you remember this.) Where would you put an office and where would you put a family room? What kind of window treatments would the kitchen windows need to keep the sun out of your eyes on a summer evening?

- Buy lots of design magazines and spend some time clipping out pictures of things you might like if you were facing this particular remodeling challenge. Choose a variety of magazines that range from the quick-fix ideas to beach-house designs to Hollywood home tours.

- Design backwards: environment—then enclosure. Figure out what would work for this family, and then design the rooms so that cabinets, beds, doors, and windows are where they need to be. Plan to leave some empty wall space in a prominent location so that you can make your favorite artwork the most important thing in the room. Figure out where the kids are going to put their muddy boots. Figure out where you would want the powder room to be. The way you lay out the home will determine how comfortable you will feel living in it. Imagine what life would be like in this space.

This is your opportunity to learn about basic home-design principles. Do some research. Cut out some furniture that is of the same scale as the floor plan and try different arrangements. Lay a piece of tracing paper over the floor plan and try moving a wall or two; imagine what that new space would feel like. Imagine moving from one activity to another; imagine entertaining the relatives on Thanksgiving Day; imagine holding a family council to decide what to do for the summer vacation; imagine getting up in the middle of the night to feed the new baby. How will all of these things work in the plan you are devising? Spend some time on this. Have some fun!

Find at least a dozen different ideas—from mild to wild—that will help you solve every high-priority problem, and put them all in a Design Ideas Box (see pages 18–23).

Careful planning will give you a great education—not only about materials, furnishings, and the language of design, but also about your lifestyle priorities.

This exercise ought to take you at least two weeks. Challenge yourself. Make believe that you are a member of this family and that you are actually going to remodel this house, because, in a sense, you are!

Then have a wine-and-design party! Get your friends in on this project and see if they agree with what you're planning to do. Listen to some of their ideas, get them on paper, and put them in the ideas box along with all of yours.

Create Your First Task Abstract List

Before you go to a designer, you have to be very clear about what you want and how you propose to get it. Are you prepared to put together a preliminary plan for Our Project?

Create your first Task Abstract List—your Master Plan—for this remodel. There is a sample form on pages 30–31. List the major tasks your contractor would have to do to complete the remodel you have in mind, and

put each task under the proper work heading. Refer to Part 1, Section 2.3, for a reminder of the construction work sequence, and try to list the tasks within each section in the order in which they will have to be done—10 bonus points if you can do that.

Now, on a second piece of lined paper, list your Alternates—at least four good alternative ways to manage everything you've listed in the Master Plan. List ideas that are both more and less expensive than those you've already included. List solutions that would change the look of a room in a different way than your first-choice ideas would. Include ideas that will inspire the designer to think outside the box. List simple solutions you could fall back on if your bids all come in high and you have to cut costs. Fill this page with ideas, and put a section number in front of each idea—for example, hanging wallpaper instead of painting the room would be a substitution of an item in the 700 section—Prep and Paint. Put 700 in front of the wallpaper alternate on the list. Finally, arrange your Alternates list in the same order as you've arranged your tasks on the Master Plan Task Abstract List.

Put your Master Plan into a spreadsheet program in your computer, just the way you will when you're working on your own project later on.

Your First Cost Estimate

Now that you have a pretty good idea of the level of work that would make this project worth doing, let's see what that work might cost you. Refer to the Preliminary Cost-Estimating Chart opposite. What do you think you'd have to spend to complete the work in your plan? Remember that this number is just a rough estimate of your predictable construction costs. Your final construction costs will depend on

PRELIMINARY COST-ESTIMATING CHART

Level	Scope of Work	Age of Home	Conditions or Extent of Work	Cost per s.f.
1	**Repair and Spruce Up** Repair exterior trim and gutters Replace damaged windows & doors Repair plumbing leaks Replace heating & air unit Replace floor finishes Paint interior and exterior	<25 yrs	Good / Simple Fair / Moderate Poor / Extensive	$15 $20 $25
2	**Repair and Remodel** Repair plumbing leaks Replace heating and air unit Replace damaged windows and doors Paint or reface kitchen cabinets Replace floor finishes Paint interior and exterior	<25 yrs	Good / Simple Fair / Moderate Poor / Extensive	$25 $30 $35
3	**Substantial Remodel** Replace heating and air unit Replace damaged plumbing pipes Repair foundation or framing Repair exterior wall finishes Replace damaged windows and doors Replace damaged wood trim on exterior Remove or build new interior walls Replace cabinets & countertops Replace floor finishes Paint interior and exterior	<25 yrs	Good / Simple Fair / Moderate Poor / Extensive	$35 $45 $55
4	**Substantial Remodel** Replace heating and air unit Replace deteriorated sections of plumbing Replace electrical panel and some wiring Remove hazardous materials Repair foundation and framing Repair exterior wall finishes Replace windows & doors Replace roof and exterior trim Remove or build new walls Replace damaged drywall or plaster Replace damaged subfloor and floor finishes Replace cabinets & countertops Paint interior and exterior	25-40 yrs	Good / Simple Fair / Moderate Poor / Extensive	$50 $65 $80
5	**Rehabilitation** Replace heating and air unit Replace entire plumbing system Replace entire electrical system Remove hazardous materials Repair or replace exterior walls, windows, & trim Repair foundation & floor framing Replace subfloor and floor finishes Strip interior to framing Replace all Sheetrock, wall, and ceiling finishes Replace all millwork, cabinets, & countertops	35+ yrs	Good / Simple Fair / Moderate Poor / Extensive	$65 $80 $95
6	**New Addition**	N/A	No plumbing w/bath w/kitchen kitchen & bath only	$100 $130 $250 $350
7	**New Deck on Foundation with Steps & Rails**	N/A		$20-25

what details you add during the design development process, and on what you find when you open up the walls.

If you're *not* planning to build an addition, just multiply the total square footage in your 30-by-62-foot existing floor plan by the cost per square foot you think would be appropriate. If you want to build an addition, multiply the number of square feet in your proposed addition by the cost per square foot of new construction, and add that to the cost of the remodeling work in the existing space.

Note: You can figure out the size of your addition by deciding what function it needs to serve. If you want to add a master suite, for example, measure master suites in model homes and see how many square feet they use. If you want an enclosed sunroom, do the same. Use existing spaces as models; then multiply that square footage by the new construction cost per square foot. Do your homework; don't just gloss over this stuff. Learn your lessons while they're free!

Remember the budget formula form in Part 1, Section 2.4 (page 49)? The preliminary cost estimate you just did represents your Initial Construction Contract Allowance, which is only 72 percent of your Total Project Budget. Divide your construction cost estimate by 0.72 to see what the job will really cost you. Write that number here: $_____, and hold that thought.

Compare the Cost With the Return

Show this book to at least one good local real estate professional. Show her the tax photo and the floor plan of this house in 1985; these represent the house your family is living in now. Then show her your preliminary Master Plan Task Abstract List and a few photos from your ideas box, which will give her a good idea of what you plan to do.

Ask her (1) What would this existing (1985) home be worth today in *your* market? And (2) What would it be worth if you did what you're planning to do? The difference between those two numbers represents your anticipated *tangible* return—your financial gain.

Ask her what she thinks of your plan. What has value and what doesn't? What would she add that you haven't thought of and what would she omit? Ask what's hot and what's not in *your* area—then decide if any of those things would matter to the family in this story.

Assume that your Realtor's numbers were right. What would your return *percentage* be? Divide the as-is market value by the anticipated after-rehab value and see. Now refer to the *Remodeling Magazine* Cost vs. Value Report in Part 1, Chapter 1 (page 9). Would your plan bring you the national average return percentage? (If you order a copy of the latest report online, you'll see what the city nearest you has reported as its average returns—that will give you a better benchmark.)

Will you change the plan to increase your tangible return? Maybe your highest priority is to make a really wonderful nest for your young family to grow in. You plan to stay for a long time; maybe financial return isn't that important.

Fiddle with your plan—go back to your real estate consultants for second opinions if you want to—until you think you've sculpted that maximum-impact, cost-effective plan you've been hoping for.

Set Your Budget

After you are through revising your plan, review your assumptions against the Preliminary Cost-Estimating Chart in Part 1, Section 2.3 (page 31). Have your changes made a significant difference?

Set the project budget. If you think that your family (new job for Dad and a third baby on the way) might set a cap on the cost of this project, start with that number as your Total Project Budget and work your way down the list. If you think they have faith in their booming real estate market and enough elbow room to do what they want, use your own estimate to fill in your Initial Construction Contract Amount first; then divide that number by 0.72 to find your Total Project Budget, and work your way down the list. If you need to remember how to calculate a remodeling budget, refer back to Part 1, Section 2.3.

What do you expect to pay for the entire project? Based on the amount of work this house needs, the design you've put together, and all the national cost data you have, does this number feel appropriate?

Give your costs one more test. Divide the total construction cost (line 3 in your budget) by the total number of heated square feet that will be in the finished house to find your remodeling cost per square foot. If you're planning an addition as well as a remodel, you will need to separate those two costs and their accompanying square footage. Now call the local chapter of the National Association of Home Builders—there is one in just about every county in the United States—and ask what they consider the average cost per square foot for the kind of work you're doing (remodeling or new construction), and see how your plan matches up.

Tweak your Master Plan until you're happy with it.

The Hard Work Is Done

It's time to find the best designer for your project. Are you ready? You won't be able to move on if you haven't done all of the planning work. If you skipped a step, please go back and finish now.

THREE

Design

This is going to be a big, complicated project. You're going to need a really good designer. Let's find one. Although in real life there are many kinds of designers, in this exercise the term *designer* and the term *architect* are used interchangeably and refer to the same person.

Get Referrals

Make a list of five or six professionals in related fields who review the work of lots of architects on a regular basis. Call two of them and ask them to provide you with at least three names of designers who can help you turn this old house into one that will fit into your great neighborhood. You're looking for someone accustomed to designing major residential remodeling projects that are substantially similar to this one. See if at least one name shows up on both lists. Go ahead. Make those calls.

Make First Contact with Your Best Candidates

Prepare a list of open questions for a telephone interview: What do you need to know? Write your questions down and practice interviewing a friend or your partner to get an idea of the best way to elicit the information you're looking for.

Here is what you might actually find if you were to do three telephone interviews:

- Candidate 1 began her career with four years in a large residential (new construction) design firm, but she has been in private practice for seven years now, doing exclusively residential remodels on older homes. She is friendly and she listened well. She is divorced with two young children to care for, and her office is in her home.
- Candidate 2 is a licensed architect and a licensed structural engineer. She is a senior partner in a practice with six younger professionals, located in an upscale office building in downtown. She has fifteen years of experience in both residential and small commercial design. She is a good listener, and while you didn't get any warm, fuzzy feelings from her, she made you comfortable by talking to you with respect.
- Candidate 3 started a private practice eight years ago when she finished architecture school at the age of thirty-seven. She is a licensed architect with past careers in interior design and fine arts as well. She seemed very self-assured. She is single and childless; her office is in her home in a chic downtown historic district. She seemed a little edgy on the phone, but she explained that she was working on a tight deadline on another project.

Who are you leaning toward and why? Do you think your project needs compatibility or expertise; art or engineering; focused experience or a varied background? What is your initial impression of these three designers? Think about the real needs of your (make-believe) family, their lifestyle, and their personalities. Whom do you think you would be most comfortable working with? Which of these three designers might be most apt to deliver the kind of design you are looking for?

Meeting the Candidates in Person

Your next move would be to make appointments to meet with each of the candidates in their own work spaces. Mom wants to do this. She wants to see their portfolios, to see how they work, and to double-check her first impressions. Develop another good set of questions for Mom's next interviews that will be a little more personal; after all, compatibility will be an important issue. Each of these professionals is very different from the others; you may have to make three different lists of questions.

Write Mom's questions down and practice interviewing a friend or your partner to get an idea of the best way to elicit the information you're looking for.

If you were Mom, and you went on these interviews, here is what might actually have happened:

• Candidate 1 had to reschedule because one of the kids got sick. When you arrived for the second appointment, everything went smoothly, and this candidate was entirely professional. She asked you lots of questions about how your family intends to use the space over the next ten years, and discussed your budget and your expectations; she was able to express a few quick ideas in sketches that you understood and liked. Her portfolio was full of remodeled homes that were similar to Our Project—or at least similar to what we hope Our Project will look like

after the remodel. While none of the designs were breathtaking, her ideas felt comfortable and familiar to you. She clearly had lots of experience doing the kind of work you wanted to do.

• Candidate 2's receptionist seated you in a glamorous conference room where the photos on the walls showed off some very attractive finished projects, although none of them resembled Our Project in any way. Shortly after this candidate joined you in the conference room, she introduced you to one of her associates. He was young, and perhaps not very experienced yet, but he specialized in residential remodeling. The senior partner stayed for the first few minutes but was soon called away. You were left to work with the younger designer, who turned out to be pretty talented. He was attentive and his sketches told you that he had both heard and could improve on your ideas. In the end, the meeting went well, even though it was not what you had expected. The young associate has replaced the senior partner as your second candidate. How did you *feel* about being passed on to someone else? Was the younger designer's experience in line with what you needed? Would you have the advantage of easy access to the other talented professionals in his firm if you needed them? Did you remember to ask him all of the prequalifying questions you had already asked his boss on the phone?

• Candidate 3 was breathless and ten minutes late for your appointment. She apologized and offered you a beverage while she spread out her portfolio; her sense of color and composition were smart and stylish; her illustrations made you drool. She was a step ahead of you in every part of the discussion, which was a little annoying, but her ideas were wonderful, and when you suggested other ideas she was able to knock out a few quick doodles that told you that she was hearing you but was already envisioning something more polished than you were thinking of. Will this spitfire be able to design to your budget? Would she listen to you if you tried to rein her in? Or would you get the most amazing project on the planet from her?

These are the top three residential remodeling architects in your area, according to other professionals who ought to know. On a scale of 1 to 10, 10 being the perfect architect for Our Project, how would you (as Mom) rate each of them? Which one do you think would be best able to coordinate the work of specialists such as a structural engineer, a kitchen designer, or a landscape architect, for example? Will you check references on all three? How many references do you want each of them to provide for you?

Checking References

Continue to play the role of Mom. Make a list of questions that you will ask the architects' *references,* and revise them until you think they will elicit the kinds of answers you are looking for.

Make your questions inviting; encourage their clients to be truthful. Don't be shy about pressing a little if they hint at a problem. Decide if you would feel the same way they did about what they're describing. For example, a client may gush about how friendly the designer was, and how responsive. Remember that designers charge by the hour; you may not want to pay for so much attention.

Imagine that you've checked references on all three now, and have uncovered a thing or

two. What do you think these designers neglected to tell you about themselves?

Now how do you feel about these candidates?

Their colleagues say they're the best. Choose somebody.

The First Meeting

You met with the designer you selected and discussed your Master Plan, and your designer looked at some of the contents of your ideas box, but asked you to hold on to it until you were ready to begin working on the finishes. Concept design is about spatial proportions, adjacencies, and other broad concepts that set the groundwork for the remainder of the details. You will work on the broad concepts first.

After an hour or so of batting ideas back and forth, you think you have the right designer and you ask her to give you a proposal for . . . what will you need? (Refer to Part 1, Section 3.2, about working with an architect if you need to refresh your memory.)

Based on your preliminary budget, what will this architect probably charge you for her services? What is 5 percent of your Initial Construction Contract Allowance, and what portion might you have to pay for concept design work? This answer is in the text too, if you need to go back and review.

Write a reiterate-and-confirm letter that outlines the services you want, the fee you'll pay, and the amount of time the designer will need to finish this work for you.

Extra Points

Do a little research and see what kinds of design contracts are available to you. Download or order them, read them carefully, and mark them up so that they give you what you need to feel comfortable. Refer to Part 1, Section 3.2, about working with an architect, and be sure to include those extra terms and conditions that are suggested there.

Concept Design— Assessing the Options

Let's see what your architect came up with. Keep in mind that what you're looking at are concept designs—freehand sketches—with few dimensions and no details.

Your designer has three options for you. Let's discuss each one separately.

Option 1

Study Option 1 carefully. Compare it to the 1985 floor plan on page 151 and make a list of all the things the designer proposes to change. (It may help if you make a photocopy of the 1985 floor plan. We're going to refer to it often.)

Let me help a little here; design drawings contain symbols that you may not be familiar with. If you understand the drawings, you'll be better able to understand how the designer is thinking.

The solid, dark lines are existing walls that will stay where they already are. This means that

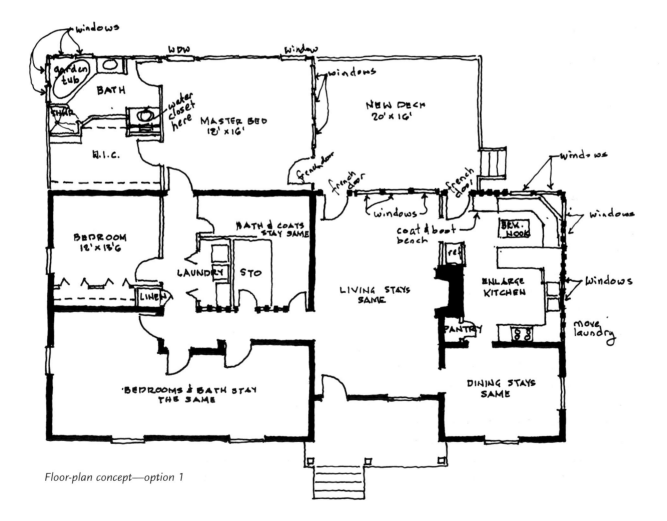

Floor-plan concept—option 1

your designer thinks they are where they need to be to work with the overall design, that they are properly supported by an existing foundation, and that the framing may still be in pretty good shape. The cost of opening up these walls to replace plumbing and wiring, and putting new drywall and paint on them, won't be nearly as expensive as building entirely new walls. This will be the least expensive area to remodel. We will refer to this area as "existing to remain."

The dotted lines represent the foundation of the original house in areas where the work *above* the foundation (the walls, doors, windows, and even perhaps the roofline) will change. In Option 1, the designer has made major changes where these dotted lines appear, and although you'll still be working on an existing foundation, this "existing to be changed" work will be more expensive than the "existing to remain" work would be.

And then there's the new addition: the master suite and the deck—all new construction. When you're calculating the cost of the new construction, remember that the construction costs apply only to enclosed, heated square feet. The deck must be handled separately.

Your Option 1 Cost Estimate

Let's work through the assessment of Option 1; you can do Options 2 and 3 on your own.

When you're estimating the cost of a remodel like Option 1, you'll need to know four numbers:

1. How many square feet are existing and will remain more or less as they are now?
2. How many square feet will sit on an existing foundation, although most of the construction above will be new?
3. How many square feet of heated space will be built from the ground up?
4. How big is your deck?

Try thinking about it this way:

1. I estimate that about 800 square feet of the original 1,860-square-foot house will remain substantially the same. That's the area along the front (east) wall: the two bedrooms and the bath on the left (south) side of the entry, the fireplace wall and some parts of the kitchen on the right (north). How would you categorize that work? Look at the Preliminary Cost-Estimating Chart in Part 1, Section 2.3. Flag that page; we'll use it a lot. We're in level 5 because of the age of the house, but where in level 5? The cost would probably fall within the lower end of the price range. Make your best guess and do the math. The cost of this part of the remodel will probably be: $_____.

2. That leaves us with 1,060 square feet (1,860 square feet – 800 square feet) of old foundation on which we will redesign the floor plan. That's more extensive work than the first section you worked on. What do you suppose this part will cost? Use a number on the higher end of the price range. Make your best guess and do the math. The "existing to be changed" section might cost you $_____.

3. The designer wants to build a master suite and a deck. The master suite is an enclosed, heated space, and although we don't have exact dimensions, we can "scale" that space against other areas that *are* dimensioned. I would guess that the new master suite is about 16 feet by 28 feet, or 448 square feet. Since this new construction will have a bathroom in it, we'll use $130 per square foot as our cost. Do the math. The cost of the enclosed portion of the addition would be about $_____.

4. The deck is 16 feet by 20 feet, and decks with foundations, steps, and rails cost about

$25 per square foot. That would add another $_____.

5. We almost forgot something. What about repairing that pitted driveway and the cracked front steps? We'll have to add a bit for paving and landscaping too. I don't know what that would cost, but I'll bet that $4,500 would cover the basics, and we can always add more landscaping later if we choose to.

When you add all five numbers together, you'll have a preliminary estimate of your predictable construction costs, a number we've been calling your Initial Construction Contract Allowance. Divide that total by 0.72 to find out what the Total Project Budget might be. Write that number down here: $_____.

Option 1—The Happiness Factor

Now forget the money and think about your family—the family in this story—and how they will grow up in this house. Does Option 1 give you everything your family needs? Go back to your list of design challenges and look at your highest priorities. Has Option 1 given you a great solution? Could you and your mate and your three kids live comfortably in this plan for the next ten years or so?

Options 2 and 3

Do the same analysis on Options 2 and 3, and see which concept you like the best. Balancing cost with happiness isn't always easy, is it?

Closing In on a Great Remodeling Concept

Gather a group of friends and family and ask for their opinions on all three options. (Don't share your cost estimates at the start.) Imagine what it would be like to live and work in each of these environments, and listen to what they observe about each layout.

Here are some things you may want to discuss with your friends.

Study the Changes the Designer Made

Look at each design carefully. Make a list of what you like and don't like about each one. Look carefully. In addition to changes in the placement of the rooms, more than twenty changes were made between Option 1 and Option 3. Look closely and make a list of all twenty-plus changes.

Decide Which of These Designs Would Be Best for Your Family

Remember to look through the eyes of the family I've described for you, and imagine going through their daily routine. Where will you keep the vacuum cleaner, the beach and picnic supplies, the step stool, the dirty laundry, the playpen, the high chair? Where will the kids and their friends play? Do you want your guests to be able to help in the kitchen? If not, where do you want them to gather while you're cooking? If the floor plan you're assessing doesn't provide a space for any of these items, what will you have to change?

After you've done a thorough assessment, make your three lists for each of the three options. List what you like, what you don't like, and what the plan doesn't have that you wish it did have.

Check your original list of goals, and see if each design solves all your problems.

Consider Cutting and Pasting

Is there a great design idea in one plan that you would like to incorporate into one of the others?

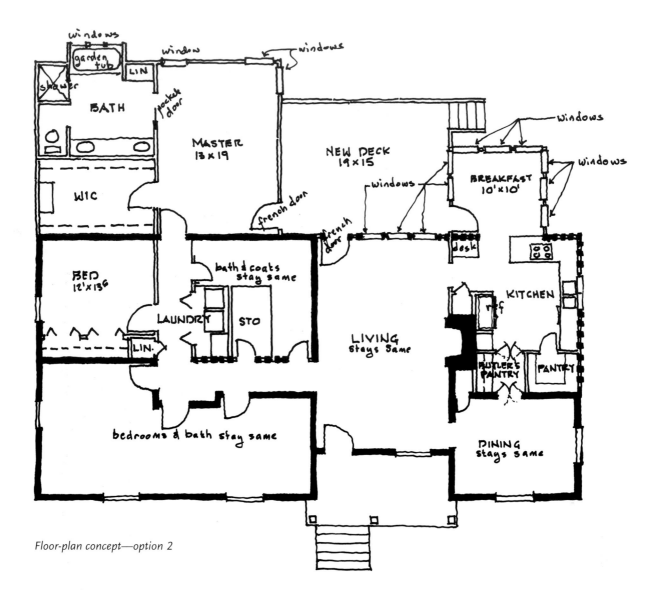

Floor-plan concept—option 2

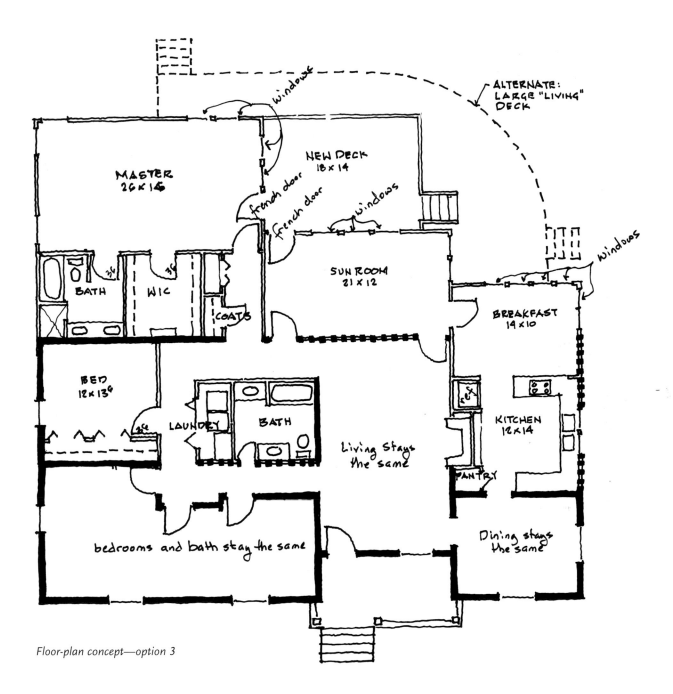

Floor-plan concept—option 3

ALTERNATE:
LARGE "LIVING"
DECK

windows

NEW DECK
18 x 14

french door

french door

windows

SUN ROOM
21 x 12

windows

MASTER
26 x 15

BATH

WIC

COATS

BREAKFAST
14 x 10

BED
12 x 13⁹

LAUNDRY

BATH

Living Stays
the same

KITCHEN
12 x 14

PANTRY

bedrooms and bath stay the same

Dining stays
the same

What's the Final Vote?

Now share your cost estimates and see if that changes anyone's mind about which design they like best.

When you're done, take a vote. Each person at the table should state which plan they like best and why. It will be interesting for you to hear their points of view.

My Opinion

Here's what I think: I've done a quick cost estimate for all three concept options (see page 176), noted the differences between each option and the 1985 floor plan, and then expressed my personal opinion about whether or not the design would accomplish what this family needs.

For the reasons I state, I think that Option 3 does the best job of addressing your design goals, and it would be a fun house to live in. I think you (the family in the story) will be able to live in it comfortably even while the kids are teenagers. Your neighborhood is great and improving; the city is thriving; you're in a really hot real estate market. I think you could justify tripling your investment in this home if you were going to get a nearly new house for the money and live there for ten years or more. What do you think?

This is one of those times where I must impose my own opinion in order to keep us moving forward. I apologize to those of you who disagree with me, but we're going to work on Option 3. I want to challenge you with a complicated project, and I want you to have a lot at stake, so Option 3 it is.

Design Development

At this point you would make an appointment to return to your architect's office to discuss the three options and begin working on the design development phase using Option 3 as your starting point.

After much brainstorming, the final floor-plan gets over a dozen changes. The revised plan is here for you. How many of the changes can you find? Make a list of them and see if you can determine why each change was made.

I'm still not convinced this design is the best it can be. Study it. If it's not absolutely perfect, what would have to be done to make it so? Make a list, but be careful about adding things that cost a lot and don't really add value.

The Design Review Meeting

Before you spend a few hundred thousand dollars, wouldn't you want to know that you weren't going to waste that money, make mistakes, or miss opportunities to optimize every square foot?

If I were Mom, I would ask the architect to set up a two-hour design review meeting and to invite a structural engineer, a kitchen designer, and an interior designer. They ought to be able to make some good suggestions. We won't actually do this, but we will imagine what it would be like.

These two hours will be expensive. (The professionals' fees will come out of your soft-costs allowance.) Use the time wisely. Bring a list of the details that still concern you. The list will serve as your agenda for the meeting.

One of the best ideas that came out of the meeting was this: The interior designer liked the circular hallway, but she added French-style pocket doors where the hall intersects with the living room so that not only can you separate the kids' and their activities from the living room when you're entertaining, but you can also keep an eye on them! That was a great idea.

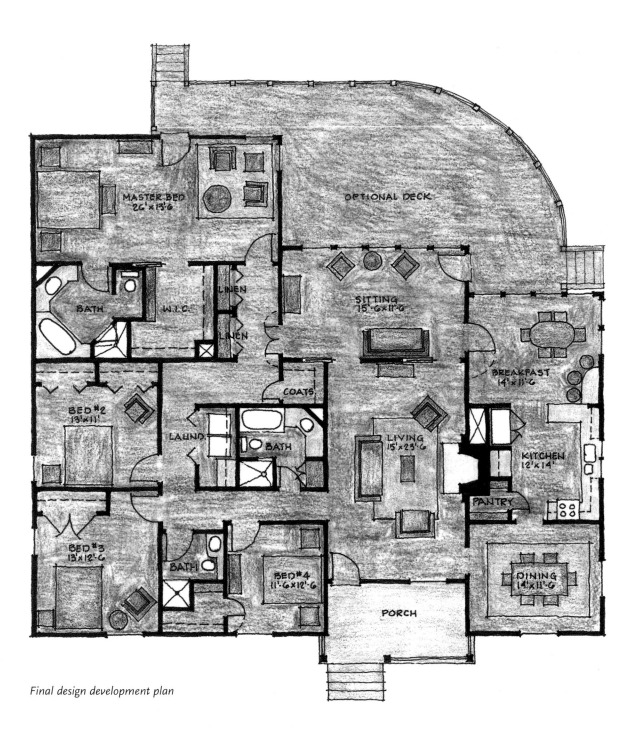

MASTER BED
26'×13'-6"

BATH

W.I.C.

LINEN

LINEN

OPTIONAL DECK

SITTING
15'-6"×11'-6"

BREAKFAST
14'×11'-6"

BED #2
13'×11'

COATS

LAUND.

BATH

LIVING
15'×23'-6"

KITCHEN
12'×14'

PANTRY

BED #3
13'×12'-6"

BATH

BED #4
11'-6"×12'-6"

PORCH

DINING
14'×11'-6"

Final design development plan

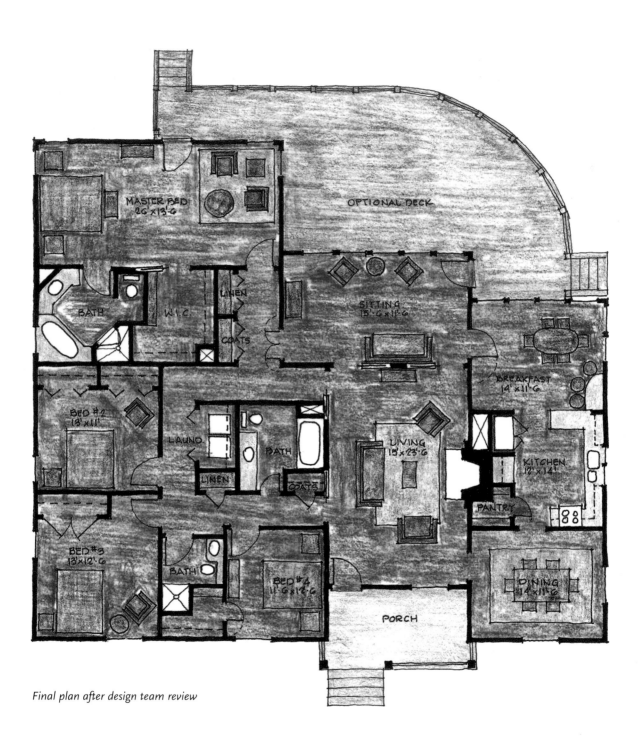

Final plan after design team review

After the meeting, the architect revised the design development drawing one more time, to incorporate all of the great ideas the review team had. Compare this final design with the last design development floor plan. Make a list of the seven changes that were made in the meeting. Revise your Task Abstract List so that it reflects all of the work in the final design development drawing shown here. Do not revise the original list; save it, copy it, and revise the copy.

Get a Professional Cost Estimate

Before you authorize the architect to go to the trouble and expense of creating the final, technical construction drawing set, let's take this last floor plan and your Task Abstract List to a cost estimator and ask for his best guesses. His numbers ought to be pretty close to what you will get from the bidders. One page 177 is what he sent you a week later. If we use the cost estimator's numbers, what will your Initial Construction Contract Allowance be?

Now set your final Total Project Budget by dividing that number by 0.72 and fill in all of the numbers on your final project budget. Shall we go ahead and finish these drawings? Or do we need to cut out some of the work to bring the price down?

Construction Drawings

It's a go! Now you must trust your architect to keep you safe by clearly defining every detail of the project, including where the light switches will be located, how to slope your roof, how the tub will abut the shower stall, and all the other minute details that the contractor has to know in order to build the space for you.

While the design team is working on your construction drawings, you have other work to do. You need to make some administrative decisions.

PROJECT BUDGET

Total Construction Budget	100%
(minus) Soft-Costs Allowance	10%
Total Construction Budget	90%
Initial Construction Contract Allowance	72%
Contingency Fund for Unanticipated Costs	18%

COMPARE THREE DESIGN CONCEPTS
Based on Preliminary Cost-Estimating Chart - Part 1, Section 2.3

Level of Work	Work Plan	Total s.f.	Est. Cost/s.f.	Total Est.Cost
Option 1	Existing to remain	800	$60	$ 48,000
	Rehab on existing foundation	1060	$80	$ 84,800
	Addition - new foundation	496	$130	$ 64,480
	Deck	320	$20	$ 6,400
	Driveway, walks, & landscaping			$ 4,500
	Estimated Initial Construction Contract (ICC)			$ 208,180
	Total Project Budget	ICC/0.72=		$ 289,139

Changes from the 1985 Floor Plan
Reconfigured kitchen. Added 33 x 16 master suite and 20 x 16 deck with lots of windows on rear wall.
Added laundry and storage in core. Rest of house is unchanged.

Thoughts
Incomplete replacement of plumbing & electric; new HVAC. Anticipate major future repairs.
Master suite is cramped and not private; no place for family time.

Level of Work	Work Plan	Total s.f.	Est. Cost/s.f.	Total Est.Cost
Option 2	Existing to remain	800	$60	$ 48,000
	Rehab on existing foundation	1060	$85	$ 90,100
	Addition - new foundation	594	$130	$ 77,220
	Deck	285	$20	$ 5,700
	Driveway, walks, & landscaping			$ 4,500
	Estimated Initial Construction Contract (ICC)			$ 221,020
	Total Project Budget	ICC/0.72=		$ 306,972

Changes from the 1985 Floor Plan
Reconfigured kitchen & breakfast. Added 26 x 19 master suite, 19 x 15 deck, and
10 x 10 breakfast room with lots of windows on rear wall. Added laundry & storage in core.

Thoughts
Incomplete replacement of plumbing & electric.
Master Bedroom too narrow No place for family time.

Level of Work	Work Plan	Total s.f.	Est. Cost/s.f.	Total Est.Cost
Option 3	Existing to remain	800	$60	$ 48,000
	Rehab on existing foundation	1060	$100	$ 106,000
	Addition - new foundation	1068	$130	$ 138,840
	Deck	252	$20	$ 5,040
	Driveway, walks, & landscaping			$ 4,500
	Estimated Initial Construction Contract (ICC)			$ 297,880
	Total Project Budget	ICC/0.72=		$ 413,722
	Substitute larger deck	500	$20	$ 10,000
	Estimated Initial Construction Contract			$ 307,880
	Total Project Budget			$ 427,611

Changed from 1985 Floor Plan
Reconfigured core and kitchen/dining. Added 26 x 26 master suite, 12 x 21 sunroom, and
10 x 14 breakfast room. Either deck will do, but the larger one suits the new windows on rear wall.

Thoughts
Complete replacement of all services means no major repairs for at least 10 years.
Master bath and closet a little small, but good trade-off for new core bath and
family room . . . and that deck!

FINAL DESIGN - PROFESSIONAL COST ESTIMATE

SEC	Item #	Task List	
0		**Hazards**	
	1	Remove windows, entry doors, all trim	$2,800
100		**Demolition and Site Work**	
	101	Remove rear wall & roof; gut interior to framing	$8,000
	102	Remove all orig. subfloor	$3,000
	103	Demo old decks, rails and steps	$1,200
200		**Foundation and Structure**	
	201	Build new fdn for add'n & deck	$7,500
	202	Install all new subfloor throughout	$5,000
	202	Frame new floors, ext.walls, ceilings, & roof	$9,500
300		**Exterior Envelope**	
	301	Weather-in entire new structure	$10,000
	302	Install all new exterior wall & roof finishes	$20,000
	303	Plywood 50% of attic floor; access stair	$3,500
	304	Build 300 s.f. deck, not 500	$6,000
400		**Doors**	
	401	3 entry (1 French)	$2,800
	402	19 interior @ $400 ea	$7,600
	403	5 interior French Doors	$6,000
500		**Windows**	
	501	9 ea. 4'0" x 4'0" square @ $500 ea	$4,500
	502	15 ea. 2'6" x 6'0" tall @ $850 ea	$12,800
600		**Interior Finishes**	
	601	Frame interior walls & blocking for cabs	$12,000
	602	Install drywall, trim, & closet shelves	$25,000
	603	Install tile floors in 3 baths & laundry	$3,000
	604	Tile wainscoting; 2 baths to 4'6"	$2,200
	605	Install pine floors	$18,000
	606	XYZ plain cabs in kitchen	$20,000
	607	Install Big Box cabinets in baths & laund	$4,000
	608	Natural stone countertops in kitchen	$9,000
	609	Man-made countertops in 3 baths & laundry	$2,000
	610	Furnish & install all appliances	$4,000
700		**Prep and Paint - Int. & Ext.**	
	701	Prime & paint interior - 6 colors	$8,500
	702	Prime & paint exterior - 3 colors	$5,500
800	801	**Plumbing:** Replace entire system	$15,000
	802	Install 1 50-gal water heater	$1,800
900	901	**HVAC:** Replace entire system; 2 zones	$6,000
1000	1001	**Electrical:** Replace entire system Incr. power/street; 250A. panel; all fixtures	$15,000
		FINAL COST ESTIMATE	**$261,200**
1100		**Alternates**	
	A1	Build 500 s.f. curved deck w/steps and rails	$10,000
	A2	Repl 15 tall windows w/8 ea 4'0" sq.	$4,000
	A3	Install ABC cabinetry in kitchen	$28,000
	A4	Man-made countertops in kitchen	$6,000
	A5	New hardwood flrs in remaining areas	$22,000
	A6	15 interior shutters - tall windows @ $250 ea.	$1,250
	A7	Buy larger refrig/freezer (add)	$1,500
	A8	Install 2 - 40-gallon water heaters in attic	$2,200
	A9	Paving	$2,500
	A10	Landscaping	$2,000

FOUR

Pre-Construction Activities

You've got about four weeks before the complete set of construction drawings will be ready. This ought to give you plenty of time to make your administrative decisions, buy some extra insurance, meet with an attorney, write your contract terms, and find three top-notch remodeling contractors so that when the drawings are done you can go out to bid. What do you intend to do about all of these issues?

Administrative Decisions

It's time to get back on the phone.

Will You Stay Put or Move Out?

Find out if you can get a nine-month lease on an apartment large enough for the four of you and a newborn baby to be comfortable in. What would such an apartment cost you? Make some calls to local apartment complexes in your area and find out.

What Will You Do With Your Houseful of Stuff?

Will you pile it all up in the bedrooms at the front of the house or store it all off-site? Call a few store-it-yourself facilities and a few local movers in your area and see what kind of deal you can make.

What About Insurance Coverage?

How much and what kind of insurance will you buy for yourself, and how much and what

kind of insurance will you ask your contractor to carry? Call your own insurance agent and find out what's available and what each kind of policy would cover. Weigh the cost against the benefits before you decide what you will require of your contractor. You will be paying for every bit of it one way or another.

What About Bonds?

Do you want to pay for the protection of payment and performance bonds? Call a bonding company and find out what they would require from your contractor and what protection their bond would give you; see if you think that extra peace of mind would be worth the price. Call a second bonding company and see if all bonds are the same. Be sure to ask about what the bond will *not* cover, and what would happen if it were to be canceled by either the agent or the contractor during the work period.

Name the Contractor's Only Boss

Put yourself in the place of the family in this story. Mom's a few months pregnant by now, but Dad's not up and running at his new job yet. Yikes. Which of these spouses would be the best one to manage the day-to-day oversight of the project? How should they set this up?

Will You Pay Your Contractor a Deposit?

If so, 15 percent of the contract value ought to be your cap. Multiply your anticipated Initial

Construction Contract Allowance by 0.15 and see what your maximum deposit would be if you felt the general contractor was justified in asking for one.

Workers' Comp

Do you know whether or not the general contractor will have to carry workers' compensation insurance? What triggers this requirement in your state, and who is responsible for enforcing the laws? Call the state department of insurance, the contractors state license board, or the local chapter of the National Association of Home Builders and find out.

Licensing Requirements

While you've got these folks on the phone, find out how general contractors are licensed under *your* state laws. What are the licensing requirements for electricians, plumbers, and heating and air-conditioning contractors, and who does your state hold responsible for ensuring that *they* are properly licensed?

Line Up the Big Guns

Find an attorney with a specialty in construction law who is willing to work on your behalf to resolve disputes. Go through the yellow pages, call the state bar association, call the contractors state license board, and get referrals to attorneys with a specialty in construction law. Don't call these attorneys during this exercise, but do keep those lists for your own project.

Setting the Terms of the Contract

We will use the Contract Terms and Conditions in the appendix so that we can all refer to the same contract if we get into trouble. Familiarize yourself with this document. Read the table of contents. Each of these subjects is covered in plain English, in one or two very short paragraphs. Let's review a few of the conditions.

In the "General Conditions" section, read "Explicit and Implied Work." Your contractor used inferior lumber on your deck—it's warped and full of knots. Would these paragraphs give you the right to ask him to revise his work? Is inferior lumber a part of the "highest standards of professional construction craftsmanship"? Is there is a paragraph that defines materials selections, and if so, would that one be a more enforceable clause?

In the "General Conditions" section, read "Anticipated Hidden Conditions." You will include a copy of this contract form in your bid package so that the bidders will know how you expect to deal with these problems. When the contractor tells you how long he expects the job to take, and your bid documents told him that you want him to open up and expose a hidden condition before he starts work in earnest, should his proposed schedule anticipate that extra ten days?

In the section "Property Owner's Rights and Responsibilities," read "Designate the Sole Decision Maker." If you tell the contractor that you will be the sole contact, and your partner calls him to ask him to change the paint color, what does the contract require the contractor to do?

Read "Create No Contractual Conflicts," a little further on in that section. If your neighbor offers to mow your lawn while the contractor is working on the inside of your house, what should your answer be? If you allow him to mow, and he falls into the plumber's ditch, who would be responsible for paying his medical bills? (Hint: It's not the plumber.)

Find the answers to the following questions (some of them are a little tricky).

- You have moved out—lock, stock, and barrel—and in the middle of the job some of the construction materials are stolen. Which clause in this contract tells you who has to pay to replace them?
- The contractor forgot to bring his ladder today; may he borrow yours? What do you do?
- The contractor asks you to pull the permits for the job. Should you do that? What does your contract say?
- The roofer is seriously injured when he falls off his ladder. Where is the statement in the contract that tells you who has to pay the roofer's medical bills?
- You would like to know how much the contractor paid the artist who painted the mural in your dining room. Where is the contract clause that determines whether or not he has to answer that question?
- Your electrician flunks three inspections in a row before you discover he isn't properly licensed. What does your contract say about who is responsible for taking action, and what does it stipulate that action should be?
- You want your kitchen countertops to be made from an exotic wood that can be found only along the banks of the Amazon River. The contractor has to have this countertop fabricated off-site by the only shop in the United States that has access to this wood. The shop will have only one shot at getting this countertop right. What does the contract say about managing off-site fabrications? How can you ensure that you are going to get exactly what the architect designed?
- You don't mind the crew working until 9 p.m. now and then—your apartment is a mile away. The blaring radio is pretty annoying to your neighbors, though. What can you point to in the contract to convince the contractor to have the guys turn off the radio?
- The contractor is preparing to pour the concrete for your new driveway; a truckload of gravel was thoughtlessly dumped into your rose garden. Is there a clause in the contract that says you can ask the contractor to move that mountain of gravel? Does the contract address whether or not you would have to pay him to do it? What about the roses? Who pays to replace them?
- Your contractor is supposed to trim back all tree limbs that are currently leaning on your roof. When the guy in the big yellow truck drives across your yard to get to the trees in the back, he mashes your son's tricycle. That sweet little boy is inconsolable. What does your contract say about who should replace the bike?
- How would you react if you found two empty beer cans on the site? What would be allowed under this contract?
- Your job will take four months to finish and the contract price is $40,000. What *portion* of the contract does the contractor have to earn in order to get his first check, and how much money would that represent?
- Your contract says that the contractor has to earn 17 percent of the contract every four weeks in order to earn a check. How long is your contract work schedule? At the end of eight weeks, the contractor has earned 32 percent. Would you issue a check?
- Your agreement says that the contractor has to earn 20 percent of the contract each time he wants a check. What does that tell you about how many payments there will be? At the end of the fourth four-week assessment period, he has earned 78 percent. Would you cut him a check?
- The cabinet manufacturer calls *you* to say that the rising cost of lumber has increased his costs of manufacturing, and he will need

an additional $6,000 before he fabricates your order. How does your contract address this sort of problem? Find more than one clause that might help you resolve this.

- The construction work is 100 percent complete. Is the job finished?

Answers to all of these questions are in the contract. Find them. If there is a misunderstanding between you and your contractor, your contract ought to help you settle it quickly. Train yourself—make it a *reflex action*—to refer to your Contract Terms and Conditions statement before you even begin a discussion.

Finding the Perfect Contractor(s)

By now I hope you know the drill. How do you find a good contractor?

List five good sources for referrals. *Call* one of them and get three names of contractors that have done consistently good work on lots of other projects *just like this one.*

Call the contractor who sounds the best to you, and ask him some of the questions from the interview logs in Part 1, Section 4.3. Be a good detective. Don't tell him anything more than that you are thinking of remodeling a 1961 brick ranch. Dodge his inquiries by telling him you're just gathering information right now. Just ask your questions and hear what he has to say.

Your last questions ought to be about how he sets his prices; then, no matter what he answers, ask if he would competitively bid. Thank him for his time and tell him that when you're ready to go, you'll be in touch. If he begs for a meeting, say no. Stand firm, but be nice. Eventually, you may find yourself calling him about your real project. He'll remember you.

Imagine that you have had telephone interviews with, and checked references on, eight contractors, all of whom appeared on three or more of the lists you obtained. All of their references were excellent. You really liked five of them, but you want to invite only three of them to bid. You ask to meet each of your favorite five in person. Here is what might actually happen.

- Candidate 1 met you at his office in a small strip mall on the outskirts of town. He comes from a big family, and his oldest brother had a contracting business. This fellow went to work at fifteen, sweeping up his brother's project sites, and quickly worked his way up to superintendent. He started his own business while he was in engineering school. By the time he graduated from college, he had already remodeled three multimillion-dollar homes. He took you to see one of them; the architecture was glorious and his work was perfect—seamless. He's proud, intelligent, talented, ambitious, very successful—and only twenty-seven years old.

- Candidate 2 met you on a job site. His hands were calloused, his boots were muddy, and when you pulled up he was hollering instructions to one of the guys on the roof. During your twenty-minute conversation, he had two materials deliveries and he watched the unloading like a hawk. The project wasn't a large one, but it was complicated. The house was at least fifty years old and had been altered several times. The purpose of this remodel was to try to bring some integrity to the appearance of the house; lots of nipping and tucking. As you headed back to your car, you noticed that there was a six-pack of beer on the floor of his truck.

- Candidate 3 invited you to lunch—that is, he made arrangements to meet you and take a short lunch break at the same time, so that there would be no distractions during your conversation. This fellow had a

PhD in art history but discovered that he liked the craft of remodeling more than the red tape of academia. You had a very enjoyable conversation about eighteenth-century literature. He seemed relaxed and friendly; he talked about his favorite hobby (fly-fishing) and about the uncle whose business he had taken over. He'd been remodeling small homes for five years and had done very well for himself.

- Candidate 4 met you in *your* office. He arrived in freshly pressed pants and a clean T-shirt with his company logo on it. He was carrying a clipboard full of neatly stacked papers. He had thirty years of experience managing remodeling projects of every size and sort; he was an officer of the contractors' association and had organized three community service projects in the last twelve months. You remember meeting him at the local home and garden trade show and you remember liking his portfolio. But he sat stick straight in the guest chair through the entire conversation, which made you a little uncomfortable.

- Candidate 5 was working in his shop when you met—an old, stark warehouse building full of beautiful custom cabinets and fireplace mantels. He had been a carpenter from the age of fifteen. His father and grandfather had also been carpenters. He continued to be a hands-on general contractor and liked to use some of the old tools when he worked. He was meticulous; the work in the shop was perfect. His office was in the front seat of his little red truck. You found an article in the local paper about great local craftsmen, and he was one of the chosen few. But when you showed him the article, you noticed that he was having a hard time reading it.

On a scale of 1 to 10, 10 being the perfect contractor for you, how do you feel about each of these contractors? Be careful not to make assumptions when you don't have all the facts. Decide which qualities you consider most important. Which three will you invite to bid your job?

If you included Candidate 1 in your short list, and he called to tell you he wouldn't competitively bid, what would you do? (Hint: Begging won't change his mind.)

At this point you would send three invitations to bid, but we won't actually do that for this exercise.

Bidding

Your architect just called. Your construction drawings are ready.

You create a Bid Form based on the final cost estimate (like the one opposite).

What other documents will you put into the bid package?

Your three bidders arrive at your home on the date and time specified in your invitation; you give them their bid packages. You and your designer stand quietly where the bidders can see you, while they climb up onto the roof, crawl around under the foundation, poke this, prod that, and discuss the highlights of last night's big game.

After about forty minutes, one of them approaches you with a question. The new electrical panel will be too large to fit on the wall the designer has placed it on. How do you want him to bid that? Your designer unrolls her drawings and flips to the electrical design sheet, then back to the floor plans. She quickly selects a new location for the panel. You immediately do something. What is it and why did you do it? If you can't recall the procedure for answering questions at the bid walk-through,

BID FORM

SEC	Item #	Task List
000		**Hazards**
	001	Remove windows, entry doors, all trim
100		**Demolition and Site Work**
	101	Remove rear wall & roof; gut interior to framing
	102	Remove all orig. subfloor
	103	Demo old decks, rails, and steps
200		**Foundation and Structure**
	201	Build new fdn for add'n & deck
	202	Install all new subfloor throughout
	203	Frame new floors, ext.walls, ceilings, & roof
300		**Exterior Envelope**
	301	Weather-in entire new structure
	302	Install all new exterior wall & roof finishes
	303	Plywood 50% of attic floor; access stair
	304	Build 300 s.f. deck, not 500
400		**Doors**
	401	3 entry (1 French)
	402	19 interior
	403	5 interior French doors
500		**Windows**
	501	9 ea. 4'0" x 4'0" square
	502	15 ea. 2'6" x 6'0" tall
600		**Interior Finishes**
	601	Frame interior walls & blocking for cabs
	602	Install drywall, trim, & closet shelves
	603	Install tile floors in 3 baths & laundry
	604	Tile wainscoting; 2 baths to 4'6"
	605	Install pine floors
	606	XYZ plain cabs in kitchen
	607	Install Big Box cabinets in baths & laund
	608	Natural stone countertops in kitchen
	609	Man-made countertops in 3 baths & laundry
	610	Furnish & install all appliances
700		**Prep and Paint - Int. & Ext.**
	701	Prime & paint interior - 6 colors
	702	Prime & paint exterior - 3 colors
800	801	**Plumbing:** Replace entire system
	802	Install 1 50-gal water heater
900	901	**HVAC:** Replace entire system; 2 zones
1000	1001	**Electrical:** Replace entire system
		Incr. power/street; 250A. panel; all fixtures

BID TOTAL $ [   ]

SEC	Item #	Task List
1100		**Alternates**
	A1	Build 500 s.f. curved deck w/steps and rails
	A2	Repl 15 tall windows w/8 ea 4'0" sq.
	A3	Install ABC cabinetry in kitchen
	A4	Man-made countertops in kitchen
	A5	New hardwood flrs in remaining areas
	A6	15 interior shutters - tall windows
	A7	Buy larger refrig/freezer (add)
	A8	Install 2 - 40-gallon water heaters in attic
	A9	Paving
	A10	Landscaping

go back to the text in the first half of the book and refresh your memory.

How will you *ensure* that all of the bidders' prices include the new location for the panel? If you can't remember, go back to the text.

Three days after the bid walk-through, one of the bidders calls and asks for a second visit. He wants to bring his electrician and have another look at the revised location of the new panel. You set a date and time for this second walk-through and call the other two contractors to tell them they are invited to do the same. They all said they could come, but only two of the bidders show up. What do you do about number three? Do you have to do anything? Could you have ensured that all three would be there?

Clarifying and Revising the Bids

The bids are back!

Open all the envelopes to be sure that all of the paperwork is there and properly signed; then copy your Final Cost Estimate Spreadsheet onto a blank computer spreadsheet and add a few columns to turn it into the Bid Comparison Spreadsheet. Record and proofread all of the bids to be sure you didn't make any mistakes.

Now study the Bid Comparison Spreadsheet opposite and circle the prices that may indicate that the contractor didn't understand something in the drawings.

How can you tell if all three contractors understood the project in the same way?

Identify any prices that appear to be out of line. Compose a query letter asking for a response within five business days. If you need to remind yourself what ought to be included in this letter, you can refer to Part 1, Section 4.4.

If this were real life, you would send a letter to each bidder, listing all of your questions and asking for answers to each one. At the end of this process, when you had all of your responses back, you would copy the original Bid Comparison Spreadsheet onto a fresh spreadsheet and make every correction the bidders sent you.

Back to the story: your adjusted Bid Comparison Spreadsheet now looks like the one on page 186.

What do you think of the final numbers?

Which contractor did you like the best? You're in the dating stage, but you're about to get married. In the long run, charm won't count for much, but integrity will be very important. Who will you invite to the table for the negotiation?

Negotiating

I have created a negotiation worksheet for you showing only the final cost estimate and the lowest adjusted bid. Please note that I've set your Initial Construction Contract Allowance at $2,000 lower than what your Total Project Budget allows. I'm concerned about how many secrets this old house is hiding from us, and I think it would be prudent to shift a few more dollars from your contract into your unanticipated costs contingency if you can. Do you think this is wise decision? If your surprises turn out to be manageable, you will have the opportunity to move this money back into the construction budget by upgrading your finishes later on. Be patient. You'll see.

Does the final price of your favorite contractor fit into your new Initial Construction Contract Allowance?

What will you choose to do to bring this figure down to your target price? You may not lower the bid price of a work item just because you think it's too high.

Think of this negotiation as a puzzle. Decide what ideas you'll bring to your meeting

BID COMPARISON SPREADSHEET - AS BID

SEC	Item #	Task List	Cost Est.	Bidder #1	Bidder #2	Bidder #3
000		**Hazards**				
	001	Remove windows, entry doors, all trim	$2,800	$2,800	by others	$2,800
100		**Demolition and Site Work**				
	101	Remove rear wall & roof; gut interior to framing	$8,000	$9,000	$9,000	$9,000
	102	Remove all orig. subfloor	$3,000	$3,000	$3,000	$3,000
	103	Demo old decks, rails, and steps	$1,200	$1,200	$1,200	$1,200
200		**Foundation and Structure**				
	201	Build new fdn for add'n & deck	$7,500	$7,500	$7,500	$7,500
	202	Install all new subfloor throughout	$5,000	$5,000	$5,000	$5,000
	203	Frame new floors, ext. walls, ceilings, & roof	$9,500	$11,000	$12,000	$11,000
300		**Exterior Envelope**				
	301	Weather-in entire new structure	$10,000	$10,000	$10,000	$10,000
	302	Install all new exterior wall & roof finishes	$20,000	$22,000	$23,000	$22,000
	303	Plywood 50% of attic floor; access stair	$3,500	$3,500	$3,500	$3,500
	304	Build 300 s.f. deck, not 500	$6,000	$6,000	$6,000	$6,000
400		**Doors**				
	401	3 entry (1 French)	$2,800	$2,800	$2,800	$2,800
	402	19 interior @ $400 ea	$7,600	$7,600	$7,600	$7,600
	403	5 interior French doors	$6,000	$6,000	$6,000	$6,000
500		**Windows**				
	501	9 ea. 4'0" x 4'0" square	$4,500	$4,500	$4,500	$4,500
	502	15 ea. 2'6" x 6'0" tall	$12,800	$12,800	$12,800	$16,000
600		**Interior Finishes**				
	601	Frame interior walls & blocking for cabs	$12,000	$12,000	$12,000	$12,000
	602	Install drywall, trim, & closet shelves	$25,000	$23,500	$23,500	$23,500
	603	Install tile floors in 3 baths & laundry	$3,000	$3,000	$3,800	$3,000
	604	Tile wainscoting; 2 baths to 4'6"	$2,200	$2,200	$2,200	$2,200
	605	Install pine floors	$18,000	$18,000	$18,000	$18,000
	606	XYZ plain cabs in kitchen	$20,000	$22,500	$20,000	$20,000
	607	Install Big Box cabinets in baths & laund	$4,000	$4,000	$4,000	$4,000
	608	Natural stone countertops in kitchen	$9,000	$9,000	$9,000	$9,000
	609	Man-made countertops in 3 baths & laundry	$2,000	$2,000	$2,000	$2,000
	610	Furnish & install all appliances	$4,000	$4,000	$4,000	$4,000
700		**Prep and Paint - Int. & Ext.**				
	701	Prime & paint interior - 6 colors	$8,500	$8,500	$8,500	$8,500
	702	Prime & paint exterior - 3 colors	$5,500	$5,500	$5,500	$5,500
800	801	**Plumbing:** Replace entire system	$15,000	$18,000	$18,000	$18,000
	802	Install 1 50-gal water heater	$1,800	$1,800	$1,800	$1,800
900	901	**HVAC:** Replace entire system; 2 zones	$6,000	$6,000	$600	$6,000
1000	1001	**Electrical:** Replace entire system	$15,000	$16,500	$16,000	$16,800
		Electrical: Replace entire system				
		FINAL COST ESTIMATE	**$261,200**	**$271,200**	**$262,800**	**$272,200**
		BUDGET & DEVIATION OF BIDS	**$259,200**	**105%**	**101%**	**105%**
1100		**Alternates**				
	A1	Build 500 s.f. curved deck w/steps and rails	$10,000	$10,000	$10,000	$10,000
	A2	Repl 15 tall windows w/8 ea 4'0" sq.	$4,000	$4,000	$4,000	$4,000
	A3	Install ABC cabinetry in kitchen	$28,000	$28,000	$28,000	$28,000
	A4	Man-made countertops in kitchen	$6,000	$6,000	$6,000	$6,000
	A5	New hardwood flrs in remaining areas	$22,000	$22,000	$22,000	$22,000
	A6	15 interior shutters - tall windows	$1,250	$1,250	$1,250	$1,250
	A7	Buy larger refrig/freezer (add)	$1,500	$1,500	$1,500	$1,500
	A8	Install 2 - 40-gallon water heaters in attic	$2,200	$2,200	$2,200	$2,200
	A9	Paving	$2,500	$2,500	$2,500	$2,500
	A10	Landscaping	$2,000	$2,000	$2,000	$2,000

ADJUSTED BID COMPARISON SPREADSHEET

SEC	Item #	Task List	Cost Est.	Bidder #1	Bidder #2	Bidder #3
000		**Hazards**				
	001	Remove windows, entry doors, all trim	$2,800	$2,800	$2,800	$2,800
100		**Demolition and Site Work**				
	101	Remove rear wall & roof; gut interior to framing	$8,000	$9,000	$9,000	$9,000
	102	Remove all orig. subfloor	$3,000	$3,000	$3,000	$3,000
	103	Demo old decks, rails, and steps	$1,200	$1,200	$1,200	$1,200
200		**Foundation and Structure**				
	201	Build new fdn for add'n & deck	$7,500	$7,500	$7,500	$7,500
	202	Install all new subfloor throughout	$5,000	$5,000	$5,000	$5,000
	203	Frame new floors, ext. walls, ceilings, & roof	**$9,500**	$11,000	$12,000	$11,000
300		**Exterior Envelope**				
	301	Weather-in entire new structure	$10,000	$10,000	$10,000	$10,000
	302	Install all new exterior wall & roof finishes	**$20,000**	$22,000	$23,000	$22,000
	303	Plywood 50% of attic floor; access stair	$3,500	$3,500	$3,500	$3,500
	304	Build 300 s.f. deck, not 500	$6,000	$6,000	$6,000	$6,000
400		**Doors**				
	401	3 entry (1 French)	$2,800	$2,800	$2,800	$2,800
	402	19 interior @ $400 ea	$7,600	$7,600	$7,600	$7,600
	403	5 interior French doors	$6,000	$6,000	$6,000	$6,000
500		**Windows**				
	501	9 ea. 4'0" x 4'0" square	$4,500	$4,500	$4,500	$4,500
	502	15 ea. 2'6" x 6'0" tall	$12,800	$12,800	$12,800	**$13,000**
600		**Interior Finishes**				
	601	Frame interior walls & blocking for cabs	$12,000	$12,000	$12,000	$12,000
	602	Install drywall, trim, & closet shelves	**$25,000**	$23,500	$23,500	$23,500
	603	Install tile floors in 3 baths & laundry	$3,000	$3,000	**$3,800**	$3,000
	604	Tile wainscoting; 2 baths to 4'6"	$2,200	$2,200	$2,200	$2,200
	605	Install pine floors	$18,000	$18,000	$18,000	$18,000
	606	XYZ plain cabs in kitchen	$20,000	**$20,000**	$20,000	$20,000
	607	Install Big Box cabinets in baths & laund	$4,000	$4,000	$4,000	$4,000
	608	Natural stone countertops in kitchen	$9,000	$9,000	$9,000	$9,000
	609	Man-made countertops in 3 baths & laundry	$2,000	$2,000	$2,000	$2,000
	610	Furnish & install all appliances	$4,000	$4,000	$4,000	$4,000
700		**Prep and Paint - Int. & Ext.**				
	701	Prime & paint interior - 6 colors	$8,500	$8,500	$8,500	$8,500
	702	Prime & paint exterior - 3 colors	$5,500	$5,500	$5,500	$5,500
800	801	**Plumbing:** Replace entire system	$15,000	$18,000	$18,000	$18,000
	802	Install 1 50-gal water heater	$1,800	$1,800	$1,800	$1,800
900	901	**HVAC:** Replace entire system; 2 zones	$6,000	$6,000	**$6,000**	$6,000
1000	1001	**Electrical:** Replace entire system	$15,000	$16,500	$16,000	$16,800
		Incr. power/street; 250A. panel; all fixtures				
		FINAL COST ESTIMATE	**$261,200**	**$268,700**	**$271,000**	**$269,200**
		BUDGET & DEVIATION OF BIDS	**$259,200**	**104%**	**105%**	**104%**
1100		**Alternates**				
	A1	Build 500 s.f. curved deck w/steps and rails	$10,000	$10,000	$10,000	$10,000
	A2	Repl 15 tall windows w/8 ea 4'0" sq.	$4,000	$4,000	$4,000	$4,000
	A3	Install ABC cabinetry in kitchen	$28,000	$28,000	$28,000	$28,000
	A4	Man-made countertops in kitchen	$6,000	$6,000	$6,000	$6,000
	A5	New hardwood flrs in remaining areas	$22,000	$22,000	$22,000	$22,000
	A6	15 interior shutters - tall windows	$1,250	$1,250	$1,250	$1,250
	A7	Buy larger refrig/freezer (add)	$1,500	$1,500	$1,500	$1,500
	A8	Install 2 - 40-gallon water heaters in attic	$2,200	$2,200	$2,200	$2,200
	A9	Paving	$2,500	$2,500	$2,500	$2,500
	A10	Landscaping	$2,000	$2,000	$2,000	

SEC	Item #	Task List	Cost Est.	Bidder #1	Notes:
000		**Hazards**			
	001	Remove windows, entry doors, all trim	$ 2,800	$ 2,800	
100		**Demolition and Site Work**			
	101	Remove rear wall & roof; gut interior to framing	$ 8,000	$ 9,000	
	102	Remove all orig. subfloor	$ 3,000	$ 3,000	
	103	Demo old decks, rails, and steps	$ 1,200	$ 1,200	
200		**Foundation and Structure**			
	201	Build new fdn for add'n & deck	$ 7,500	$ 7,500	
	601	Install all new subfloor throughout	$ 5,000	$ 5,000	
	202	Frame new floors, ext.walls, ceilings, & roof	$ 9,500	$ 11,000	
300		**Exterior Envelope**			
	301	Weather-in entire new structure	$ 10,000	$ 10,000	
	302	Install all new exterior wall & roof finishes	$ 20,000	$ 22,000	
	303	Plywood 50% of attic floor; access stair	$ 3,500	$ 3,500	
	304	Build 300 s.f. deck, not 500	$ 6,000	$ 6,000	
400		**Doors**			
	401	3 entry (1 French)	$ 2,800	$ 2,800	
	402	19 interior @ $400 ea	$ 7,600	$ 7,600	
	403	5 interior French doors	$ 6,000	$ 6,000	
500		**Windows**			
	501	9 ea. 4'0" x 4'0" square	$ 4,500	$ 4,500	
	502	15 ea. 2'6" x 6'0" tall	$ 12,800	$ 12,800	
600		**Interior Finishes**			
	601	Frame interior walls & blocking for cabs	$ 12,000	$ 12,000	
	602	Install drywall, trim, & closet shelves	$ 25,000	$ 23,500	
	603	Install tile floors in 3 baths & laundry	$ 3,000	$ 3,000	
	604	Tile wainscoting; 2 baths to 4'6"	$ 2,200	$ 2,200	
	605	Install pine floors	$ 18,000	$ 18,000	
	606	XYZ plain cabs in kitchen	$ 20,000	$ 20,000	
	607	Install Big Box cabinets in baths & laund	$ 4,000	$ 4,000	
	608	Natural stone countertops in kitchen	$ 9,000	$ 9,000	
	609	Man-made countertops in 3 baths & laundry	$ 2,000	$ 2,000	
	610	Furnish & install all appliances	$ 4,000	$ 4,000	
700		**Prep and Paint - Int. & Ext.**			
	701	Prime & paint interior - 6 colors	$ 8,500	$ 8,500	
	702	Prime & paint exterior - 3 colors	$ 5,500	$ 5,500	
800	801	**Plumbing:** Replace entire system	$ 15,000	$ 18,000	
	802	Install 1 50-gal water heater	$ 1,800	$ 1,800	
900	901	**HVAC:** Replace entire system; 2 zones	$ 6,000	$ 6,000	
1000	1001	**Electrical:** Replace entire system Incr. power/street; 250A. panel; all fixtures	$ 15,000	$ 16,500	
		FINAL COST ESTIMATE	**$ 261,200**	**$ 268,700**	

Signatures:

SEC	Item #	Task List	Cost Est.	Bidder #1	
1100		**Contract Alternates**			
	A1	Build 500 s.f. curved deck w/steps and rails	$ 10,000	$ 10,000	
	A2	Repl 15 tall windows w/8 ea 4'0" sq.	$ 4,000	$ 4,000	
	A3	Install ABC cabinetry in kitchen	$ 28,000	$ 28,000	
	A4	Man-made countertops in kitchen	$ 6,000	$ 6,000	
	A5	New hardwood flrs in remaining areas	$ 22,000	$ 22,000	
	A6	15 interior shutters - tall windows	$ 1,250	$ 1,250	
	A7	Buy larger refrig/freezer (add)	$ 1,500	$ 1,500	
	A8	Install 2 - 40-gallon water heaters in attic	$ 2,200	$ 2,200	
	A9	Paving	$ 2,500	$ 2,500	
	A10	Landscaping	$ 2,000	$ 2,000	

that might lower the cost of the job without sacrificing any of the more important details of the design.

Now sit down with your contractor. Discuss your ideas. Discuss his ideas. Mark changes you can agree to on the negotiations spreadsheet, and change the line-item prices and the bottom line as you go.

When you and the contractor are both happy with the final scope of work, you should both sign the negotiation spreadsheet. This will represent your mutual commitment until you can put together the complete, edited, contract package.

Set your work start date and schedule the pre-construction meeting for about three weeks before work is scheduled to start.

My Opinion

If I were negotiating on behalf of your family, this is what the final Contract Agreement Form would look like. I apologize for interrupting your train of thought; you may have had a better idea. But in order for us to continue to work on the project together, we'll have to be working from the same contract prices, and since I don't know what you're thinking, we'll use my best guess.

Closing the Deal

Please fill in the blanks:

Your final Initial Construction Contract price is $_____.

Your contractor submitted a Bid Summary form with his bid that said that he thought the project would take twenty-eight weeks to complete.

• How much does he have to earn each week to stay on schedule? $_____

• How much would he have to earn in every four-week pay period to be eligible to receive a check? $_____

• If you plan to do progress evaluations every two weeks, and hope to pay him at the end of each four-week assessment period, you will be issuing him (how many?) _____ checks by the time he's finished?

Copy the last page of the contract form in the appendix and fill in the payment schedule and the contract amount. Anticipated payment dates ought to represent the end of each four-week assessment period. Let's assume that work will start on June 12. Remember that there are thirty or thirty-one days in a calendar month, but only twenty-eight days in a four-week pay period. Don't let this confuse you. Use the four-week time periods.

The designer just called. Your marked-up construction drawings are ready!

If this were a real project, you would pick up the drawings, assemble one complete, original set of construction contract documents—the Terms and Conditions Statement from the appendix and the complete set of clearly marked drawings and specifications—and trot down to the local blueprint shop and have ten copies prepared.

What would you do with the original contract document set?

Who gets the rest of the sets?

Completing the Contract Details

Bidder 1, the fellow you negotiated your contract with, initially submitted a price of $261,200, with an anticipated work schedule of twenty-eight weeks.

During the negotiation you were able to reduce the cost of the project to $259,500 by omitting the tile wainscoting in the bathrooms,

AUTHOR'S NEGOTIATIONS

SEC	Item #	Task List	Cost Est.	Bidder #1
000		**Hazards**		
	001	Remove windows, entry doors, all trim	$2,800	$2,800
100		**Demolition and Site Work**		
	101	Remove rear wall & roof; gut interior to framing	$8,000	$9,000
	102	Remove all orig. subfloor	$3,000	$3,000
	103	Demo old decks, rails, and steps	$1,200	$1,200
	SwEq	Owner to demo deck; contractor to haul		$ (1000)
200		**Foundation and Structure**		
	201	Build new fdn for add'n & deck	$7,500	$7,500
	601	Install all new subfloor throughout	$5,000	$5,000
	202	Frame new floors, ext.walls, ceilings, & roof	$9,500	$11,000
300		**Exterior Envelope**		
	301	Weather-in entire new structure	$10,000	$10,000
	302	Install all new exterior wall & roof finishes	$20,000	$22,000
	303	Plywood 50% of attic floor; access stair	$3,500	$3,500
	SwEq	Owner to install-only plywood in attic		$ (1000)
	304	Build 300 s.f. deck, not 500	$6,000	$6,000
400		**Doors**		
	401	3 entry (1 French)	$2,800	$2,800
	402	19 interior @ $400 ea	$7,600	$7,600
	403	5 interior French doors	$6,000	$6,000
500		**Windows**		
	501	9 ea. 4'0" x 4'0" square	$4,500	$4,500
	502	15 ea. 2'6" x 6'0" tall	$12,800	$12,800
600		**Interior Finishes**		
	601	Frame interior walls & blocking for cabs	$12,000	$12,000
	602	Install drywall, trim, & closet shelves	$25,000	$23,500
	603	Install tile floors in 3 baths & laundry	$3,000	$3,000
	605	Install pine floors	$18,000	$18,000
	606	XYZ plain cabs in kitchen	$20,000	$20,000
	607	Install Big Box cabinets in baths & laund	$4,000	$4,000
	A4	Man-made countertops in kitchen	$6,000	$6,000
	609	Man-made countertops in 3 baths & laundry	$2,000	$2,000
700		**Prep and Paint - Int. & Ext.**		
	701	Prime & paint interior - 6 colors	$8,500	$8,500
	702	Prime & paint exterior - 3 colors	$5,500	$5,500
800	801	**Plumbing:** Replace entire system	$15,000	$18,000
	802	Install 1 50-gal water heater	$1,800	$1,800
900	901	**HVAC:** Replace entire system; 2 zones	$6,000	$6,000
1000	1001	**Electrical:** Replace entire system	$15,000	$16,500
		Incr. power/street; 250A. panel; all fixtures		
		FINAL COST ESTIMATE	$252,000	$257,500

Signatures:	**D. Contractor**	**D. Homeowner**

1100		**Contract Alternates**		
	A1	Build 500 s.f. curved deck w/steps and rails	$10,000	$10,000
	A2	Repl 15 tall windows w/8 ea 4'0" sq.	$4,000	$4,000
	A3	Install ABC cabinetry in kitchen	$28,000	$28,000
	608	Natural stone countertops in kitchen	$9,000	$9,000
	604	Tile wainscoting; 2 baths to 4'6"	$2,200	$2,200
	A5	New hardwood flrs in remaining areas	$22,000	$22,000
	A6	15 interior shutters - tall windows	$1,250	$1,250
	A7	Buy larger refrig/freezer (add)	$1,500	$1,500
	A8	Install 2 - 40-gallon water heaters in attic	$2,200	$2,200
	A9	Paving	$2,500	$2,500
	A10	Landscaping	$2,000	$2,000
	610	Furnish & install all appliances	$4,000	$4,000

FINAL CONTRACT AGREEMENT

SEC	Item #	Task List	Bidder #1
000		**Hazards**	
	001	Remove windows, entry doors, all trim	$2,800
100		**Demolition and Site Work**	
	101	Remove rear wall & roof; gut interior to framing	$9,000
	102	Remove all orig. subfloor	$3,000
	103	Demo old decks, rails, and steps	$1,200
	SwEq	Owner to demo deck; contractor to haul	$(1000)
200		**Foundation and Structure**	
	201	Build new fdn for add'n & deck	$7,500
	202	Install all new subfloor throughout	$5,000
	203	Frame new floors, ext.walls, ceilings, & roof	$11,000
300		**Exterior Envelope**	
	301	Weather-in entire new structure	$10,000
	302	Install all new exterior wall & roof finishes	$22,000
	303	Plywood 50% of attic floor; access stair	$3,500
	SwEq	Owner to install-only plywood in attic	$(1000)
	304	Build 300 s.f. deck, not 500	$6,000
400		**Doors**	
	401	3 entry (1 French)	$2,800
	402	19 interior @ $400 ea	$7,600
	403	5 interior French doors	$6,000
500		**Windows**	
	501	9 ea. 4'0" x 4'0" square	$4,500
	502	15 ea. 2'6" x 6'0" tall	$12,800
600		**Interior Finishes**	
	601	Frame interior walls & blocking for cabs	$12,000
	602	Install drywall, trim, & closet shelves	$23,500
	603	Install tile floors in 3 baths & laundry	$3,000
	605	Install pine floors	$18,000
	606	XYZ plain cabs in kitchen	$20,000
	607	Install Big Box cabinets in baths & laund	$4,000
	A4	Man-made countertops in kitchen	$6,000
	609	Man-made countertops in 3 baths & laundry	$2,000
700		**Prep and Paint - Int. & Ext.**	
	701	Prime & paint interior - 6 colors	$8,500
	702	Prime & paint exterior - 3 colors	$5,500
800	801	Plumbing: Replace entire system	$18,000
	802	Install 1 50-gal water heater	$1,800
900	901	**HVAC: Replace entire system; 2 zones**	$6,000
1000	1001	Electrical: Replace entire system	$16,500
		Incr. power/street; 250A. panel; all fixtures	
		FINAL CONTRACT AMOUNT	**$257,500**

Signatures:	D. Contractor	D. Homeowner

SEC	Item #	Task List	Bidder #1
1100		**CONTRACT ALTERNATES**	
	A1	Build 500 s.f. curved deck w/steps and rails	$10,000
	A2	Repl 15 tall windows w/8 ea 4'0" sq.	$4,000
	A3	Install ABC cabinetry in kitchen	$28,000
	608	Natural stone countertops in kitchen	$9,000
	A5	Tile wainscoting; 2 baths to 4'6"	$2,200
	605	New hardwood flrs in remaining areas	$22,000
	A6	15 interior shutters - tall windows	$1,250
	A7	Buy larger refrig/freezer (add)	$1,500
	A8	Install 2 - 40-gallon water heaters in attic	$2,200
	A9	Paving	$2,500
	A10	Landscaping	$2,000
	610	Furnish & install all appliances	$4,000

the stone countertops in the kitchen, and the purchase and installation of your new appliances.

Then you volunteered to do $2,000 worth of sweat equity and put a little extra back into the contingency fund. Your final contract amount was $257,500.

To set the work schedule, divide the *initial bid* by the twenty-eight weeks he thought the work would take to complete. This will tell you that your contractor anticipated being able to earn $_____ a week.

Now divide that weekly earnings number into your new negotiated contract price and see if a twenty-eight-week schedule is still a reasonable expectation. What do you think?

Record the projected pay dates on the contract. In a minute, you will record the weekly earnings target on both your Progress Evaluation Spreadsheets and your Construction Accounting Sheet.

FIVE

Construction Phase 1—Demolition

Time to get this job moving! Your pre-construction meeting went very smoothly. You both (Mom and Dad) attended, and you got to meet the crew chief (the superintendent) and a few of the key subcontractors. Dad and the general contractor signed every set of the construction documents after you had all reviewed every detail of the project as a team. The contractor confirmed that he could start on the date he had promised.

You hired a mover, got everything out of the house and into a small storage facility, and took your favorite and most comforting things to a small three-bedroom house you rented about a mile away.

Mom is six months pregnant now and a little cranky but feeling fine; the little guys are acting up because they don't understand what's going on; and Dad is feeling the stress and praying for peace.

You (Mom and Dad) have agreed that since Dad has to work so many hours in his new position, Mom should be the contractor's contact until Dad's acclimated and she's getting uncomfortable. It was the best you could come up with under the circumstances.

You have reserved one hour of your general contractor's time on Friday afternoons from 3 to 4 p.m. every other week for your formal progress evaluations. This is your chance to ask all your questions. Catching him, or his superintendent, on the fly is not a good idea—it will distract them from their work.

When you do your informal site visits, it will be best if you don't actually talk to anyone. Take your pictures, make your notes, and go home. The crew will get used to your being there; they'll pay their respects and get right back to work.

You are as prepared as you can be. Here we go!

Setting Up the Site

The contractor has pulled his permit and posted his inspections data card for the inspectors to sign.

The electrical subcontractor will be removing your old electrical system entirely, and the subs will need power for their tools, so the general contractor has erected a temporary power pole in the front yard, and the local power company has hooked it up to the transformer at the street for him.

The plumber will be demolishing all of the existing plumbing, so the crew has arranged for a temporary source of water.

One of your special conditions was that the big shade tree in your yard be protected, so the superintendent has draped an orange plastic mesh fence on posts around that tree for protection.

The general has ordered large containers, the first of which has been delivered and will be filled with debris in no time.

Temporary power pole

Permit box

Temporary water supply

Tree protection

Large waste bin

All of that took about a week, but the demolition crew is now ready to begin.

Week 2

It's Friday at 3 p.m.—the end of the second week since the work start date—and it's time for your first formal progress evaluation.

We'll take the first few evaluations one step at a time. We can move more quickly once you get the hang of this.

Prepare the Paperwork

Before you leave the house, you must prepare your first Progress Evaluation Spreadsheet.

Copy your Final Contract Agreement Form onto a fresh spreadsheet, remove the Alternates, and add the four additional columns. Since you haven't made any changes yet, there won't be revisions to put in the "Changes" column, so you can copy the original contract prices into the *third* column too. Bring two copies of this spreadsheet with you to the site: one for you and one for the general contractor. If you need help, refer to the example opposite.

Show Up (On Time)

As you drive up to the house, you can hear the banging of the demolition work inside the house. This is what the site looks like.

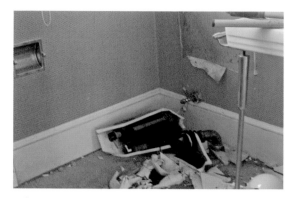
Taking apart the bathroom

Disassembling the roof

Demolishing the deck

Removing kitchen cabinets

Opening the walls

Dropping the ceilings

PROGRESS EVALUATION SPREADSHEET - Setup

SEC	Item #	Task List	Initial Contract	Changes	Revised Contract	%-Compl	Earned to Date
				(none yet)			
000		**Hazards**					
	001	Remove windows, entry doors, all trim	$2,800		$2,800		
100		**Demolition and Site Work**					
	101	Demo rear wall & roof; gut int. to framing	$9,000		$9,000		
	102	Remove all orig. subfloor	$3,000		$3,000		
	103	Demo old decks, rails, and steps	$200		$200		
200		**Foundation and Structure**					
	201	Build new fdn for add'n & deck	$7,500		$7,500		
	202	Install all new subfloor throughout	$5,000		$5,000		
	203	Frame new floors,ext.walls,ceilings, & roof	$11,000		$11,000		
300		**Exterior Envelope**					
	301	Weather-in entire new structure	$10,000		$10,000		
	302	Install new exterior wall & roof finishes	$22,000		$22,000		
	303	Plywood 50% of attic floor; access stair	$2,500		$2,500		
	304	Build 300 s.f. deck, not 500	$6,000		$6,000		
400		**Doors:** 3 Entry; 19 Int; 5 Int. Fr.	$16,400		$16,400		
500		**Windows:** 9@4'0" sq; 15@2'-6"x6"0"	$17,300		$17,300		
600		**Interior Finishes**					
	601	Frame int. walls & blocking for cabs	$12,000		$12,000		
	602	Install drywall, trim, & closet shelves	$23,500		$23,500		
	603	Install tile floors in 3 baths & laundry	$3,000		$3,000		
	605	Install pine floors	$18,000		$18,000		
	606	XYZ plain cabs in kitchen	$20,000		$20,000		
	607	Install Big Box cabs in baths & laund	$4,000		$4,000		
	A4	Man-made countertops in kitchen	$6,000		$6,000		
	609	Man-made ctrtps in 3 baths & laund	$2,000		$2,000		
700		**Prep and Paint - Int. & Ext.**					
	701	Prime & paint interior - 6 colors	$8,500		$8,500		
	702	Prime & paint exterior - 3 colors	$5,500		$5,500		
800	801	**Plumbing:** Replace entire system	$18,000		$18,000		
	802	Install 1 50-gal water heater	$1,800		$1,800		
900	901	**HVAC:** Replace entire system	$6,000		$6,000		
1000	1001	**Electrical:** Replace entire system	$16,500		$16,500		
		Incr. power/street; 25A. panel; all fix's					
		TOTALS	**$257,500**		**$257,500**		

Next Pay Avail. At __ Weeks x $9200 $

Signatures:

The general contractor smiles as he picks his way through the rubble, asks how you're feeling (remember, you're Mom, six months pregnant), then he guides you carefully through the debris, and you are now standing in front of your first challenge—the floor repairs. Three areas of the floor will need work. Your contractor doesn't think you need to call a structural engineer; the damage is confined in each case to an area not more than 3 feet square, and the remaining framing looks just fine.

You begin to ask about the cost, and the general tells you to hold on; there's more.

The Real Surprises

You anticipated the floor-framing repairs. But you never anticipated any of these . . .

- The contractor points to something fuzzy above your broken ceiling drywall. Pigeons have nested in your attic crawl space for years. There is an entire colony of birds up there—nests, eggs, chicks, adult birds, dead birds, and all of the accompanying mess. It will all have to be removed by a hazard abatement contractor and his specially licensed crew.
- There is black mold on the framing around the original bathrooms. It may be toxic. It needs to be tested, and the contaminated lumber may have to be treated or removed by that same hazard removal contractor.

The general has already called in an environmental consultant; both the removal of the birds and the treatment of the mold can be scheduled for next week. He tells you what this will cost. Since there is only one hazard removal company in a twenty-mile radius, there won't be any room for haggling on this one—not if you want the work done immediately.

- The termite damage observed by the home inspector turned out to be pretty extensive.

Most of your wall framing in one or two areas will have to be replaced.
- The mortar in some of the original foundation piers has deteriorated and the bricks are beginning to compress. The damaged mortar will have to be replaced before you can put any weight on these piers.
- Then your contractor shows you a section of the main waste line that the plumber is in the process of removing from a trench in your front yard. What a mess! You had planned to replace all of the plumbing anyway, so you're grateful that this problem won't cost you extra, but it's seems there's more to the story than that.

The city's main line in the street was installed in the 1940s, and it is now cracked and leaking. The Public Utilities Department inspector argued that the crack in the main line was the plumber's fault because he tried to remove a branch line from a rusty connection. The general argued that the main line was cracked before the plumber got there and the repair would have been necessary in any case. The general won—not necessarily because he was right, but because you picked the right contractor: he's been around the block a few times, and he has friends where he needs them.

The inspector said that the public utilities crew wouldn't be able to make the repair for about three weeks.

What did the general contractor do? He made a personal appearance in the Public Utilities Department, chatted up his buddies, and politely asked what the status of your job was. He sweet-talked the guy that schedules the work crews, and he got the city to repair the hookups the next day, last Wednesday. The new connection ended up 3 feet from where the original one was, so there will be a charge

Termite damage

Bird nest in wall framing   *Bird nest inside wall*

Water rot in subfloor under bathroom

Bird nest in ceiling insulation

Crumbling mortar in foundation wall

Termite damage in wall framing

Toxic mold in bathroom wall

Clogged plumbing in waste line

for the plumber to dig a new trench in your front yard, but no more than that.

You've made notes of all of the surprises and negotiated fair prices for each one. Thank goodness for that contingency fund! You will prepare a change order in a minute.

The Evaluation

It's time for that formal progress evaluation now.

You and your contractor will work collaboratively to establish what portion of each task he has completed. If you look at the Week 2 Progress Evaluation Spreadsheet on page 199, you'll see that you've agreed that he is finished removing all of the lead paint, that the back wall of the house is about 60 percent down, and that the plumber, the HVAC sub, and the electrician have completed much of their demolition work. (Demolition of an item may account for as much as 15 percent of a subcontractor's costs.)

Your hour is up. You and the contractor both sign the evaluation sheet and you agree to deliver the change order early Monday morning. What you'll walk away from the meeting with is shown opposite.

As you leave, you notice that there are tire marks where the protective fence around your shade tree was crushed by one of the work trucks, and you remind the contractor that the contract prohibits damaging the area around this tree; he apologizes and resets the stakes as you speak.

As you continue walking toward your car, you realize that the entire back wall of your house is now open to the weather. You call back to the general to remind him that the contract requires him to provide continuous protection. He nods, smiles, and waves good-bye.

How Much Has He Earned?

Calculate the amount of money he's earned by multiplying the percent-complete by the total value of each task he's worked on and add the subtotals together to find out the total amount he's earned to date. (Isn't this easy?) Now your spreadsheet should look like the one on page 200.

How Is His Momentum?

He's got a twenty-eight-week schedule, and a total contract worth $_____ (not including the change order that you have not executed yet).

How much should he have earned in the first two weeks in order to start the project with the right momentum?

What Percentage of the Schedule Has Elapsed?

Divide two weeks by the total schedule of twenty-eight weeks, and the answer is _____ percent.

Now see if he's working to his schedule. Multiply his total contract value (not including the change order you haven't executed yet) by the percentage of the schedule that has elapsed and see what he should have earned by now. The answer to this question is that he should have earned $_____.

Has he earned that much yet? Is he working within his schedule?

If he's not, what do you think is the reason? How should you respond? What might be the outcome of your contractor getting behind schedule this early in the project? What do contractors do when they begin to worry about losing money?

PROGRESS EVALUATION SPREADSHEET - Week 2 Walk-Through

SEC	Item #	Task List	Initial Contract	Changes	Revised Contract	%-Compl	Earned to Date
000		**Hazards**					
	001	Remove windows, entry doors, all trim	$2,800		$2,800	100%	
100		**Demolition and Site Work**					
	101	Demo rear wall & roof; gut int. to framing	$9,000		$9,000	60%	
	102	Remove all orig. subfloor	$3,000		$3,000		
	103	Demo old decks, rails, and steps	$200		$200		
200		**Foundation and Structure**					
	201	Build new fdn for add'n & deck	$7,500		$7,500		
	202	Install all new subfloor throughout	$5,000		$5,000		
	203	Frame new floors,ext.walls,ceilings, & roof	$11,000		$11,000		
300		**Exterior Envelope**					
	301	Weather-in entire new structure	$10,000		$10,000		
	302	Install new exterior wall & roof finishes	$22,000		$22,000		
	303	Plywood 50% of attic floor; access stair	$2,500		$2,500		
	304	Build 300 s.f. deck, not 500	$6,000		$6,000		
400		**Doors:** 3 Entry; 19 Int; 5 Int. Fr.	$16,400		$16,400		
500		**Windows:** 9@4'0" sq; 15@2'6"x6"0"	$17,300		$17,300		
600		**Interior Finishes**					
	601	Frame int. walls & blocking for cabs	$12,000		$12,000		
	602	Install drywall, trim, & closet shelves	$23,500		$23,500		
	603	Install tile floors in 3 baths & laundry	$3,000		$3,000		
	605	Install pine floors	$18,000		$18,000		
	606	XYZ plain cabs in kitchen	$20,000		$20,000		
	607	Install Big Box cabs in baths & laund	$4,000		$4,000		
	A4	Man-made countertops in kitchen	$6,000		$6,000		
	609	Man-made ctrtps in 3 baths & laund	$2,000		$2,000		
700		**Prep and Paint - Int. & Ext.**					
	701	Prime & paint interior - 6 colors	$8,500		$8,500		
	702	Prime & paint exterior - 3 colors	$5,500		$5,500		
800	801	**Plumbing:** Replace entire system	$18,000		$18,000	5%	
	802	Install 1 50-gal water heater	$1,800		$1,800		
900	901	**HVAC:** Replace entire system	$6,000		$6,000	10%	
1000	1001	**Electrical:** Replace entire system Incr. power/street; 250A. panel; all fix's	$16,500		$16,500	10%	
		TOTALS	**$257,500**		**$257,500**		

Next Pay Avail. At 4 Weeks x $9200 $ 36,800

Signatures:	**D. Contractor**	**D. Homeowner**

PROGRESS EVALUATION SPREADSHEET - Week 2 Calculations

SEC	Item #	Task List	Initial Contract	Changes	Revised Contract	%-Compl	Earned to Date
000		**Hazards**					
	001	Remove windwos, entry doors, all trim	$2,800		$2,800	100%	$2,800
100		**Demolition and Site Work**					
	101	Demo rear wall & roof; gut int. to framing	$9,000		$9,000	60%	$5,400
	102	Remove all orig. subfloor	$3,000		$3,000		$ -
	103	Demo old decks, rails, and steps	$200		$200		$ -
200		**Foundation and Structure**					
	201	Build new fdn for add'n & deck	$7,500		$7,500		$ -
	202	Install all new subfloor throughout	$5,000		$5,000		$ -
	203	Frame new floors,ext.walls,ceilings, & roof	$11,000		$11,000		$ -
300		**Exterior Envelope**					
	301	Weather-in entire new structure	$10,000		$10,000		$ -
	302	Install new exterior wall & roof finishes	$22,000		$22,000		$ -
	303	Plywood 50% of attic floor; access stair	$2,500		$2,500		$ -
	304	Build 300 s.f. deck, not 500	$6,000		$6,000		$ -
400		**Doors:** 3 Entry; 19 Int; 5 Int. Fr.	$16,400		$16,400		$ -
500		**Windows:** 9@4'0" sq; 15@2'6"x6'0"	$17,300		$17,300		$ -
600		**Interior Finishes**					
	601	Frame int. walls & blocking for cabs	$12,000		$12,000		$ -
	602	Install drywall, trim, & closet shelves	$23,500		$23,500		$ -
	603	Install tile floors in 3 baths & laundry	$3,000		$3,000		$ -
	605	Install pine floors	$18,000		$18,000		$ -
	606	XYZ plain cabs in kitchen	$20,000		$20,000		$ -
	607	Install Big Box cabs in baths & laund	$4,000		$4,000		$ -
	A4	Man-made countertops in kitchen	$6,000		$6,000		$ -
	609	Man-made ctrtps in 3 baths & laund	$2,000		$2,000		$ -
700		**Prep and Paint - Int. & Ext.**					
	701	Prime & paint interior - 6 colors	$8,500		$8,500		$ -
	702	Prime & paint exterior - 3 colors	$5,500		$5,500		$ -
800	801	**Plumbing:** Replace entire system	$18,000		$18,000	5%	$900
	802	Install 1 50-gal water heater	$1,800		$1,800		$ -
900	901	**HVAC:** Replace entire system	$6,000		$6,000	10%	$600
1000	1001	**Electrical:** Replace entire system Incr. power/street; 250A. panel; all fix's	$16,500		$16,500	10%	$1,650
		TOTALS	**$257,500**		**$257,500**		**$11,350**

First PayA vail. At 4 wks x $9200 $36,800

Signatures:	D.Contractor	D.Homeowner

Setting Up Bookkeeping

There are samples of two accounting worksheets at the end of Chapter 4 in Part One, pages 117 and 119. The Soft-Costs Accounting Sheet is self-explanatory. The Construction Accounting Sheet is a little more complicated.

After every progress evaluation—immediately after you've finished calculating the amount your contractor has earned—complete the Construction Accounting Sheet. I promised you a simple system. This is as simple as it gets. Setting it up for the first entries is the hardest part.

CONSTRUCTION ACCOUNTING - Week 2

CHANGE ORDER LOG

CO#	Change Date	A Contract Amount	B Net Change	C=A+B Revised Contract	D=In.Con.-B Remaining Conting.	E Current Sched	F Days Added	G=E+F Revised Schedule
				Initial Contingency:	$69,000			
1								
2								
3								
4								

PROGRESS EVALUATIONS

Wk#	Eval. Date	A # Days in Sched.	B # Days Lapsed	C=B/A %-Sched Lapsed	D Contract Amount	E T.Amt. Earned	F=E/D %-Contr. Earned	Target: $9,200 per wk.
2	(Day 14)	196	14	7%	$257,500	$11,350	4%	$36,800
4			28					
6			42					
8			56					
12			84					
16			112					
20			140					
24			168					
28			196					
32			224					
36			252					

CONTRACTOR PAYMENTS

	A T.Earned to Date	B Minus 10% Retain.	C=A-B Balance #1	D Minus All Prev.Pay'ts	E=C-D Balance #2	F Minus Late Fees	G=E-F AMOUNT PAID	Check Date & Number
DEP	$ -	$ -	$ -	$ -	$ -	$ -	$15,000	d / n
Ck 1								
Ck 2								
Ck 3								
Ck 4								
Ck 5								
Ck 6								
Ck 7								
Ck 8								
Ck 9								

Start with a clean, blank worksheet and set up the nine columns as they are set up here.

Note that there are three different boxes, each box has different column headings, and each has its own unique set of calculations.

- The first box is the Change Order Log, which will keep track of your changes, their costs, the diminishment of the contingency fund, and revisions to both the schedule and the contract amount. That's a lot of information, but it's all on the change order form. When the time comes to record this information, you'll have what you need right in front of you.
- The second box is for progress evaluation calculations. The number of the columns is the same, but the headings are a little different. Nearly everything you need you already have on the Progress Evaluation Spreadsheet. Note that the *formula* for each calculation is indicated in the heading over each column. If you follow these abbreviated instructions, you can't go wrong.
- The third box will help you calculate and keep track of contractor payments. The number of columns is the same, but the headings changed again. Follow the formulas.

Set the Construction Funds Budget

Your construction funds—the contract amount and the contingency set-aside—work a little differently than your soft-costs allowance. They have to be more fluid.

When you negotiated your contract, you were a little cautious, and you signed a contract worth $257,500 instead of the $261,200 you had in your budget. This will allow you to put the *difference* ($3,700) into the contingency fund so you'll have a little larger safety net. That was wise. You anticipated having a fund of $65,300, but with the added $3,700 it's going to be $69,000. Was that clear? Fill in the total contingency fund amount as $69,000.

Do you remember the metaphor of the water in the locks in the Erie Canal and how that water can flow from one lock into another but there can never be more or less total water after the change than you had when you started? You will move money from the contingency fund into the contract every time you add work to the job with a change order, but at any point you should be able to add your revised contract amount to the remainder in your contingency fund and they should always add up to the same Total Construction Budget amount.

The contract negotiation set the starting points, which turned out to be a little different than you anticipated. That's okay. You've still got the same amount of money in both funds combined, and that's the acid test.

The Accounting Sheet

Although you determined what your costs would be for your first change order during the Week 2 walk-through, you did not *execute* the change order yet, so there is nothing to record in the Change Order Log box on the top of your accounting sheet except to note the starting amount of the contingency fund—$69,000.

Budget	Contract	+	Contingency	=	Total Construction Budget
Original Budget	$261,200	+	$65,300	=	$326,500
Adjusted Contract	$257,500	+	$69,000	=	$326,500

In the Progress Evaluations box—the middle box on the Construction Accounting Sheet—you can fill in the numbers from your signed Progress Evaluation Spreadsheet—the date of the walk-through, the number of calendar days (not work days or weekdays) in the total contract schedule, the number of calendar days that have lapsed since the start date in the contract (whether or not the contractor actually started work on that date), the total current value of the construction contract, and the amount the contractor has earned to date. That part is easy.

You have to figure out C and F, and to establish a progress target to complete the work in this portion of the accounting sheet.

In this middle box, column C asks you to divide B (the number of days lapsed) by A (the total number of days in the schedule). The result of this division will give you the percentage of the schedule that has lapsed: $14 \div 196 = 7\%$.

Column F asks you to divide E (the amount the contractor has earned) by D (the total contract amount). The result of this division will give you the percentage of the contract that he's earned: $\$11,350 \div \$257,500 = 4\%$.

Remember the maxim that if you want the project to be 100 percent complete when the schedule is 100 percent elapsed—that is, if you want him to finish on time—then you want the project to be 20 percent complete when the schedule is 20 percent elapsed. Comparing the percentages in columns C and F will tell you at a glance how he's doing. If the percentage in column C *matches* the percentage in column F, then all is right with the world. How is your contractor doing so far?

Setting Momentum Targets

To set the pace for this job, divide the number of weeks in his contract schedule into the total

contract amount. This will give you a weekly earnings rate that will move him along as fast as the schedule is passing him by ($\$257,500 \div 28 = \$9,196.43$—round that off and call it $\$9,200$). He has to earn $\$9,200$ a week to finish on time. If that wasn't clear, read it again.

Write $\$9,200$ at the head of the last column in the Progress Evaluations box.

Now figure out how much he ought to earn in each four-week pay period in order to get a check. This is easy too—if he has to earn $\$9,200$ in one week, he has to earn four times that in four weeks. $4 \times \$9,200 = \$36,800$. He has to earn $\$36,800$ in the four-week pay period or he does not get a check.

And . . . if you execute a change order for $\$9,200$ in extra work, you'll have to add a week to his contract schedule to be fair. Is that clear?

Payments

The calculations in the third box will tell you whether it's time to pay your contractor or not. Is your general ready for his first check? No. Why not?

Your contract says that he must be working on schedule (which he is not—he's completed 4 percent of the job, but 7 percent of the schedule has elapsed) and that he has to earn $\$36,800$ in order to earn his first check; he has earned only $\$11,350$ so far. He doesn't get a check in Week 2. That's no surprise, and in this case it's nothing to worry about either. We know what slowed him down.

You have paid him a deposit. That may be a payment, but it's not money earned. We've recorded your deposit of $\$15,000$ in the Contractor Payments box, but nothing in the Ck 1 line yet.

Your accounting sheet is now ready for action. From now on, all you have to do is fill in the blanks.

File a hard copy of this spreadsheet so that it stays clean and safe. This accounting spreadsheet will be the only one you'll need from now until you pay the contractor his last check. Keep the spreadsheet on the computer. You won't need to copy and edit it each time you make a progress evaluation; you can just continue to complete each line as the project progresses—just be sure you keep a backup copy. With each evaluation, complete the spreadsheet on the computer and print out a new hard copy. Keep the hard copies in your project file under Contractor Payments.

The Change Order

You owe your contractor a change order. If this agreement isn't fully executed (signed by the two of you) and in his hands by early Monday morning, the hazard removal crew won't be able to start on Tuesday or finish their work by the end of the week. That deadline is critical to the general contractor because the hazard removal work requires that the site be abandoned by the construction crew, which will put him even further behind schedule.

Have a Good Look at the Change Order

Read the paragraph under the heading. Any work on a fully executed change order becomes a part of the contract—the contractor must do the work and you must pay for it. This means that the *value* of this change will move from your contingency fund into your contract fund when the form is signed.

Notice that the items on the change order are listed in the same *order* as they would be listed on the Task Abstract List.

Notice that there are two boxes at the bottom of the sheet for you to show clearly how this change order will revise your construction contract amount and your contract schedule.

Your signatures make this a legal agreement and incorporate the agreement into your construction contract "by reference"—which means that this piece of paper doesn't necessarily have to be stapled to anything, but that it is binding and that all of the contract terms and conditions will apply to this new work just as if it had been in the contract all along.

Accounting Updates

You and your contractor would execute two copies of Change Order #1 on Monday morning, as planned. You can take two copies of the change order to the site, and you would each have an original signed copy, or you can take one copy on Monday morning, take the signed order home, and make the contractor a photocopy for his files—whichever you like. My preference is to have only one set of original signatures, and I always like to be the one holding those original documents.

Pull out that Construction Accounting Sheet, and add this change order to the sheet. Here's how.

In the Change Order Log, in the top box, copy the information from signed change order #1, right across the first line, next to "1." When you're done with that, all you ought to have left to do is to calculate the answer to column D, the Revised Contingency amount: $69,000 (the current contingency amount) minus $24,700 (the value of the change order that must move into the contract now) leaves a balance of $44,300 in your contingency fund. Write that number in column D; that's what you have left for other unanticipated costs.

You're now officially done with the Week 2 progress evaluation.

CHANGE ORDER #1

Date: (Monday - Week 3)

Project   (address)
Owner   D.Homeowner
GC   D.Contractor

This Change Order is hereby incorporated into the Contract by reference and shall be subject to all stipulations and covenants of that Contract, once it is fully executed.

Section	List of Changes	Cost
000	Treat black mold on framing near kit and baths, and remove birds, nests, and debris from attic	$12,000
	Note: Hazard remediation will take one week, and site must be abandoned except for trained workers	
200	Repair and repoint mortar in existing foundation	$2,600
200	Replace rotten floor framing in three locations	$3,400
200	Replace only rotten or termite-damaged framing in front section of house; remainder of house will be all new	$4,500
800	City water line connection broke; repair under way Plumber must dig new trench to hit new connection	$2,200
	Net Change to Contract Value	**$24,700**

Current Contract Value	$257,500
Plus/Minus This Change Order	$24,700
Equals New Contract Value	**$282,200**

Total Calendar Days in Schedule	196
Time Added by This Change Order (@ $9,200/wk)	18
Revised Total Calendar Days in Schedule	**214**
Number of Four-Week Pay Periods in Revised Schedule	7.6

Signatures	**Date**
D.Contractor	d
D.Homeowner	d

SIX

Construction Phase 2—Structure and Framing

Week 4

It's time for your second formal biweekly progress evaluation. Update the Progress Evaluation Spreadsheet before you head for the job site.

Don't break the perfect paper trail. Copy the completed Week 2 spreadsheet onto a clean worksheet and add Change Order #1 to the second column on the new spreadsheet. Review your change order and look at how we've incorporated it into the Week 4 Progress Evaluation Spreadsheet (page 208). Column 1, Initial Contract, never changes. Changes will appear in column 2 and be carried over into column 3, Revised Contract.

Take two copies of this revised spreadsheet to the site on Friday at 3 p.m. sharp.

Progress Evaluation

Opposite are photos of what you saw when you walked through the house at the end of week four.

The mold and the birds are gone; all areas affected by either problem have been treated and tested for safety. Make a note to pay your environmental consultant his fee, and to record that on the Soft-Costs Accounting Sheet. (The fee for the consultant who did the assessment and the clearance testing will be paid out of soft costs. The remediation contractor's work is a part of your general contractor's obligations; it is covered in Change Order #1.)

The large container is full. There's a muddy backhoe parked in your side yard, track marks all around the new foundation area, and a stack of concrete blocks in the front yard ready for the mason to build the piers that will hold up the new addition.

The demolition is nearly done, so you and your contractor agree on some percentages in sections 000 and 100, but it's no surprise when you calculate his earnings and he hasn't hit his mark (page 209). He took a week to set up (that's normal); then he lost his plumber in Week 2 while the city crew worked in the street; then he had to move all his men off the site in Week 3 for the removal of the hazardous materials; so his only productive week has been Week 4. He's worked really hard and earned $32,135, but he needed to earn $36,800 if he wanted you to release his first check. What will you do?

Here's what I'd do. Your contractor signed a contract stating that he accepted your terms of payment. He doesn't get a check yet. But you could agree to pay him when he hits $36,800, whenever that is. How's that for a compromise?

Discarded lumber

Secret panel in the fireplace

Water damage on foundation wall

Gutting the hallway

Opening interior walls

Service trench for cabling and plumbing

Preparing to replumb the bathroom

PROGRESS EVALUATION SPREADSHEET - Week 4 Setup

SEC	Item #	Task List	Initial Contract	Changes	Revised Contract	%-Compl	Earned to Date
000		**Hazards**					
	001	Remove windows, entry doors, all trim	$2,800		$2,800		
	CO1	**Treat black mold & remove birds**		$12,000	$12,000		
100		**Demolition and Site Work**					
	101	Demo rear wall & roof; gut int. to framing	$9,000		$9,000		
	102	Remove all orig. subfloor	$3,000		$3,000		
	103	Demo old decks, rails, and steps	$200		$200		
200		**Foundation and Structure**					
	201	Build new fdn for add'n & deck	$7,500		$7,500		
	CO1	**Repair mortar in existing fdn**		$2,600	$2,600		
	CO1	**Replace floor framing - 3 locations**		$3,400	$3,400		
	202	Install all new subfloor throughout	$5,000		$5,000		
	203	Frame new floors,ext.walls,ceilings, & roof	$11,000		$11,000		
	CO1	**Replace bad wall framing in front**		$4,500	$4,500		
300		**Exterior Envelope**					
	301	Weather-in entire new structure	$10,000		$10,000		
	302	Install new exterior wall & roof finishes	$22,000		$22,000		
	303	Plywood 50% of attic floor; access stair	$2,500		$2,500		
	304	Build 300 s.f. deck, not 500	$6,000		$6,000		
400		**Doors:** 3 Entry; 19 Int; 5 Int. Fr.	$16,400		$16,400		
500		**Windows:** 9@4'0" sq; 15@2'6"x6"0"	$17,300		$17,300		
600		**Interior Finishes**					
	601	Frame int. walls & blocking for cabs	$12,000		$12,000		
	602	Install drywall, trim, & closet shelves	$23,500		$23,500		
	603	Install tile floors in 3 baths & laundry	$3,000		$3,000		
	605	Install pine floors	$18,000		$18,000		
	606	XYZ plain cabs in kitchen	$20,000		$20,000		
	607	Install Big Box cabs in baths & laund	$4,000		$4,000		
	A4	Man-made countertops in kitchen	$6,000		$6,000		
	609	Man-made ctrtps in 3 baths & laund	$2,000		$2,000		
700		**Prep and Paint - Int. & Ext.**					
	701	Prime & paint interior - 6 colors	$8,500		$8,500		
	702	Prime & paint exterior - 3 colors	$5,500		$5,500		
800	801	**Plumbing:** Replace entire system	$18,000		$18,000		
	CO1	**New trench for lines to street**		$2,200	$2,200		
	802	Install 1 50-gal water heater	$1,800		$1,800		
900	901	**HVAC:** Replace entire system	$6,000		$6,000		
1000	1001	**Electrical:** Replace entire system	$16,500		$16,500		
		Incr. power/street; 250A. panel; all fix's					
		TOTALS	$257,500	$24,700	$282,200		

Next Pay Avail. At 4 Weeks x $9200 $36,800

Signatures:

PROGRESS EVALUATION SPREADSHEET - Week 4 Calculations

SEC	Item #	Task List	Initial Contract	Changes	Revised Contract	%-Compl	Earned to Date
000		**Hazards**					
	001	Remove windows, entry doors, all trim	$2,800		$2,800	100%	**$2,800**
	CO1	**Treat black mold & remove birds**		$12,000	$12,000	100%	**$12,000**
100		**Demolition and Site Work**					
	101	Demo rear wall & roof; gut int. to framing	$9,000		$9,000	80%	**$7,200**
	102	Remove all orig. subfloor	$3,000		$3,000		$ -
	103	Demo old decks, rails, and steps	$200		$200	100%	**$200**
200		**Foundation and Structure**					
	201	Build new fdn for add'n & deck	$7,500		$7,500		$ -
	CO1	**Repair mortar in existing fdn**		$2,600	$2,600		$ -
	CO1	**Replace floor framing - 3 locations**		$3,400	$3,400		$ -
	202	Install all new subfloor throughout	$5,000		$5,000		$ -
	203	Frame new floors,ext.walls,ceilings, & roof	$11,000		$11,000		$ -
	CO1	**Replace bad wall framing in front**		$4,500	$4,500	40%	**$1,800**
300		**Exterior Envelope**					
	301	Weather-in entire new structure	$10,000		$10,000		$ -
	302	Install new exterior wall & roof finishes	$22,000		$22,000		$ -
	303	Plywood 50% of attic floor; access stair	$2,500		$2,500		$ -
	304	Build 300 s.f. deck, not 500	$6,000		$6,000		$ -
400		**Doors:** 3 Entry; 19 Int; 5 Int. Fr.	$16,400		$16,400		$ -
500		**Windows:** 9@4'0" sq; 15@2'6"x6"0"	$17,300		$17,300		$ -
600		**Interior Finishes**					
	601	Frame int.walls & blocking for cabs	$12,000		$12,000		$ -
	602	Install drywall, trim, & closet shelves	$23,500		$23,500		$ -
	603	Install tile floors in 3 baths & laundry	$3,000		$3,000		$ -
	605	Install pine floors	$18,000		$18,000		$ -
	606	XYZ plain cabs in kitchen	$20,000		$20,000		$ -
	607	Install Big Box cabs in baths & laund	$4,000		$4,000		$ -
	A4	Man-made countertops in kitchen	$6,000		$6,000		$ -
	609	Man-made ctrtps in 3 baths & laund	$2,000		$2,000		$ -
700		**Prep and Paint - Int. & Ext.**					
	701	Prime & paint interior - 6 colors	$8,500		$8,500		$ -
	702	Prime & paint exterior - 3 colors	$5,500		$5,500		$ -
800	801	**Plumbing:** Replace entire system	$18,000		$18,000	15%	**$2,700**
	CO1	**New trench for lines to street**		$2,200	$2,200	80%	**$1,760**
	802	Install 1 50-gal water heater	$1,800		$1,800		$ -
900	901	**HVAC:** Replace entire system	$6,000		$6,000	20%	**$1,200**
1000	1001	**Electrical:** Replace entire system	$16,500		$16,500	15%	**$2,475**
		Incr. power/street; 250A. panel; all fix's					$ -
		TOTALS	**$257,500**	**$24,700**	**$282,200**		**$32,135**

Next Pay Avail. At 4 Weeks x $9200   **$36,800**

Signatures:	**D. Contractor**	**D. Homeowner**

CONSTRUCTION ACCOUNTING - Week 4

CHANGE ORDER LOG

CO#	Change Date	A Contract Amount	B Net Change	C=A+B Revised Contract	D=In.Con.-B Remaining Conting.	E Current Sched	F Days Added	G=E+F Revised Schedule
				Initial Contingency:	$69,000			
1	(Day 15)	$257,500	$24,700	**$282,200**	$44,300	196	18	**214**
2								
3								
4								

PROGRESS EVALUATIONS

Wk#	Eval. Date	A # Days in Sched.	B # Days Lapsed	C=B/A %-Sched Lapsed	D Contract Amount	E T.Amt. Earned	F=E/D %-Contr. Earned	Target: $9,200 per wk.
2	(Day 14)	196	14	7%	$257,500	$11,350	4%	
4	(Day 28)	**214**	28	13%	**$282,200**	**$32,135**	11%	**$36,800**
6			42					
8			56					$73,600
12			84					
16			112					
20			140					
24			168					
28			196					
32			224					
36			252					

CONTRACTOR PAYMENTS

	A T.Earned to Date	B Minus 10% Retain.	C=A-B Balance #1	D Minus All Prev.Pay'ts	E=C-D Balance #2	F Minus Late Fees	G=E-F AMOUNT PAID	Check Date & Number
DEP	$ -	$ -		$ -		$ -	$15,000	d / n
Ck 1	$54,450	$5,445	$49,005	$15,000	$34,005	$ -	$34,005	d / n
Ck 2								
Ck 3								
Ck 4								
Ck 5								
Ck 6								
Ck 7								
Ck 8								
Ck 9								

Salvaging the old hardwood floorboards

Repairing rotten floor framing

Opposite is the accounting sheet you completed for Week 4. The contractor still has not earned his first check.

Week 6

Please update your Progress Evaluation Spreadsheet. Remove the *earned* amounts from the last column. The percentages in the fourth column stay in place, so you won't make the mistake of thinking he's earned less this time than you agreed to last time. When you walk the site, you'll cross out the old percentages and write the new percentages next to them and sign that corrected form. Take two copies of this sheet to the site with you.

You arrive promptly at 3 p.m. and the place looks like an anthill; you hear hammering, banging, sawing, hollering, loud radios—all the sounds of a happy, productive work site. These photos show some of what you see.

Laying new floor framing for the addition

Removing the old roof

Laying the subfloor in the addition

Brick delivery

Masons building new foundation

The electrician has pulled the additional power from the street to the new panel on the side of your house. Inside the remains of the old house, the carpenters have stripped the drywall and trim off the walls that will remain in the original position ("existing to remain") and exposed all of the in-the-wall services. They have already demolished the walls in the area we are referring to as "existing to be changed" and have torn up the original flooring throughout. They have repaired the three damaged areas of the floor and the termite-ridden wall framing.

The roofers are tearing plywood and shingles off in chunks.

The most exciting thing of all is that some of the new construction has begun. The ground in the backyard has been graded in preparation for the setting of the new foundation, and the masons have nearly finished their work already.

The heating and air crew have removed the old unit and all of the old ductwork, the plumber has finished the new trench and the new connections at the street, and the electrician has removed the old panel and hung the new box on the interior wall.

You and your happy contractor walk all around the site and evaluate every task on the Progress Evaluation Spreadsheet, listing the percent-complete numbers that you agree to.

The completed Progress Evaluation Spreadsheet is on page 213. Please complete the Construction Accounting Sheet on page 214.

Is it time to cut your contractor a check? This is Week 6, so he's past due, and you agreed to pay him for the first benchmark of $36,800 whenever he hit that number. Has he earned at least $36,800?

Yes! Let's cut him a check.

Calculating a Payment

You can do your calculations on the Construction Accounting Sheet. Follow the abbreviated instructions in the column headings:

1. In the bottom box, marked Contractor Payments, next to "Ck 1" in column A, write the total amount of money he has earned to date: $54,450.
2. Deduct 10 percent retainage from this total on every check except his last one; in this case we'll deduct $5,445.
3. Establish Balance #1 in column C. C = A − B, so C is $54,450 − $5,445 = $49,005.
4. Now deduct all previous payments. In this case all you've paid him so far is the $15,000 deposit.
5. Establish Balance #2 in column E. E = C − D, so E is $49,005 − $15,000 = $34,005.
6. Deduct any late fees—this applies only to the very last check, so in this and all other cases, the value of column F is $0.00.
7. Establish the amount you have to pay him, which is Balance #2 minus late fees ($0) = $34,005.

Write the man a check for $34,005, and deliver it on Monday morning if you can. If the bank is issuing the checks, follow their procedures, but don't hold up your contractor's money. Submit your request Monday morning and follow up with a call every day until you know that the check is ready for the contractor to pick up; then call the contractor and meet him at the bank.

If your contractor is doing a great job for you, the only appropriate thank-you is the speedy release of his check. He'll really appreciate it.

PROGRESS EVALUATION SPREADSHEET - Week 6

SEC	Item #	Task List	Initial Contract	Changes	Revised Contract	%-Compl	Earned to Date
000		**Hazards**					
	001	Remove windows, entry doors, all trim	$2,800		$2,800	100%	$2,800
	CO1	Treat black mold & remove birds		$12,000	$12,000	100%	$12,000
100		**Demolition and Site Work**					
	101	Demo rear wall & roof; gut int. to framing	$9,000		$9,000	95%	$8,550
	102	Remove all orig. subfloor	$3,000		$3,000	100%	$3,000
	103	Demo old decks, rails, and steps	$200		$200	100%	$200
200		**Foundation and Structure**					
	201	Build new fdn for add'n & deck	$7,500		$7,500	80%	$6,000
	CO1	Repair mortar in existing fdn		$2,600	$2,600	100%	$2,600
	CO1	Replace floor framing - 3 locations		$3,400	$3,400	100%	$3,400
	202	Install all new subfloor throughout	$5,000		$5,000	40%	$2,000
	203	Frame new floors,ext.walls,ceilings, & roof	$11,000		$11,000		$ -
	CO1	Replace bad wall framing in front		$4,500	$4,500	100%	$4,500
300		**Exterior Envelope**					
	301	Weather-in entire new structure	$10,000		$10,000		$ -
	302	Install new exterior wall & roof finishes	$22,000		$22,000		$ -
	303	Plywood 50% of attic floor; access stair	$2,500		$2,500		$ -
	304	Build 300 s.f. deck, not 500	$6,000		$6,000		$ -
400		**Doors:** 3 Entry; 19 Int; 5 Int. Fr.	$16,400		$16,400		$ -
500		**Windows:** 9@4'0" sq; 15@2'6"x6"0"	$17,300		$17,300		$ -
600		**Interior Finishes**					
	601	Frame int.walls & blocking for cabs	$12,000		$12,000		$ -
	602	Install drywall, trim, & closet shelves	$23,500		$23,500		$ -
	603	Install tile floors in 3 baths & laundry	$3,000		$3,000		$ -
	605	Install pine floors	$18,000		$18,000		$ -
	606	XYZ plain cabs in kitchen	$20,000		$20,000		$ -
	607	Install Big Box cabs in baths & laund	$4,000		$4,000		$ -
	A4	Man-made countertops in kitchen	$6,000		$6,000		$ -
	609	Man-made ctrtps in 3 baths & laund	$2,000		$2,000		$ -
700		**Prep and Paint - Int. & Ext.**					
	701	Prime & paint interior - 6 colors	$8,500		$8,500		$ -
	702	Prime & paint exterior - 3 colors	$5,500		$5,500		$ -
800	801	**Plumbing:** Replace entire system	$18,000		$18,000	15%	$2,700
	CO1	New trench for lines to street		$2,200	$2,200	100%	$2,200
	802	Install 1 50-gal water heater	$1,800		$1,800		$ -
900	901	**HVAC:** Replace entire system	$6,000		$6,000	20%	$1,200
1000	1001	**Electrical:** Replace entire system	$16,500		$16,500	20%	$3,300
		Incr. power/street; 250A. panel; all fix's					$ -
		TOTALS	**$257,500**	**$24,700**	**$282,200**		**$54,450**
		Next Pay Avail. At 6 Weeks x $9200					$73,600

Signatures: **D. Contractor**   **D. Homeowner**

CONSTRUCTION ACCOUNTING - Week 6

CHANGE ORDER LOG

CO#	Change Date	A Contract Amount	B Net Change	C=A+B Revised Contract	D=In.Con.-B Remaining Conting.	E Current Sched	F Days Added	G=E+F Revised Schedule
				Initial Contingency:	$69,000			
1	(Day 15)	$257,500	$24,700	**$282,200**	$44,300	196	18	**214**
2								
3								
4								

PROGRESS EVALUATIONS

Wk#	A Eval. Date	B # Days in Sched.	B # Days Lapsed	C=B/A %-Sched Lapsed	D Contract Amount	E T.Amt. Earned	F=E/D %-Contr Earned	Pay every 4 weeks @ $9,200 per wk.
2	(Day 14)	196	14	7%	$257,500	$11,350	4%	
4	(Day 28)	**214**	28	13%	**$282,200**	$32,135	11%	$36,800
6	(Day 42)	214	42	20%	$282,200	$54,450	19%	
8			56					$73,600
12			84					
16			112					
20			140					
24			168					
28			196					
32			224					
36			252					

CONTRACTOR PAYMENTS

	A T.Earned to Date	B Minus 10% Retain.	C=A-B Balance #1	D Minus All Prev.Pay'ts	E=C-D Balance #2	F Minus Late Fees	G=E-F AMOUNT PAID	Check Date & Number
DEP	$ -	$ -		$ -		$ -	$15,000	d / n
Ck 1								
Ck 2								
Ck 3								
Ck 4								
Ck 5								
Ck 6								
Ck 7								
Ck 8								
Ck 9								

Releasing a Payment

When the check is ready, whether you've got it or the bank has it, you and the contractor both have to be there in order for it to be released to him.

Whatever the circumstances, you want to get a photocopy of the check before he takes it, and you want him to sign the photocopy indicating that he got the check. You also want an upstanding citizen, not a spouse or family member, to sign that photocopy, indicating that he or she saw him get the check.

Now the contractor can have his money. You take the photocopy home and put it in your payments file. Staple it to the Progress Evaluation Spreadsheet that caused you to cut it in the first place. If there's ever a question of what you paid for with that check—if one of the subcontractors complains that he was never paid—you have evidence of exactly what you paid for on the Progress Evaluation Spreadsheet. Clever, no?

Week 8

Almost two months have passed since your contractor started work. Mom is now eight months pregnant and having a harder and harder time climbing around the site. Luckily Dad is pretty well settled into his new job. He knows the day has come for him to take over, so he's going to come with Mom on this walk-through.

Your contractor earned his first check in Week 6, but he's eligible for another check this week—every four weeks, according to the contract, if he's earned his target amount. Let's see what you find.

You (Mom and Dad together) update your Progress Evaluation Spreadsheet before you leave the house, and take *three* copies to the site with you. You ask Dad to please just listen. He agrees.

Here is what you see when you arrive:

Street maintenance patch

Patching the subfloor around the chimney

Construction drawings on the site

Carpenter completely focused on his work

Tying the new roofline into the old

After the rainstorm

Framing the addition

Removing a wall to create a great room

Trying to protect the exposed interior

There is (finally) a tarp draped over the gaping hole that used to be your roof, but it's flapping in the wind. There was a storm last night, and there are large puddles on the new wood subfloor. Dad has a fit. "Where's the contractor?" he hollers to the crew; so much for watching and learning.

The two of you are standing in the middle of the old house. The general approaches from behind the fireplace wall. A lot of work has gotten done, and he expected you to be pleased, but all Dad can see is the puddles and the damage they may be leaving behind on his brand-new subfloors. The contractor, you can tell, is a little confused about who is in charge. You (Mom) have to do something. If the relationship between the contractor and Dad starts off on the wrong foot, the rest of the project will be in trouble, and Mom wants to be worry free when the new baby comes. What will she do? (You tell me!)

Here's what I would do. I would introduce my charming husband to the contractor and explain why he's so upset; the contractor (if he was as good as everybody told you he was) would apologize for the mess, and he'd ask someone to begin sweeping the water off the floor onto the ground and to re-anchor the tarp—something he should have done first thing in the morning so that everything would have been in order when you arrived.

As soon as I (Mom) got home, I would call a lumberyard and find out if the subfloor boards (the brand name is stamped on them in bright green) would likely be warped or otherwise damaged by the standing water. If they would be, I would ask the contractor to replace them at no cost to me. Which contract clause gives me this option?

If the boards are designed to handle water (which turns out to be the case), I (Mom) would write the contractor a letter restating the requirement for constant protection, and telling him that I will charge him a penalty of $500 if this happens again.

If I use the reiterate-and-confirm letter format, and he doesn't respond with an argument against that penalty, we would have an agreement, and I could charge him for damages in the future.

Write that letter.

Now let's continue with the progress evaluation:

The demolition and the new foundation are complete, and about 60 percent of the new structural framing (exterior and other load-bearing walls, ceilings, and roof framing) is done. Forty percent of the new inside walls are framed, and the mechanical, plumbing, and electrical subcontractors are hot on the heels of the framing crew, weaving ducts, pipes, and wires through the grid of the framing.

Any More Surprises?

As you are leaving, the contractor reminds you of something you discussed briefly at the pre-construction meeting. When he hits 40 percent complete—which he expects to do in the next few weeks—he will have to have all of your final decisions about materials and finishes—all of your discretionary changes. Remember them? After that it will be hard—and expensive—to make any changes. He asks you to be prepared with your wish list and to bring a blank change order form to the next walk-through so you can execute the change order at the site and he can order any long-lead items right away. The two of you—Mom and Dad, that is—will put your heads together and decide what you want to do. You have plenty of money in the contingency fund, and you have passed the point where you expect to find any more surprises.

Here's your completed Progress Evaluation Spreadsheet (pages 218–219). Please complete the Construction Accounting Sheet and see whether or not your contractor has earned his second check. He's at the end of Week 8, so he has to have earned 8 × $9,200 to get that check. How did he do?

If he earned a check, how much will you pay him?

Note: You would continue to do formal progress evaluations every *two* weeks on Friday afternoon promptly at 3 p.m. so that you can keep your eye on his momentum, but from now on we'll review only the evaluations that ought to trigger a check—the *four*-week intervals.

PROGRESS EVALUATION SPREADSHEET - Week 8

SEC	Item #	Task List	Initial Contract	Changes	Revised Contract	%-Compl	Earned to Date
000		**Hazards**					
	001	Remove windows, entry doors, all trim	$2,800		$2,800	100%	$2,800
	CO1	Treat black mold & remove birds		$12,000	$12,000	100%	$12,000
100		**Demolition and Site Work**					
	101	Demo rear wall & roof; gut int. to framing	$9,000		$9,000	100%	$9,000
	102	Remove all orig. subfloor	$3,000		$3,000	100%	$3,000
	103	Demo old decks, rails, and steps	$200		$200	100%	$200
200		**Foundation and Structure**					
	201	Build new fdn for add'n & deck	$7,500		$7,500	100%	$7,500
	CO1	Repair mortar in existing fdn		$2,600	$2,600	100%	$2,600
	CO1	Replace floor framing - 3 locations		$3,400	$3,400	100%	$3,400
	202	Install all new subfloor throughout	$5,000		$5,000	100%	$5,000
	203	Frame new floors,ext.walls,ceilings, & roof	$11,000		$11,000	60%	$6,600
	CO1	Replace bad wall framing in front		$4,500	$4,500	100%	$4,500
300		**Exterior Envelope**					
	301	Weather-in entire new structure	$10,000		$10,000		$ -
	302	Install new exterior wall & roof finishes	$22,000		$22,000		$ -
	303	Plywood 50% of attic floor; access stair	$2,500		$2,500		$ -
	304	Build 300 s.f. deck, not 500	$6,000		$6,000		$ -
400		**Doors:** 3 Entry; 19 Int; 5 Int. Fr.	$16,400		$16,400		$ -
500		**Windows:** 9@4'0" sq; 15@2'6"x6"0"	$17,300		$17,300		$ -
600		**Interior Finishes**					
	601	Frame int.walls & blocking for cabs	$12,000		$12,000	40%	$4,800
	602	Install drywall, trim, & closet shelves	$23,500		$23,500		$ -
	603	Install tile floors in 3 baths & laundry	$3,000		$3,000		$ -
	605	Install pine floors	$18,000		$18,000		$ -
	606	XYZ plain cabs in kitchen	$20,000		$20,000		$ -
	607	Install Big Box cabs in baths & laund	$4,000		$4,000		$ -
	A4	Man-made countertops in kitchen	$6,000		$6,000		$ -
	609	Man-made ctrtps in 3 baths & laund	$2,000		$2,000		$ -
700		**Prep and Paint - Int. & Ext.**					
	701	Prime & paint interior - 6 colors	$8,500		$8,500		$ -
	702	Prime & paint exterior - 3 colors	$5,500		$5,500		$ -
800	801	**Plumbing:** Replace entire system	$18,000		$18,000	30%	$5,400
	CO1	New trench for lines to street		$2,200	$2,200	100%	$2,200
	802	Install 1 50-gal water heater	$1,800		$1,800		$ -
900	901	**HVAC:** Replace entire system	$6,000		$6,000	25%	$1,500
1000	1001	**Electrical:** Replace entire system	$16,500		$16,500	25%	$4,125
		Incr. power/street; 250A. panel; all fix's					$ -
		TOTALS	**$257,500**	**$24,700**	**$282,200**		**$74,625**

Next Pay Avail. At 8 Weeks x $9200 — $73,600

Signatures:	**D. Contractor**	**D. Homeowner**

CONSTRUCTION ACCOUNTING - Week 8

CHANGE ORDER LOG

CO#	Change Date	A Contract Amount	B Net Change	C=A+B Revised Contract	D=In.Con.-B Remaining Conting.	E Current Sched	F Days Added	G=E+F Revised Schedule
				Initial Contingency:	$69,000			
1	(Day 15)	$257,500	$24,700	**$282,200**	$44,300	196	18	**214**
2								
3								
4								

PROGRESS EVALUATIONS

Wk#	Eval. Date	A # Days in Sched.	B # Days Lapsed	C=B/A %-Sched Lapsed	D Contract Amount	E T.Amt. Earned	F=E/D %-Contr. Earned	Pay every 4 weeks @ $9,200 per wk.
2	(Day 14)	196	14	7%	$257,500	$11,350	4%	
4	(Day 28)	**214**	28	13%	**$282,200**	**$32,135**	11%	$36,800
6	(Day 42)	214	42	20%	$282,200	$54,450	19%	
8	(Day 56)	214	56	**26%**	$282,200	**$74,625**	**26%**	**$73,600**
12			84					
16			112					
20			140					
24			168					
28			196					
32			224					
36			252					

CONTRACTOR PAYMENTS

	A T.Earned to Date	B Minus 10% Retain.	C=A-B Balance #1	D Minus All Prev.Pay'ts	E=C-D Balance #2	F Minus Late Fees	G=E-F AMOUNT PAID	Check Date & Number
DEP	$ -	$ -		$ -		$ -	$15,000	Week 0 - #
Ck 1	$54,450	$5,445	$49,005	$15,000	$34,005	$ -	$34,005	Week 6 - #
Ck 2								
Ck 3								
Ck 4								
Ck 5								
Ck 6								
Ck 7								
Ck 8								
Ck 9								

SEVEN

Construction Phase 3—Services and Finishes

Week 12

Dad is in charge now. Let's see how he does.

The Crisis

Early on the Wednesday morning prior to Friday's walk-through, Dad gets a call at work. The contractor tells him that the good news is that all of the doors, including the six French doors, have arrived safely. The bad news is that two of the interior French pocket doors were stolen last night. Dad says he'll be over at midday to talk, and he pulls the construction contract out of his desk drawer to see what his options are.

Which clause in the contract will help him resolve the question of who pays to replace the two French pocket doors?

The clause that addresses site security says that if the family has vacated the site, the contractor is entirely and solely responsible for site security. This would imply, even if it didn't actually state, that the theft of these French doors was the contractor's problem, not the owner's.

When you (Dad) arrive to talk about the problem, you're armed and ready, but the contractor read his contract too and already knows what the outcome will be. He greets you with a smile and the news that the replacement doors will be on the site within forty-eight hours, which should not cause a scheduling delay. You are relieved, your shoulders relax, and you are beginning to actually like this contractor. He

seems to have some integrity. All the hours you and Mom spent on the phone checking references may actually have paid off.

The Walk-through

Dad has updated the Progress Evaluation Spreadsheet and has brought two copies of both that form and the blank change order to the site.

This is what he sees when he gets there. Demolition is done, the new foundation is in, and the crew has completed the framing of the floors and laid the new plywood (or something like it) subfloor. Exterior walls are framed and they're "weathered-in" with sheets of plywood (or something like it) and a plastic sheet that serves as a moisture barrier. Insulation is also installed between the wall-framing members on the inside of the weather barrier. Ninety percent of the windows are in, and the new roof is framed and sheathed in plywood (or something like it) and covered with sheets of tar paper or another moisture barrier. We're weather safe now, except for the entry doors, which are on order and due next week.

As the contractor approaches, he notices that you (Dad) are looking at the spots where the puddles were. He shakes your hand and asks what you think of the progress. Frankly, you say, you are impressed.

With a little extra discussion during which the contractor brings you up to speed on how

Preparing window openings   *Break time*

Windows and insulation installed

New window delivery

Plumbing in the ceiling

Wiring new electrical panel   *Installing new outlet*

the evaluation system works, you and the contractor walk the site. You agree on the percent-complete numbers, and you both sign the spreadsheet.

The project is moving along pretty quickly. What is your contractor's overall percent complete? (___%.) What should you be asking the contractor that may prompt him to stay on top of upcoming deadlines?

The Change Order
Last night you and Mom put your heads together and reviewed the list of Alternates you had the contractor price when he bid, to see

Finishing the new roof shingles

PROGRESS EVALUATION SPREADSHEET - Week 12

SEC	Item #	Task List	Initial Contract	Changes	Revised Contract	%-Compl	Earned to Date
000		**Hazards**					
	001	Remove windows, entry doors, all trim	$2,800		$2,800	100%	$2,800
	CO1	Treat black mold & remove birds		$12,000	$12,000	100%	$12,000
100		**Demolition and Site Work**					
	101	Demo rear wall & roof; gut int. to framing	$9,000		$9,000	100%	$9,000
	102	Remove all orig. subfloor	$3,000		$3,000	100%	$3,000
	103	Demo old decks, rails, and steps	$200		$200	100%	$200
200		**Foundation and Structure**					
	201	Build new fdn for add'n & deck	$7,500		$7,500	100%	$7,500
	CO1	Repair mortar in existing fdn		$2,600	$2,600	100%	$2,600
	CO1	Replace floor framing - 3 locations		$3,400	$3,400	100%	$3,400
	202	Install all new subfloor throughout	$5,000		$5,000	100%	$5,000
	203	Frame new floors,ext.walls,ceilings, & roof	$11,000		$11,000	100%	$11,000
	CO1	Replace bad wall framing in front		$4,500	$4,500	100%	$4,500
300		**Exterior Envelope**					
	301	Weather-in entire new structure	$10,000		$10,000	100%	$10,000
	302	Install new exterior wall & roof finishes	$22,000		$22,000		–
	303	Plywood 50% of attic floor; access stair	$2,500		$2,500	100%	$2,500
	304	Build 300 s.f. deck, not 500	$6,000		$6,000		–
400		**Doors:** 3 Entry; 19 Int; 5 Int. Fr.	$16,400	ordered	$16,400		–
500		**Windows:** 9@4'0" sq; 15@2'6"x6'0"	$17,300	delivered	$17,300	90%	$15,570
600		**Interior Finishes**					
	601	Frame int. walls & blocking for cabs	$12,000		$12,000	70%	$8,400
	602	Install drywall, trim, & closet shelves	$23,500		$23,500		–
	603	Install tile floors in 3 baths & laundry	$3,000		$3,000		–
	605	Install pine floors	$18,000		$18,000		–
	606	XYZ plain cabs in kitchen	$20,000		$20,000		–
	607	Install Big Box cabs in baths & laund	$4,000		$4,000		–
	A4	Man-made countertops in kitchen	$6,000		$6,000		–
	609	Man-made ctrtps in 3 baths & laund	$2,000		$2,000		–
700		**Prep and Paint - Int. & Ext.**					
	701	Prime & paint interior - 6 colors	$8,500		$8,500		–
	702	Prime & paint exterior - 3 colors	$5,500		$5,500		–
800	801	**Plumbing:** Replace entire system	$18,000		$18,000	30%	–
	CO1	New trench for lines to street		$2,200	$2,200	100%	–
	802	Install 1 50-gal water heater	$1,800		$1,800		–
900	901	**HVAC:** Replace entire system	$6,000		$6,000	25%	–
1000	1001	**Electrical:** Replace entire system	$16,500		$16,500	25%	–
		Incr. power/street; 250A. panel; all fix's					
		TOTALS	**$257,500**	**$24,700**	**$282,200**		–
		Next Pay Avail. At 12 Weeks x $9200					**$110,400**

Signatures:	D.Contractor	D.Homeowner

what additional work or upgrades you might want to spend some of the remaining contingency money on. You keep in mind that you would like to set enough of this money aside to pay for your temporary furniture storage and the cost of the rental house, but even if you deduct that, you've still got a nice allowance for improvements.

What would you choose to do? What would you add or upgrade? And how would those changes affect the scope of work that is already in the contract?

How about this?

- Add paving and landscaping for $4,500. There's none in the contract, the driveway is a mess, and your yard is embarrassing. This will take care of the curb appeal you need so badly.
- Omit the construction of the smaller deck, and build the larger one. It's nearly twice the size and will provide a much nicer outdoor environment for the kids, and a great place to entertain in warm weather. That will add $4,000 to the contract.
- Add the tile to the walls of the bathrooms that the kids will use. This will make cleaning up a little easier, and we're all for that, aren't we? Add another $2,200.
- The kitchen will be so wonderful with all of those huge windows along the back wall that you choose to go back to the natural stone countertops. Add $3,000.
- Painted wood shutters would be really nice on the inside of the big windows along the back walls. Remember that the rear of the house faces west and the afternoon sun can be brutal in the summer months. Add $1,250.
- Let's ask the contractor to furnish and install all of the appliances (add $4,000), and while you're at it, upgrade the refrigerator to the larger, side-by-side model (add another $1,500).

- Install those two 40-gallon water heaters with linked water circulation in place of one 50-gallon tank. With three kids, there will be lots of dishes and clothes to wash, and lots of bathtubs to fill. This ought to keep you in hot water no matter what happens. Add $400.

Total amount added to the contract: $20,850. If you agree to this, we'll proceed.

You had $41,800 left in the contingency; you've now spent about half, and with a little luck you've still got enough left to pay for most or all of your temporary housing costs. We'll have to see what kind of trouble you and the contractor have between now and the end of the project to know for sure.

You didn't execute this change order before the walk-through, so it won't show up on the Progress Evaluation Spreadsheet, but when you complete the Accounting Spreadsheet, be sure to carry down both the change in contract value and the change in the number of days in the schedule into the Progress Evaluations box for Week 16, and to update the next spreadsheet so it reflects the upcoming changes.

The discretionary change order is on page 225. You were fair to the contractor and added time to his schedule to allow him to accomplish all of this added work.

The contractor says that all of the changes are manageable, but he is concerned about the stone countertop. He has held off ordering the cabinets until you decided whether or not to upgrade to the ABC manufacturer's model—which you chose not to do. But the countertops can't be ordered until the cabinets are in and set so that the manufacturer can get precise measurements before he cuts the stone. There is a long lead time on stone countertops, and the contractor worries that he won't have enough time in the

Copy of the Original CONTRACT AGREEMENT

SEC	Item #	Task List	Bidder #1
0		**Hazards**	
	1	Remove windows, entry doors, all trim	$2,800
100		**Demolition and Site Work**	
	101	Remove rear wall & roof; gut interior to framing	$9,000
	102	Remove all orig. subfloor	$3,000
	103	Demo old decks, rails, and steps	$1,200
	SwEq	Owner to demo deck; contractor to haul	$(1,000)
200		**Foundation and Structure**	
	201	Build new fdn for add'n & deck	$7,500
	202	Install all new subfloor throughout	$5,000
	203	Frame new floors, ext.walls, ceilings, & roof	$11,000
300		**Exterior Envelope**	
	301	Weather-in entire new structure	$10,000
	302	Install all new exterior wall & roof finishes	$22,000
	303	Plywood 50% of attic floor; access stair	$3,500
	SwEq	Owner to install-only plywood in attic	$(1,000)
	304	Build 300 s.f. deck, not 500	$6,000
400		**Doors**	
	401	3 entry (1 French)	$2,800
	402	19 interior @ $400 ea	$7,600
	403	5 interior French Doors	$6,000
500		**Windows**	
	501	9 ea. 4'0" x 4'0" square	$4,500
	502	15 ea. 2'6" x 6'0" tall	$12,800
600		**Interior Finishes**	
	601	Frame interior walls & blocking for cabs	$12,000
	602	Install drywall, trim, & closet shelves	$23,500
	603	Install tile floors in 3 baths & laundry	$3,000
	605	Install pine floors	$18,000
	606	XYZ plain cabs in kitchen	$20,000
	607	Install Big Box cabinets in baths & laund	$4,000
	A4	Man-made countertops in kitchen	$6,000
	609	Man-made countertops in 3 baths & laundry	$2,000
700		**Prep and Paint - Int. & Ext.**	
	701	Prime & paint interior - 6 colors	$8,500
	702	Prime & paint exterior - 3 colors	$5,500
800	801	Plumbing: Replace entire system	**$18,000**
	802	Install 1 50-gal water heater	$1,800
900	901	HVAC: Replace entire system; 2 zones	$6,000
1000	1001	Electrical: Replace entire system	$16,500
		Incr. power/street; 25A. panel; all fixtures	
		FINAL CONTRACT AMOUNT	**$257,500**

Signatures:	D.Contractor	D.Homeowner

1100		**CONTRACT ALTERNATES**	
	A1	Build 500 s.f. curved deck w/ steps and rails	$10,000
	A2	Repl 15 tall windows w/ 8 ea 4'0" sq.	$4,000
	A3	Install ABC cabinetry in kitchen	$28,000
	608	Natural stone countertops in kitchen	$9,000
	A5	Tile wainscoting; 2 baths to 4'6"	$2,200
	605	New hardwood flrs in remaining areas	$22,000
	A6	15 interior shutters - tall windows	$1,250
	A7	Buy larger refrig/freezer (add)	$1,500
	A8	Install 2 - 40-gallon water heaters in attic	$2,200
	A9	Paving	$2,500
	A10	Landscaping	$2,000
	612	Furnish & install all appliances	$4,000

CHANGE ORDER #2

Date: (Week 12)

Project	(address)
Owner	D.Homeowner
GC	D.Contractor

This Change Order is hereby incorporated into the Contract by reference and shall be subject to all stipulations and covenants of that Contract, once it is fully executed.

Section	List of (Discretionary) Changes	Cost
	(pressed by plumber!)	
100	A9 Paving	$2,500
100	A10 Landscaping	$2,000
304	**OMIT:** Build 300 s.f. deck, not 500	$(6,000)
304	**ADD:** A1 Build 500 s.f. curved deck	$10,000
	Net Change = ADD	$4,000
600	Tile wainscoting; 2 baths to 4'6"	$2,200
A4	**OMIT:** A4 Man-made countertops in kitchen	$(6,000)
A4	**ADD:** Natural stone countertops in kitchen	$9,000
	Net Change = ADD	$3,000
600	A6 15 interior shutters - tall windows	$1,250
600	Furnish & install all appliances	$4,000
600	A7 Buy larger refrig/freezer (add)	$1,500
802	**OMIT:** Install 1 50-gal water heater	$(1,800)
802	**ADD:** A8 Install 2 - 40-gallon water heaters	$2,200
	Net Change = ADD	$400
	Net Change to Contract Value	**$20,850**

Current Contract Value	$282,200
Plus/Minus This Change Order	$20,850
Equals New Contract Value	**$303,050**

Total Calendar Days in Schedule	214
Time Added by This Change Order (@ $9,200 / wk)	16
Revised Total Calendar Days in Schedule	**230**
Number of Four-Week Pay Periods in Revised Schedule	**8.2**

Signatures	Date
D. Contractor	d
D. Homeowner	d

schedule. You consider this, and how much Mom wants the stone countertops, and you tell the contractor you'll deal with the schedule when you find out whether or not the countertops will be a problem. You want the stone, so you'll hope for the best.

Was that the right answer? Was that fair to the contractor? Will it help you to keep just a little pressure on him or will that damage your relationship and maybe the quality of his work?

The Accounting

You (Dad) complete the Construction Accounting Sheet (on page 228) for the first time, with a little coaching from Mom, and determine that it's time to cut another check. Mom talks you through the process of calculating and releasing the check. Please complete all sections of the Construction Accounting Sheet now.

The Baby

The baby arrives the next week—lucky Week 13. You name her Hope. Mom's out of the picture now for at least six weeks. Dad's just going to have to cope with both his own job and the construction project, sleep or no sleep.

Week 16

We're at the end of the fourth four-week pay period, and the schedule is now 230 days long—extended by the change orders—which means there will be (230 ÷ 28 days per four-week pay period =) eight-plus pay periods and eight or nine checks, not seven as you originally planned. As long as the contractor continues to earn $9,200 a week, he'll finish on the new completion date, because we calculated the number of days we added for each change order based on the contractor's crew being able

to continue to earn an average of $9,200 a week. Was that clear? If you add $9,200 in work, then you must, to be fair, add seven days to his work period, to keep his schedule and his contract amount in balance.

Update the Spreadsheet

You executed a change order at your last walk-through, and those items and their costs must be added to the Progress Evaluation Spreadsheet for Week 16 before you can do your walk-through. The revised sheet is on page 229.

The Walk-through

The framing crew is working on the inside now, tying the new framing to the old. Some of the walls are drywalled. A radio is blasting rock-and-roll music with an energizing beat and the guys are shouting out and singing along as they work. This crew looks happy and productive; here's what you see when you look around.

French doors ready for installation

Applying new roof finishes

Hooking up the new HVAC unit in the attic

Installing new double water heaters in the attic

Waterproofing the shower enclosure

Finishing the drywall

Cutting the ceramic tile for the bathroom

Finished bathroom flooring

The new water heaters and the new HVAC unit are both installed in the attic, the ceramic tile is finished, the exterior finishes are nearly done, and the tape and spackle are going on the drywall.

Here are the percentages you agreed on. Please complete the Progress Evaluation Spreadsheet (page 230), and then the Construction Accounting Sheet (page 231) and see whether the contractor is working on schedule, whether or not he's earned a check, and if he has, how much you will pay him.

Week 20

It's the end of the fifth four-week pay period. Hope is seven weeks old and absolutely delightful. Mom hasn't been to the site since the baby was born, but she's dying to know what's going on. You bring pictures home for her after every visit, and discuss any concerns with her before you talk to the contractor. You and the contractor seem to be getting along just fine now.

You're trying to remember who it was that thought you'd lost your mind when you decided to take on this huge project. You must call them and tell them how well this is going!

The Crisis

The site is noisy and busy. There's no sign of the contractor, but once you enter the house you do see a fellow in a business suit joking with the electrician as if this were a cocktail party.

You introduce yourself and discover that this is the contractor's brother-in-law. He's been filling in for the last two weeks while your contractor took a trip out of state.

Why didn't you know this? Your contractor should have told you he was going away! The painful truth is that you should have known anyway; you didn't because you haven't slept for weeks, your new job has you on the run, and the project has been going so well that you haven't made an informal site visit since your last progress evaluation two weeks ago. Now you'll pay for it.

You try to be cordial. When does the brother-in-law expect the contractor to return home? He shrugs and says he expects him home in a few days.

CONSTRUCTION ACCOUNTING - Week 13

CHANGE ORDER LOG

CO#	Change Date	A Contract Amount	B Net Change	C=A+B Revised Contract *Initial Contingency:*	D=Last Bal.-B Remaining Conting. *$69,000*	E Current Sched	F Days Added	G=E+F Revised Schedule
1	(Day 15)	$257,500	$24,700	$282,200	$44,300	196	18	214
2	(Day 84)	$282,200	$20,850	**$303,050**	$23,450	214	16	**230**
3								
4								

PROGRESS EVALUATIONS

Wk#	Eval. Date	A # Days in Sched.	B # Days Lapsed	C=B/A %-Sched Lapsed	D Contract Amount	E T.Amt. Earned	F=E/D %-Contr Earned	Pay every 4 weeks @ $9,200 per wk.
2	(Day 14)	196	14	7%	$257,500	$11,350	4%	
4	(Day 28)	**214**	28	13%	**$282,200**	$32,135	11%	$36,800
6	(Day 42)	214	42	20%	$282,200	$54,450	19%	
8	(Day 56)	214	56	26%	$282,200	$74,625	26%	$73,600
12	(Day 84)	214	84	39%	$282,200	–		$110,400
16			112					$147,200
20			140					$184,000
24			168					$220,800
28			196					$257,600
32			224					$294,400
36			252					$331,200

CONTRACTOR PAYMENTS

	A T.Earned to Date	B Minus 10% Retain.	C=A-B Balance #1	D Minus All Prev.Pay'ts	E=C-D Balance #2	F Minus Late Fees	G=E-F AMOUNT PAID	Check Date & Number
DEP	–	–		–		–	$15,000	Week 0 - #
Ck 1	$54,450	$5,445	$49,005	$15,000	$34,005	–	$34,005	Week 6 - #
Ck 2	$74,625	$7,463	$67,163	$49,005	$18,158	–	$18,158	Week 8 - #
Ck 3								Week 12 - #
Ck 4								
Ck 5								
Ck 6								
Ck 7								
Ck 8								
Ck 9								

PROGRESS EVALUATION SPREADSHEET - Week 16 Setup

SEC	Item #	Task List	Initial Contract	Changes	Revised Contract	%-Compl	Earned to Date
000		**Hazards**					
	001	Remove windows, entry doors, all trim	$2,800		$2,800		
	CO1	Treat black mold & remove birds		$12,000	$12,000		
100		**Demolition and Site Work**					
	101	Demo rear wall & roof; gut int. to framing	$9,000		$9,000		
	102	Remove all orig. subfloor	$3,000		$3,000		
	103	Demo old decks, rails, and steps	$200		$200		
	CO2	**A9 Paving**		**$2,500**	**$2,500**		
	CO2	**A10 Landscaping**		**$2,000**	**$2,000**		
200		**Foundation and Structure**					
	201	Build new fdn for add'n & deck	$7,500		$7,500		
	CO1	Repair mortar in existing fdn		$2,600	$2,600		
	CO1	Replace floor framing - 3 locations		$3,400	$3,400		
	202	Install all new subfloor throughout	$5,000		$5,000		
	203	Frame new floors,ext.walls,ceilings, & roof	$11,000		$11,000		
	CO1	Replace bad wall framing in front		$4,500	$4,500		
300		**Exterior Envelope**					
	301	Weather-in entire new structure	$10,000		$10,000		
	302	Install new exterior wall & roof finishes	$22,000		$22,000		
	303	Plywood 50% of attic floor; access stair	$2,500		$2,500		
	304	Build 300 s.f. deck, not 500	$6,000		$6,000		
	CO2	ADD: A1 Build 500 sf deck (net add)		$4,000	$4,000		
400		**Doors:** 3 Entry; 19 Int; 5 Int. Fr.	$16,400	ordered	$16,400		
500		**Windows:** 9@4'0" sq; 15@2'6"x6"0"	$17,300	delivered	$17,300		
600		**Interior Finishes**					
	601	Frame int.walls & blocking for cabs	$12,000		$12,000		
	602	Install drywall, trim, & closet shelves	$23,500		$23,500		
	603	Install tile floors in 3 baths & laundry	$3,000		$3,000		
	CO2	**Tile wainscoting; 2 baths to 4'6"**		**$2,200**	**$2,200**		
	605	Install pine floors	$18,000		$18,000		
	606	XYZ plain cabs in kitchen	$20,000		$20,000		
	607	Install Big Box cabs in baths & laund	$4,000		$4,000		
	A4	Man-made countertops in kitchen	$6,000		$6,000		
	CO2	**ADD: Stone ctrtops (net add)**		**$3,000**	**$3,000**		
	609	Man-made ctrtps in 3 baths & laund	$2,000		$2,000		
	CO2	**A6 15 interior shutters - tall windows**		**$1,250**	**$1,250**		
	CO2	**Furnish & install all appliances**		**$4,000**	**$4,000**		
	CO2	**A7 Buy larger refrig/freezer (net add)**		**$1,500**	**$1,500**		
700		**Prep and Paint - Int. & Ext.**					
	701	Prime & paint interior - 6 colors	$8,500		$8,500		
	702	Prime & paint exterior - 3 colors	$5,500		$5,500		
800	801	**Plumbing:** Replace entire system	$18,000		$18,000		
	CO1	New trench for lines to street		$2,200	$2,200		
	802	Install 1 50-gal water heater	$1,800		$1,800		
	CO2	ADD: A8 Install 2 - 40-gallon water heaters (net add)		$400	$400		
900	901	**HVAC:** Replace entire system	$6,000		$6,000		
1000	1001	**Electrical:** Replace entire system	$16,500		$16,500		
		Incr. power/street; 250A. panel; all fix's					
		TOTALS	**$257,500**	**$45,550**	**$303,050**		
		Next Pay Avail. At 16 Weeks x $9200					**$147,200**

Signatures: D.Contractor   D.Homeowner

PROGRESS EVALUATION SPREADSHEET - Week 16

SEC	Item #	Task List	Initial Contract	Changes	Revised Contract	%-Compl	Earned to Date
000		**Hazards**					
	001	Remove windows, entry doors, all trim	$2,800		$2,800	100%	$2,800
	CO1	Treat black mold & remove birds		$12,000	$12,000	100%	$12,000
100		**Demolition and Site Work**					
	101	Demo rear wall & roof; gut int. to framing	$9,000		$9,000	100%	$9,000
	102	Remove all orig. subfloor	$3,000		$3,000	100%	$3,000
	103	Demo old decks, rails, and steps	$200		$200	100%	$200
	CO2	A9 Paving		$2,500	$2,500	20%	$500
	CO2	A10 Landscaping		$2,000	$2,000	20%	$400
200		**Foundation and Structure**					
	201	Build new fdn for add'n & deck	$7,500		$7,500	100%	$7,500
	CO1	Repair mortar in existing fdn		$2,600	$2,600	100%	$2,600
	CO1	Replace floor framing - 3 locations		$3,400	$3,400	100%	$3,400
	202	Install all new subfloor throughout	$5,000		$5,000	100%	$5,000
	203	Frame new floors,ext.walls, ceilings, & roof	$11,000		$11,000	100%	$11,000
	CO1	Replace bad wall framing in front		$4,500	$4,500	100%	$4,500
300		**Exterior Envelope**					
	301	Weather-in entire new structure	$10,000		$10,000	100%	$10,000
	302	Install new exterior wall & roof finishes	$22,000		$22,000	70%	$15,400
	303	Plywood 50% of attic floor; access stair	$2,500		$2,500	100%	$2,500
	304	Build 300 s.f. deck, not 500	$6,000		$6,000		
	CO2	ADD: A1 Build 500 s.f. curved deck		$4,000	$4,000		
400		**Doors:** 3 Entry; 19 Int; 5 Int. Fr.	$16,400	delivered	$16,400	30%	$4,920
500		**Windows:** 9@4'0" sq; 15@2'6"x6'0"	$17,300		$17,300	100%	$17,300
600		**Interior Finishes**					
	601	Frame int.walls & blocking for cabs	$12,000		$12,000	100%	$12,000
	602	Install drywall, trim, & closet shelves	$23,500		$23,500	30%	$7,050
	603	Install tile floors in 3 baths & laundry	$3,000		$3,000	100%	$3,000
	CO2	Tile wainscoting; 2 baths to 4'6"		$2,200	$2,200	100%	$2,200
	605	Install pine floors	$18,000		$18,000		
	606	XYZ plain cabs in kitchen	$20,000	Due Wk.20	$20,000		
	607	Install Big Box cabs in baths & laund	$4,000		$4,000		
	A4	Man-made countertops in kitchen	$6,000		$6,000		
	CO2	ADD: Natural stone countertops in kitchen		$3,000	$3,000		
	609	Man-made ctrtps in 3 baths & laund	$2,000		$2,000		
	CO2	A6 15 interior shutters - tall windows		$1,250	$1,250		
	CO2	Furnish & install all appliances		$4,000	$4,000		
	CO2	A7 Buy larger refrig/freezer (add)		$1,500	$1,500		
700		**Prep and Paint - Int. & Ext.**					
	701	Prime & paint interior - 6 colors	$8,500		$8,500		
	702	Prime & paint exterior - 3 colors	$5,500		$5,500		
800	801	**Plumbing:** Replace entire system	$18,000		$18,000	60%	
	CO1	New trench for lines to street		$2,200	$2,200	100%	
	802	Install 1 50-gal water heater	$1,800		$1,800	80%	
	CO2	ADD: A8 Install 2 - 40-gallon water heaters		$400	$400	80%	
900	901	**HVAC:** Replace entire system	$6,000		$6,000	75%	
1000	1001	**Electrical:** Replace entire system Incr. power/street; 250A. panel; all fix's	$16,500		$16,500	75%	
		TOTALS	$257,500	$45,550	$303,050		
		Next Pay Avail. At 16 Weeks x $9200					$147,200

Signatures:	D.Contractor	D.Homeowner

CONSTRUCTION ACCOUNTING - Week 16

CHANGE ORDER LOG

CO#	Change Date	A Contract Amount	B Net Change	C=A+B Revised Contract	D=Last Bal.-B Remaining Conting.	E Current Sched	F Days Added	G=E+F Revised Schedule
				Initial Contingency:	*$69,000*			
1	(Day 15)	$257,500	$24,700	$282,200	$44,300	196	18	214
2	(Day 84)	$282,200	$20,850	**$303,050**	$23,450	214	16	**230**
3								
4								

PROGRESS EVALUATIONS

Wk#	Eval. Date	A # Days in Sched.	B # Days Lapsed	C=B/A %-Sched Lapsed	D Contract Amount	E T.Amt. Earned	F=E/D %-Contr Earned	Pay every 4 weeks @ $9,200 per wk.
2	(Day 14)	196	14	7%	$257,500	$11,350	4%	
4	(Day 28)	**214**	28	13%	**$282,200**	$32,135	11%	$36,800
6	(Day 42)	214	42	20%	$282,200	$54,450	19%	
8	(Day 56)	214	56	26%	$282,200	$74,625	26%	$73,600
12	(Day 84)	214	84	39%	$282,200	$110,695	39%	$110,400
16	(Day 112)	**214**	112	52%	**$303,050**			$147,200
20			140					$184,000
24			168					$220,800
28			196					$257,600
32			224					$294,400
36			252					$331,200

CONTRACTOR PAYMENTS

	A T.Earned to Date	B Minus 10% Retain.	C=A-B Balance #1	D Minus All Prev.Pay'ts	E=C-D Balance #2	F Minus Late Fees	G=E-F AMOUNT PAID	Check Date & Number
DEP	–	–	$49,005	–	$34,005	–	$15,000	Week 0 - #
Ck 1	$54,450	$5,445	$49,005	$15,000	$34,005	–	$34,005	Week 6 - #
Ck 2	$74,625	$7,463	$67,163	$49,005	$18,158	–	$18,158	Week 8 - #
Ck 3	$110,695	$11,070	$99,626	$67,163	$32,463	–	$32,463	Week 12 - #
Ck 4								
Ck 5								
Ck 6								
Ck 7								
Ok 8								
Ck 9								

The Other Crisis

The cabinets were due this week—the contractor told you on Week 12 when he ordered them that he had a commitment from the factory—but they haven't arrived yet. This will also delay the stone countertops. If the contractor were here, he would be on the phone.

The brother-in-law didn't even know that the cabinets *should* have been here, so he hasn't taken any action at all. You're steaming, but there's no sense yelling at the brother-in-law.

The Walk-through

You have updated the Progress Evaluation Spreadsheet and incorporated the change order costs. You brought two copies of this sheet to the site and you were feeling pretty upbeat until you met the brother-in-law. Now you're upset and worried.

Here is what you see, and here are the percent-complete numbers you and the brother-in-law agree on. Please complete the Progress Evaluation Spreadsheet (page 233) and the Construction Accounting Sheet (page 234) and see if you're going to cut a check, and if so, for how much. And, by the way, who would you give that check to?

Wiring the electronic controls

Sanding the ceiling

Extending the deck

Installing the bathroom vanity

Finishing the new deck

Finishing the sunroom

Installing wood trim moldings

Finishing the closet interiors

PROGRESS EVALUATION SPREADSHEET - Week 20

SEC	Item #	Task List	Initial Contract	Changes	Revised Contract	%-Compl	Earned to Date
000		**Hazards**					
	001	Remove windows, entry doors, all trim	$2,800		$2,800	100%	$2,800
	CO1	Treat black mold & remove birds		$12,000	$12,000	100%	$12,000
100		**Demolition and Site Work**					
	101	Demo rear wall & roof; gut int. to framing	$9,000		$9,000	100%	$9,000
	102	Remove all orig. subfloor	$3,000		$3,000	100%	$3,000
	103	Demo old decks, rails, and steps	$200		$200	100%	$200
	CO2	A9 Paving		$2,500	$2,500	20%	$500
	CO2	A10 Landscaping		$2,000	$2,000	20%	$400
200		**Foundation and Structure**					
	201	Build new fdn for add'n & deck	$7,500		$7,500	100%	$7,500
	CO1	Repair mortar in existing fdn		$2,600	$2,600	100%	$2,600
	CO1	Replace floor framing - 3 locations		$3,400	$3,400	100%	$3,400
	202	Install all new subfloor throughout	$5,000		$5,000	100%	$5,000
	203	Frame new floors,ext.walls,ceilings, & roof	$11,000		$11,000	100%	$11,000
	CO1	Replace bad wall framing in front		$4,500	$4,500	100%	$4,500
300		**Exterior Envelope**					
	301	Weather-in entire new structure	$10,000		$10,000	100%	$10,000
	302	Install new exterior wall & roof finishes	$22,000		$22,000	85%	$18,700
	303	Plywood 50% of attic floor; access stair	$2,500		$2,500	100%	$2,500
	304	Build 300 s.f. deck, not 500	$6,000		$6,000	50%	$3,000
	CO2	ADD: A1 Build 500 s.f. curved deck		$4,000	$4,000	50%	$2,000
400		**Doors:** 3 Entry; 19 Int; 5 Int. Fr.	$16,400		$16,400	60%	$9,840
500		**Windows:** 9@4'0" sq; 15@2'6"x6'0"	$17,300		$17,300	100%	$17,300
600		**Interior Finishes**					$ -
	601	Frame int.walls & blocking for cabs	$12,000		$12,000	100%	$12,000
	602	Install drywall, trim, & closet shelves	$23,500		$23,500	80%	$18,800
	603	Install tile floors in 3 baths & laundry	$3,000		$3,000	100%	$3,000
	CO2	Tile wainscoting; 2 baths to 4'6"		$2,200	$2,200	100%	$2,200
	605	Install pine floors	$18,000		$18,000		$ -
	606	XYZ plain cabs in kitchen	$20,000	delayed	$20,000		$ -
	607	Install Big Box cabs in baths & laund	$4,000		$4,000	50%	$2,000
	A4	Man-made countertops in kitchen	$6,000		$6,000		$ -
	CO2	ADD: Natural stone countertops in kitchen		$3,000	$3,000		$ -
	609	Man-made ctrtps in 3 baths & laund	$2,000		$2,000		$ -
	CO2	A6 15 interior shutters - tall windows		$1,250	$1,250		$ -
	CO2	Furnish & install all appliances		$4,000	$4,000		$ -
	CO2	A7 Buy larger refrig/freezer (add)		$1,500	$1,500		$ -
700		**Prep and Paint - Int. & Ext.**					
	701	Prime & paint interior - 6 colors	$8,500		$8,500	15%	$ -
	702	Prime & paint exterior - 3 colors	$5,500		$5,500		$ -
800	801	**Plumbing:** Replace entire system	$18,000		$18,000	50%	$ -
	CO1	New trench for lines to street		$2,200	$2,200	100%	$ -
	802	Install 1 50-gal water heater	$1,800		$1,800	80%	$ -
	CO2	ADD: A8 Install 2 - 40-gallon water heaters		$400	$400	80%	$ -
900	901	**HVAC:** Replace entire system	$6,000		$6,000	75%	$ -
1000	1001	**Electrical:** Replace entire system	$16,500		$16,500	75%	$ -
		Incr. power/street; 250A. panel; all fix's					$ -
		TOTALS	**$257,500**	**$45,550**	**$303,050**		**$ -**

Next Pay Avail. At 20 Weeks x $9200   **$184,000**

Signatures:	D.Contractor	D.Homeowner

CONSTRUCTION ACCOUNTING - Week 20

CHANGE ORDER LOG

CO#	Change Date	A Contract Amount	B Net Change	C=A+B Revised Contract	D=Last Bal.-B Remaining Conting.	E Current Sched	F Days Added	G=E+F Revised Schedule
					Initial Contingency: $69,000			
1	(Day 15)	$257,500	$24,700	$282,200	$44,300	196	18	214
2	(Day 84)	$282,200	$20,850	**$303,050**	$23,450	214	16	**230**
3								
4								

PROGRESS EVALUATIONS

Wk#	Eval. Date	A # Days in Sched.	B # Days Lapsed	C=B/A %-Sched Lapsed	D Contract Amount	E T.Amt. Earned	F=E/D %-Contr Earned	Pay every 4 weeks @ $9,200 per wk.
2	(Day 14)	196	14	7%	$257,500	$11,350	4%	
4	(Day 28)	**214**	28	13%	**$282,200**	$32,135	11%	$36,800
6	(Day 42)	214	42	20%	$282,200	$54,450	19%	
8	(Day 56)	214	56	26%	$282,200	$74,625	26%	$73,600
12	(Day 84)	214	84	39%	$282,200	$110,695	39%	$110,400
16	(Day 112)	**230**	112	49%	**$303,050**	$150,605	50%	$147,200
20	(Day 140)	230	140	61%	$303,050	–		$184,000
24			168					$220,800
28			196					$257,600
32			224					$294,400
36			252					$331,200

CONTRACTOR PAYMENTS

	A T.Earned to Date	B Minus 10% Retain.	C=A-B Balance #1	D Minus All Prev.Pay'ts	E=C-D Balance #2	F Minus Late Fees	G=E-F AMOUNT PAID	Check Date & Number
DEP	–	–		–		–	$15,000	Week 0 - #
Ck 1	$54,450	$5,445	$49,005	$15,000	$34,005	–	$34,005	Week 6 - #
Ck 2	$74,625	$7,463	$67,163	$49,005	$18,158	–	$18,157	Week 8 - #
Ck 3	$110,695	$11,070	$99,626	$67,163	$32,463	–	$32,463	Week 12 - #
Ck 4	$150,605	$15,061	$135,545	$99,626	$35,919	–	$35,919	Week 16 - #
Ck 5	**$194,350**	$19,435	$174,915	$135,545	$39,371	–	**$39,371**	Week 20 - #
Ck 6								
Ck 7								
Ck 8								
Ck 9								

When you finish the spreadsheets, you decide to leave a message on the contractor's answering machine. You're brief and to the point. The cabinets didn't arrive last week; would he please get in touch with the manufacturer immediately and call you on Monday morning?

Monday of Week 21

Your contractor calls you at the office to report that the cabinets will probably be delayed another week or two, and he asks when he can pick up his check . . . just as if nothing was wrong. You tell him you have to talk to him and would like a short meeting at midday. You'll come to the site.

The work area is so dusty and full of wet paint that you decide to sit in his truck.

"Why didn't you let me know you were going out of town?" you ask. He answers that he had a death in the family and when he got the call he packed a bag and headed for the airport. It completely slipped his mind to call you.

"Why were you gone for two weeks?" you ask. He answers that there were complications—his mother had a stroke. He chose to spend an extra week with her to make arrangements for a housekeeper/cook to come for an hour each day to help.

"Does your brother-in-law have any experience running a construction site?" you ask. He answers that his brother-in-law is an insurance salesman and knows very little about construction.

What Would You Do If You Were Dad?

You would tell him that you are very sorry to hear his news, and equally sorry to tell him that before you will cut him a check you will need *his* signature—not his brother-in-law's—on the Progress Evaluation Spreadsheet. Your contract is with him, not his brother-in-law.

You do a walk-through and the contractor affirms the percentages, and signs next to his brother-in-law's name on the form.

That was a great relief. If he had chosen to contest the numbers, or to claim that his brother-in-law had no right to sign this sheet, you might have found yourself facing a serious dispute. You dodged a bullet, but your chest still feels a little tight. You're not sure you trust the contractor anymore.

And you do owe him a check. Go home and cut it, and bring it to him early tomorrow (Tuesday) morning.

He's been through a lot, if his tale is true, and now you withheld his check. Even though it was only for a day, it has now made him wary of you.

You have to continue to work with this contractor for another two months. You have to rebuild the trust between you or the rest of the job will be pretty hard going.

Let's see what happens next.

Week 24

The cabinets have arrived! They came last week—Week 23 instead of Week 20. The contractor tells you that he has called the countertop guy to come tomorrow and measure, by which time he expects his crew to have the base cabinets laid out and ready for final measurements. There's a little tension in the air as the contractor waits for your response.

"Great!" you say. "Call and tell me what he anticipates the countertop delivery date will be and we'll settle the issue of the change order then." The two of you have already discussed that your contractor will need at least two weeks to finish after the countertops are installed. The way he sees it, this is the second time you've put off the change order and gambled with his money, and he's not entirely happy about that.

The Walk-through

All of the other work is going along quite well. The crew is at full capacity and working on finishes. Wood floors are being polished, exterior trim is done and being painted, and it's time to make final paint-color selections for the interior of the house. For this, you need Mom. You put that decision off until Monday morning, when you promise that the two of you (Mom and Dad) will spend just fifteen minutes to make your final selections. The contractor agrees to paint some color samples on the wall to help you decide.

The Crisis

At the end of your walk-through, while the contractor is signing the Progress Evaluation Spreadsheet, you notice an empty beer can in a pile of scraps. Has one of the workers been drinking on the job?

The kitchen cabinets arrive

Laying out the kitchen cabinets

Preparing the bedroom for paint

Choosing a paint color

Sanding the new wood floors

Spray painting the exterior

Detailed wood moldings around the roof

What would you do about this? Scan your contract for a clause about drinking (and drugs) to find out whether you have any options. What will it allow you to do, and what will it require of the general contractor?

What would you *choose* to do?

Do the Math

The meeting is over. It is time to go home and complete the Progress Evaluation Spreadsheet (page 238) and the Construction Accounting Sheet (page 239) for Week 24, and see whether or not you will cut him a check, and if so, for how much.

Afterthoughts

Over the weekend, it occurred to you that if you have an alcohol problem on the site, which you would have a hard time proving, you may be at risk for a construction accident. You make a mental note to check your insurance coverage, and the contractor's as well.

On Monday morning you (Dad) pick up the phone and call your agent. Would your insurance cover the medical bills or the lifetime disability checks if one of the workers had an accident?

Call your own insurance agent and find out who would be responsible if this happened to you.

You (Dad) call the general contractor's agent next. The contractor's agent says he isn't carrying the workers' comp policy anymore. That policy lapsed a month ago, and the contractor never renewed it.

Now what? Read your contract. What are your rights and obligations? What are the contractor's rights and obligations? What will you do? This is a serious lapse in your protection, a breach of the terms of the contract, and a break in the trust between you and the contractor, whether it was intentional or not.

If this contractor had earned a check, and you had cut it over the weekend and had it in your wallet, would you release it to him on Monday morning knowing that he had let his insurance lapse? What does your contract say about this?

Picking Colors

You almost forgot. You and Mom have to get over to the site right away to pick paint colors. You're hardly in the mood, but you haven't shared the latest news with Mom, so she's happy to go, and she brings Hope to show her off.

Work pretty much stops when the baby arrives. All of the contractors reach out with their calloused hands to touch the baby's fingers and toes. This is Hope's first day out, so Mom is ready to pick her colors quickly.

A Quick Discussion About a Big Problem

While Mom is walking through the site and mulling over the color samples, you ask the contractor about the workers' comp policy. He apologizes for his oversight, but he has changed agents and it slipped his mind to bring you a new certificate; he'll have one on site for you as soon as the new agent can fax him one.

Was that a satisfactory answer? You refer him to the contract clause about maintaining continuous insurance, and then to the clause about remedial action in the case of insufficient insurance coverage, and you tell him you will hold his check (if he has earned one) until you have an *original* certificate, not a fax, in hand, and can verify that there was no break in the coverage.

If he has the insurance, and there was no gap between the end of the first policy and the start of the second, he has maintained continuous coverage and you'll release the check. If you find that he was not continuously covered, what does the contract say your rights are? Look it up. What action would you take?

Week 28

Four weeks ago the work was okay, but the relationship between the owner and the contractor was on the skids. Let's see what happened, then move on to the next progress evaluation.

On the Wednesday after Mom selected her paint colors—let's see, that would have been . . . Week 25—the contractor appeared in your office with the original insurance certificate for the new workers' comp policy. You checked the start date and were happy to see that he *had* managed to keep continuous coverage. You made a photocopy of his check and had him sign it. One of your colleagues witnessed; then you gave your contractor his check.

PROGRESS EVALUATION SPREADSHEET - Week 24

SEC	Item #	Task List	Initial Contract	Changes	Revised Contract	%-Compl	Earned to Date
000		**Hazards**					
	001	Remove windows, entry doors, all trim	$2,800		$2,800	100%	$
	CO1	Treat black mold & remove birds		$12,000	$12,000	100%	$
100		**Demolition and Site Work**					
	101	Demo rear wall & roof; gut int. to framing	$9,000		$9,000	100%	$
	102	Remove all orig. subfloor	$3,000		$3,000	100%	$
	103	Demo old decks, rails, and steps	$200		$200	100%	$
	CO2	A9 Paving		$2,500	$2,500	20%	$
	CO2	A10 Landscaping		$2,000	$2,000	20%	$
200		**Foundation and Structure**					
	201	Build new fdn for add'n & deck	$7,500		$7,500	100%	$
	CO1	Repair mortar in existing fdn		$2,600	$2,600	100%	$
	CO1	Replace floor framing--3 locations		$3,400	$3,400	100%	$
	202	Install all new subfloor throughout	$5,000		$5,000	100%	$
	203	Frame new floors,ext.walls, ceilings, & roof	$11,000		$11,000	100%	$
	CO1	Replace bad wall framing in front		$4,500	$4,500	100%	$
300		**Exterior Envelope**					
	301	Weather-in entire new structure	$10,000		$10,000	100%	$
	302	Install new exterior wall & roof finishes	$22,000		$22,000	95%	$
	303	Plywood 50% of attic floor; access stair	$2,500		$2,500	100%	$
	304	Build 300 s.f. deck, not 500	$6,000		$6,000	50%	$
	CO2	ADD: A1 Build 500 s.f. curved deck		$4,000	$4,000	50%	$
400		**Doors:** 3 Entry; 19 Int; 5 Int. Fr.	$16,400		$16,400	60%	$
500		**Windows:** 9@4'0" sq; 15@2'6"x6'0"	$17,300		$17,300	100%	$
600		**Interior Finishes**					
	601	Frame int.walls & blocking for cabs	$12,000		$12,000	100%	$
	602	Install drywall, trim, & closet shelves	$23,500		$23,500	95%	$
	603	Install tile floors in 3 baths & laundry	$3,000		$3,000	100%	$
	CO2	Tile wainscoting; 2 baths to 4'6"		$2,200	$2,200	100%	$
	605	Install pine floors	$18,000		$18,000	60%	$
	606	XYZ plain cabs in kitchen	$20,000	**Arr Wk 23**	$20,000	40%	$
	607	Install Big Box cabs in baths & laund	$4,000		$4,000	100%	$
	A4	Man-made countertops in kitchen	$6,000		$6,000		$
	CO2	ADD: Natural stone countertops in kitchen	**Ord.Wk 24**	$3,000	$3,000		$
	609	Man-made ctrtps in 3 baths & laund	$2,000		$2,000		$
	CO2	A6 15 interior shutters - tall windows		$1,250	$1,250		$
	CO2	Furnish & install all appliances		$4,000	$4,000		$
	CO2	A7 Buy larger refrig/freezer (add)		$1,500	$1,500		$
700		**Prep and Paint - Int. & Ext.**					
	701	Prime & paint interior - 6 colors	$8,500		$8,500	35%	$
	702	Prime & paint exterior - 3 colors	$5,500		$5,500	40%	$
800	801	**Plumbing:** Replace entire system	$18,000		$18,000	50%	$
	CO1	New trench for lines to street		$2,200	$2,200	100%	$
	802	Install 1 50-gal water heater	$1,800		$1,800	80%	$
	CO2	ADD: A8 Install 2 - 40-gallon water heater		$400	$400	80%	$
900	901	**HVAC:** Replace entire system	$6,000		$6,000	75%	$
1000	1001	**Electrical:** Replace entire system	$16,500		$16,500	75%	$
		Incr. power/street; 250A. panel; all fix's					
		TOTALS	$257,500	$45,550	$303,050		$

Next Pay Avail. At 24 Weeks x $9200 $ 220,800.00

Signatures:	D.Contractor	D.Homeowner

CONSTRUCTION ACCOUNTING - Week 24

CHANGE ORDER LOG

		A	B	C=A+B	D=Last Bal.-B	E	F	G=E+F
CO#	Change Date	Contract Amount	Net Change	Revised Contract	Remaining Conting.	Current Sched	Days Added	Revised Schedule
				Initial Contingency:	*$69,000*			
1	(Day 15)	$257,500	$24,700	$282,200	$44,300	196	18	214
2	(Day 84)	$282,200	$20,850	**$303,050**	$23,450	214	16	**230**
3								
4								

PROGRESS EVALUATIONS

		A	B	C=B/A	D	E	F=E/D	Pay every 4 weeks @ $9,200 per wk.
Wk#	Eval. Date	# Days in Sched.	# Days Lapsed	%-Sched Lapsed	Contract Amount	T.Amt. Earned	%-Contr Earned	
2	(Day 14)	196	14	7%	$257,500	$11,350	4%	
4	(Day 28)	**214**	28	13%	**$282,200**	$32,135	11%	$36,800
6	(Day 42)	214	42	20%	$282,200	$54,450	19%	
8	(Day 56)	214	56	26%	$282,200	$74,625	26%	$73,600
12	(Day 84)	214	84	39%	$282,200	$110,695	39%	$110,400
16	(Day 112)	**230**	112	49%	**$303,050**	$150,605	50%	$147,200
20	(Day 140)	230	140	61%	$303,050	$194,350	64%	$184,000
24	(Day 168)	230	168	**73%**	$303,050			**$220,800**
28			196					$257,600
32			224					$294,400
36			252					$331,200

CONTRACTOR PAYMENTS

	A	B	C=A-B	D	E=C-D	F	G=E-F	
	T.Earned to Date	Minus 10% Retain.	Balance #1	Minus All Prev.Pay'ts	Balance #2	Minus Late Fees	AMOUNT PAID	Check Date & Number
DEP	–	–		–		–	$15,000	Week 0 - #
Ck 1	$54,450	$5,445	$49,005	$15,000	$34,005	–	$34,005	Week 6 - #
Ck 2	$74,625	$7,463	$67,163	$49,005	$18,158	–	$18,158	Week 8 - #
Ck 3	$110,695	$11,070	$99,626	$67,163	$32,463	–	$32,463	Week 12 - #
Ck 4	$150,605	$15,061	$135,545	$99,626	$35,919	–	$35,919	Week 16 - #
Ck 5	$194,350	$19,435	$174,915	$135,545	$39,371	–	$39,371	Week 20 - #
Ck 6	**$224,770**	$22,478	$202,298	$174,916	$27,382	–	**$27,382**	Week 24 - #
Ck 7								
Ck 8								
Ck 9								

He sat silently in your office for a minute before he spoke. He apologized for neglecting to phone you before he went to his family funeral and he apologized for neglecting to inform you that he'd changed insurance agents. He said he hoped that the two of you could go forward from here without any further problems. You said you couldn't agree more, and the two of you shook hands. His apology broke the tension between you; you even joked a bit about only having five weeks left . . . what the heck else could go wrong in the last five weeks? Ha-ha-ha.

The Week 28 Evaluation

It's Week 28 and all of the major materials except the stone countertop are on-site, installed, and being hooked up or finished; the crew was working hard and the quality of the work is excellent. There had not been another sign of alcohol, and you hadn't mentioned anything to the contractor.

Hope, born in lucky Week 13, was growing like a weed. Both you and Mom were grateful that she was beginning to sleep through the night. Mom could hardly contain herself; she really wanted to see the work in progress.

You began doing your informal site visits about twice a week.

The Progress Evaluation

The contractor informed you that the last items were now on the schedule: Paving and landscaping would be last, after there was no more risk of a worker pulling his truck up onto the lawn or driving across the wet cement. The deck was about 50 percent finished; they wouldn't put the rails on or paint it until there was no chance any of the crew would walk in the wet paint by mistake. A few closet shelves needed to be hung, the appliance delivery date had been set, and the painters were touching up the trim work. Unfortunately, the three service subs—plumbing, HVAC, and electric—would be unable to finish until the stone countertop comes in. Here is what you saw.

Painting the trim

Blowing hot air to dry paint more quickly

Protecting the bathroom tile with a plastic tarp

Leveling kitchen cabinets

Working in the attic crawl space

Installing the bath vanity countertop

New deck rail

Painting trim in the family room

The contractor seemed really nervous.

He's not confident he'll finish on time, and he doesn't want to pay late penalties. He's already paid a thousand dollars out of pocket to replace the stolen French pocket doors. He can't afford to lose any more money.

He asked for a moment of your time after the walk-through, and told you that the countertop wasn't due until Week 30 and he was supposed to be finished, paperwork and all, by Week 32. He had little confidence in the delivery date; he knew the manufacturer. Would you please give him that change order you'd been discussing for the last six weeks?

Do the Math

You decide to have a closer look at the problem, and here's what you find:

You want to know how much he's been earning each week on average, so you divide his total earnings as of the last walk-through by the twenty-four weeks that had passed at that point.

$_____ (total earnings through Week 24), divided by 24 weeks = $_____.

Has he been holding up his end of the bargain? Has he been earning his $9,200/week?

Next you want to know how many weeks beyond Week 24 he would need to finish the job, if he could keep up his current earnings rate, so you divide his weekly earnings rate into the amount of money that remained in the contract as of the Week 24 progress evaluation.

$_____ (remaining contract value), divided by $_____ (average weekly earnings rate), and you thought he could probably finish in _____ (how many?) weeks. If this was true, he probably (could, or could not) finish on time.

The problem was that you were both unsure of the delivery date of the stone countertop.

You decided to . . . What *would* you

decide? He's getting tense. Should you keep the pressure on?

Accounting—Week 28

The completed Progress Evaluation Spreadsheet for the Week 28 walk-through is on pages 242–243. Please complete the Construction Accounting Sheet, and then decide what to do about your contractor's dilemma.

The Advantages of Poetic License

I've suspended the contractor in time (poof!) so he won't have any hard feelings about you putting this decision off.

Here's what's going through your mind . . .

Maybe this is entirely your fault. That big discretionary change order you executed when the job was 40 percent complete may have come too late. Maybe you should have made those decisions two weeks earlier and benefited from that extra lead time now. But then again, didn't you act when the contractor asked you to?

Now that you've done the accounting for Week 28, run that math again and see if the contractor is maintaining the same earnings rate. If so, he's doing a great job for you! How can you help him out? If you extend his time without offering to share in the cost of keeping the men on the site for that extra week or so, you haven't done him any favors.

You decide not to issue the change order, but to see when the countertop actually comes in and then to decide, with his input, how to handle this.

(Poof!) We're back in real time.

You cut the check for this pay period and tell him your decision on Monday morning when you deliver the check. He says he's okay with that, but you can feel him tightening up again.

PROGRESS EVALUATION SPREADSHEET - Week 28

SEC	Item #	Task List	Initial Contract	Changes	Revised Contract	%-Compl	Earned to Date
000		**Hazards**					
	001	Remove windows, entry doors, all trim	$2,800		$2,800	100%	$2,800
	CO1	Treat black mold & remove birds		$12,000	$12,000	100%	$12,000
100		**Demolition and Site Work**					
	101	Demo rear wall & roof; gut int. to framing	$9,000		$9,000	100%	$9,000
	102	Remove all orig. subfloor	$3,000		$3,000	100%	$3,000
	103	Demo old decks, rails, and steps	$200		$200	100%	$200
	CO2	A9 Paving		$2,500	$2,500	20%	$500
	CO2	A10 Landscaping		$2,000	$2,000	20%	$400
200		**Foundation and Structure**					
	201	Build new fdn for add'n & deck	$7,500		$7,500	100%	$7,500
	CO1	Repair mortar in existing fdn		$2,600	$2,600	100%	$2,600
	CO1	Replace floor framing - 3 locations		$3,400	$3,400	100%	$3,400
	202	Install all new subfloor throughout	$5,000		$5,000	100%	$5,000
	203	Frame new floors,ext.walls, ceilings, & roof	$11,000		$11,000	100%	$11,000
	CO1	Replace bad wall framing in front		$4,500	$4,500	100%	$4,500
300		**Exterior Envelope**					
	301	Weather-in entire new structure	$10,000		$10,000	100%	$10,000
	302	Install new exterior wall & roof finishes	$22,000		$22,000	95%	$20,900
	303	Plywood 50% of attic floor; access stair	$2,500		$2,500	100%	$2,500
	304	Build 300 s.f. deck, not 500	$6,000		$6,000	50%	$3,000
	CO2	ADD: A1 Build 500 s.f. curved deck		$4,000	$4,000	50%	$2,000
400		**Doors:** 3 Entry; 19 Int; 5 Int. Fr.	$16,400		$16,400	100%	$16,400
500		**Windows:** 9@4'0" sq; 15@2'6"x6'0"	$17,300		$17,300	100%	$17,300
600		**Interior Finishes**					–
	601	Frame int.walls & blocking for cabs	$12,000		$12,000	100%	$12,000
	602	Install drywall, trim, & closet shelves	$23,500		$23,500	95%	$22,325
	603	Install tile floors in 3 baths & laundry	$3,000		$3,000	100%	$3,000
	CO2	Tile wainscoting; 2 baths to 4'6"		$2,200	$2,200	100%	$2,200
	605	Install pine floors	$18,000		$18,000	100%	$18,000
	606	XYZ plain cabs in kitchen	$20,000		$20,000	80%	$16,000
	607	Install Big Box cabs in baths & laund	$4,000		$4,000	100%	$4,000
	A4	Man-made countertops in kitchen	$6,000		$6,000		–
	CO2	ADD: Natural stone countertops in kitchen	Due Wk 30	$3,000	$3,000		–
	609	Man-made ctrtps in 3 baths & laund	$2,000		$2,000	100%	$2,000
	CO2	A6 15 interior shutters - tall windows		$1,250	$1,250	100%	$1,250
	CO2	Furnish & install all appliances		$4,000	$4,000		–
	CO2	A7 Buy larger refrig/freezer (add)		$1,500	$1,500		–
700		**Prep and Paint - Int. & Ext.**					
	701	Prime & paint interior - 6 colors	$8,500		$8,500	75%	$6,375
	702	Prime & paint exterior - 3 colors	$5,500		$5,500	95%	$5,225
800	801	**Plumbing:** Replace entire system	$18,000		$18,000	75%	$13,500
	CO1	New trench for lines to street		$2,200	$2,200	100%	$2,200
	802	Install 1 50-gal water heater	$1,800		$1,800	100%	$1,800
	CO2	ADD: A8 Install 2 - 40-gallon water heaters		$400	$400	100%	$400
900	901	**HVAC:** Replace entire system	$6,000		$6,000	85%	$5,100
1000	1001	**Electrical:** Replace entire system	$16,500		$16,500	85%	$14,025
		Incr. power/street; 250A. panel; all fix's					–
		TOTALS	$257,500	$45,550	$303,050		$263,400

Next Pay Avail. At 28 Weeks x $9200 $257,600

Signatures: D.Contractor   D.Homeowner

CONSTRUCTION ACCOUNTING - Week 28

CHANGE ORDER LOG

CO#	Change Date	A Contract Amount	B Net Change	C=A+B Revised Contract	D=Last Bal.-B Remaining Conting.	E Current Sched	F Days Added	G=E+F Revised Schedule
				Initial Contingency:	*$69,000*			
1	(Day 15)	$257,500	$24,700	$282,200	$44,300	196	18	214
2	(Day 84)	$282,200	$20,850	**$303,050**	$23,450	214	16	**230**
3								
4								

PROGRESS EVALUATIONS

Wk#	Eval. Date	A # Days in Sched.	B # Days Lapsed	C=B/A %-Sched Lapsed	D Contract Amount	E T.Amt. Earned	F=E/D %-Contr Earned	Pay every 4 weeks @ $9,200 per wk.
2	(Day 14)	196	14	7%	$257,500	$11,350	$0.04	
4	(Day 28)	**214**	28	13%	**$282,200**	$32,135	$0.11	$36,800
6	(Day 42)	214	42	20%	$282,200	$54,450	$0.19	
8	(Day 56)	214	56	26%	$282,200	$74,625	$0.26	$73,600
12	(Day 84)	214	84	39%	$282,200	$110,695	$0.39	$110,400
16	(Day 112)	230	112	49%	$303,050	$150,605	$0.50	$147,200
20	(Day 140)	230	140	61%	$303,050	$194,350	$0.64	$184,000
24	(Day 168)	230	168	73%	$303,050	$224,775	$0.74	$220,800
28			196					$257,600
32			224					$294,400
36			252					$331,200

CONTRACTOR PAYMENTS

	A T.Earned to Date	B Minus 10% Retain.	C=A-B Balance #1	D Minus All Prev.Pay'ts	E=C-D Balance #2	F Minus Late Fees	G=E-F AMOUNT PAID	Check Date & Number
DEP	–	–	–			–	$15,000	Week 0 - #
Ck 1	$54,450	$5,445	$49,005	$15,000	$34,005	–	$34,005	Week 6 - #
Ck 2	$74,625	$7,463	$67,163	$49,005	$18,158	–	$18,158	Week 8 - #
Ck 3	$110,695	$11,070	$99,626	$67,163	$32,463	–	$32,463	Week 12 - #
Ck 4	$150,605	$15,061	$135,545	$99,626	$35,919	–	$35,919	Week 16 - #
Ck 5	$194,350	$19,435	$174,915	$135,545	$39,371	–	$39,371	Week 20 - #
Ck 6	$224,775	$22,478	$202,298	$174,916	$27,382	–	$27,382	Week 24 - #
Ck 7	**$263,400**	$26,340	$237,060	$202,298	$34,763	–	**$34,763**	Week 28 - #
Ck 8								
Ck 9								

EIGHT

Finishing Up

The stone countertops arrived on Monday of Week 30. You squeaked through another one. The contractor called to tell you, and asked that you be prepared to write him a punch list when you come for the biweekly progress evaluation at the end of the week. He wants to know what you see that his crew might have overlooked, so that in two more weeks, when he is, hopefully, completely finished, he can meet you in the notary's office and sign the lien waiver for the final check with no strings attached.

Another Crisis

Your mother-in-law has been begging for your permission to come see the new baby, and she's just chomping at the bit to see that house. When you first bought it she thought you were crazy, but you've been sending progress photos and she's had lots to say about what they should have done and how they should have done it. She gave her kitchen a face-lift a few years ago—installed new cabinet doors, changed the vinyl flooring, and painted—so she considers herself somewhat of an expert when it comes to remodeling.

You've been dreading this, but she would not be put off any longer. It's Tuesday of Week 30, and here she is.

On the second day of her five-day visit, the Wednesday before the punch-list walk-through, she took it upon herself to drive over to the project site. The construction crew was on lunch break at some local fast-food place, but there was one lonely painter working on the trim in the bathroom when Mom's mom arrived, so she had a nice long chat with him—what a lovely boy— and had him give her the tour.

She asked about everything. Had they thought about the energy bills that all those tall windows would generate? Had they considered that the deck ought to have a roof over it? What did they intend to do about that tiny little laundry closet? How could they expect her daughter—with three little children—to manage all that laundry in that tiny little laundry closet?

The painter did his best and said a lot of yes-ma'ams, but he was in no position—nor did he wish to be—to do anything about her requests. She left the site a bit miffed.

The next day—Thursday—while Mom and Hope were down for their afternoon nap, she drove to the site and caught the general contractor's ear. She introduced herself and showed him her driver's license as if it were a sheriff's badge, then told him that her daughter had decided to change the color of the paint in the living room. You see, she explained, the artwork would show better against this nice purple color. Why, he could see that himself, if he could see the paintings she intended to hang in that room. Mom's mom had even stopped by the local home improvement store and pulled a paint chip she liked, which she offered to the contractor now, saying that this was the color her daughter had chosen.

He thanked her for bringing this to his attention and promised to see what he could do.

You're lucky you found and chose this contractor. He *knew* what to do. He called you (Dad, his boss) at the office and asked if any such change had been authorized. You, of course, had not the faintest idea.

You called home and woke Mom with the news that the contractor was going to paint the living room purple on her mother's say-so. She told you she'd take care of her mother if he would call the contractor back and ask him to continue with the colors she had originally selected. No purple!

When her mother returned home shortly thereafter, pleased as punch to have made such an important decision, and eager to tell her daughter of the surprise that awaited her, she was crestfallen to see her daughter scowling.

There was silence, and nobody moved for a few minutes. Then Mom softened and said, "Thank you, Mom, but we really like the colors we chose. Maybe we can use that great purple in another room." And that was the end of it. For the remainder of her visit, Mom's mom concentrated on playing with little Hope, now fifteen weeks old and bursting with energy. Another crisis averted!

The Punch List

The next day was Friday, and you and Mom were due at the site to write up a punch list for the contractor. Mom walked around the site as if she had been transported to fairyland. She was thrilled with the work, and hugged the contractor and thanked him. He winked at you over her shoulder, and grinned.

Staple in bifold doors

Unsealed exterior wall penetration

Concrete backsplash at driveway

Missing cover plate at duplex outlet

Missing cover on doorbell chime

Scratches on new cooktop

After a few tearful moments, Mom got it together and you started your inspection in earnest. Here is what you saw.

Now you need to prepare a punch list for the contractor. List problems you can see in the photos, but also list anything else that you think might not have been completed at this point.

Assign an estimated cost to each item. For example, it might take the painter an hour to scrape and paint over the paving marks on the side of the house, or it might take a laborer an hour to pull the staple out of the folding doors or the nail out of the wall, patch the holes, and touch up the paint. Assume that their time is worth $30 an hour to the general contractor. That's not what they earn, mind you, but that may cover what it costs him to keep them on the job.

What will you do about the cooktop? It's an expensive item with a lead time of about two weeks. You can't accept a scratched appliance. How would you handle the cost of replacing the cooktop? Who would you hold responsible?

Complete the punch list, add up the costs, and see if the total is greater than or less than 1 percent of the final, total construction contract value.

What do you think? Is the job "substantially complete"?

Week 32

Theoretically, if the contractor needed it, he could have another week to finish. He has 230 days in his construction schedule, which is the same as 32.8 weeks.

But he promised his next client he would start her job next week, and he's ordered some of her materials. He's ready to shift his crew to their next job.

Preparing to pour the new driveway

Laying out the new garden

Installing the new light fixtures

Finishing the electronic controls

Finishing the plumbing fixture installation

The new laundry room

PUNCH LIST

Date: (2 weeks before anticipated completion date)

Item #	Item	Approx. Value
1	Scrape and paint over concrete splashes on painted foundation wall	$ 30.00
2	Remove staple from bifold closet doors without damaging the finish. Remove nail from bedroom wall; spackle and touch up the paint.	$ 30.00
3	Seal all penetrations in exterior walls against weather and bug infiltrations	$ 30.00
4	Install all missing face plates on outlets and switches	$ 30.00
5	Install cover on doorbell chime in front entry foyer	$ 15.00
6	Replace scratched stovetop with new	$ 2,500.00
7	etc…	
8		
9		
10		
11		
12		

ESTIMATED VALUE OF ALL ITEMS: $

Signatures: **D.Contractor**   **D.Homeowner**

The Final Walk-through

Outside, the cement truck is making the last deep tracks in what will soon be your front yard; they're pouring your new driveway. Your front walk will be set by hand once the yard has been filled and graded. The paving and landscaping ought to be done within forty-eight hours.

Inside, the electricians are installing switches, outlets, and switch plates and checking and labeling the new electrical panel, installing the exterior security lights, installing light fixtures and chandeliers, and putting in the lighting under the wall-hung cabinets. The plumbers are installing final hookups to the sinks and the faucets and other doodads that go with them, checking water pressure and temperature against the settings on the water heaters, and installing the exterior hose bibs (the spigot you hook your outside hose to). The HVAC technicians are installing the thermostats and testing the system, making sure that the right amount of air will be pushed into each room, and that the right amount of fresh air will be brought into the home with each circulation. Carpenters are installing closet shelving, cabinet doors and shelves, and quarter-round trim moldings along the bottoms of the bathtubs. When things settle down a bit, the flooring installers will come back to touch up the wood floors.

Everything looks great, and you can't wait to move back in. *But wait* . . .

The Crisis

The appliances have arrived. Remember that bigger refrigerator you ordered? Well, the model you specified has been discontinued. The manufacturer has another model, very similar, so they shipped that one to the vendor, who delivered it without checking the tag. The new model is an inch wider than the old one was, and it won't fit into the space provided for it. The general contractor will have to send it back, and you will have to postpone your move. Now what!

The contractor says he will personally return this refrigerator to the vendor, whom he knows well, find you that other model or an equivalent one, bring it back to the house, and install it himself, if you will agree to waive all late fees. He makes it clear that although he can't guarantee he'll find the perfect replacement in forty-eight hours, he doesn't think it will take more than a week or so; his vendor has lots of connections. You make it clear that he won't get his final check, the fat one with all of the retainage in it, until the refrigerator is in place and full of groceries.

It's a deal, and you sit down and write a change order on the back of one of the filthy construction drawings that are sitting on the kitchen counter, so that it can be signed today. You plan to take that frayed, rumpled, muddy piece of paper home with you and frame it. An official change order would look like the form on page 249.

Now you check absolutely everything to be sure the contractor's really 99.9 percent complete, and he begins the ceremony of the handing over of the paperwork.

- The inspections data card has been signed by all of the appropriate inspectors. He hands that to you.
- There are three pounds of owner's manuals for the water heaters, the thermostat, and all the new appliances, including the garbage disposal, and all of the warranty pages have been completed in a legible hand.
- He gives you an original copy of the certificate of occupancy from the inspections department.

CHANGE ORDER #3

Date: (at Week 32 Progress Evaluation)

Project	(address)
Owner	D.Homeowner
GC	D.Contractor

This Change Order is hereby incorporated into the Contract by reference and shall be subject to all stipulations and covenants of that Contract, once it is fully executed.

Section	List of Changes	Cost
600	Manufacturer no longer makes the model we ordered. The model he shipped to the vendor doesn't fit into the opening.	$0.00
	Contractor will personally replace the unsuitable fridge with a proper substitute, on his own time and at his own expense.	
	Owner will not charge late fees, but will also not release contractor's final check until the new refrigerator is in place and the contractor joins the family for lunch to celebrate.	
	Net Change to Contract Value	$ -

Current Contract Value	$	303,050
Plus/Minus This Change Order	$	-
Equals New Contract Value	**$**	**303,050**

Total Calendar Days in Schedule	230
Time Added by This Change Order (@ $9,200 / wk)	0
Revised Total Calendar Days in Schedule	**230**

Signatures	Date
D.Contractor	d
D.Homeowner	d

- And he's carefully prepared a complete list of all of the subcontractors that worked on this job—not the individuals—the companies.

Then he gives you a nice little bonus. He's prepared a materials list with the manufacturer, model number, serial number, color number, pattern number, and so on of everything that might need repair in the years that follow his warranty period. Wasn't that nice?

Lucky You!

As luck would have it, the contractor's appliance vendor had just the right refrigerator in his warehouse, and the contractor was able to have it delivered and set within forty-eight hours. He even put a bottle of champagne in it, tied with a curly pink ribbon and dangling a note that said "Welcome Home!"

You and Mom cheered, and the three of you shared a toast as if your favorite team had just won the pennant.

When you are absolutely sure that the work is completely done, fill in the final Progress Evaluation Spreadsheet, and all three of you sign the bottom of it.

Go home and complete your final Construction Accounting Sheet to be sure the books are balanced, and then call the bank.

Even if you didn't borrow their money, you'll need their notary. Meet the contractor at the bank the next morning and trade him a signed and notarized lien waiver for his final check.

Then call the mover and set a date for him to bring all your furniture back to the house and start packing up your temporary home.

Congratulations—you, reader, did a *great* job!

- You selected a great contractor and managed him well.
- You avoided all disputes despite your frustrations.
- You were in control from start to finish.
- You did not exceed your budget.
- You got exactly what you wanted, and more.
- You have a really wonderful home to raise your family in, and you can be proud that you were the one that made it all happen.
- And lastly, you have a home that fits nicely in your lovely neighborhood, and you didn't have to invest more than the market value of the finished product to get it.

Final Accounting

Your final project accounting is on pages 251 and 252. Finally, let's take a tour of the finished house; just turn to page 253. You're going to be very proud of yourself!

FINAL SOFT-COSTS ACCOUNTING

				PAYMENT LOG		
Total Construction Budget	100%	$ 360,000				
Soft-Costs Allowance	10%	$ 36,000				
		Allowances		Amount	Ck.Dt.	Ck.No.
Planning:						
Home Inspection		$ 600		$ 600	d	c
Wine-and-Design Party		$ 300		$ 250	cash	cash
Additional Insurance		$ 300		$ 380	d	c
Design:						
Concept Design		$ 3,000		$ 4,000	d	c
Design Development		$ 4,500		$ 5,500	d	c
Construction Documents		$ 7,500		$ 8,000	d	c
Post-Bid Final Payment				$ 1,500	d	c
Architect at Meetings @ $150/hr	6 hrs	$ 900		$ 300	d	c
Structural Engineer @ $100/hr	5 hrs	$ 500		$ 200	d	c
Kitchen Designer @ $65/hr	3 hrs	$ 200		$ 130	d	c
Interior Designer @ $65/hr	3 hrs	$ 200		$ 130	d	c
Professional Cost Estimate		$ 600		$ 600	d	c
Pre-Construction:						
Environmental Consult		$ 500		$ 500	d	c
Loan Closing Costs		$ 500		$ 500	d	c
Furniture Storage - @150/mo.	8 mo's	$ 1,500		$ 1,200	d	c
Rental House - @ $1,000/mo.	8 mo's	$ 10,000		$ 8,000	d	c
(as available - reimburse at end of job)		$ 11,500		$ 9,200		
Construction:						
Attorney - Document Review @ $150/hr		$ 300		$ 150	d	c
Structural Engineer @ $100/hr		$ 400		$ 400	d	c
Environmental Consult		$ 1,000		$ 1,000		
Attorney - Disputes @ $150/hr		$ 1,000		$ -		
Remodeling Coach @$50/hr						
Planning Phase	4 hrs	$ 200		$ 200	d	c
Design Review	3 hrs	$ 150		$ 150	d	c
Construction Phase	10 hrs	$ 500		$ 850	d	c
Total Soft Costs =		**$ 21,750**		**$ 43,740**		

FINAL CONSTRUCTION ACCOUNTING

CHANGE ORDER LOG

CO#	Change Date	A Contract Amount	B Net Change	C=A+B Revised Contract	D=Last Bal.-B Remaining Conting.	E Current Sched	F Days Added	G=E+F Revised Schedule
				Initial Contingency:	*$69,000*			
1	(Day 15)	$257,500	$24,700	$282,200	$44,300	196	18	214
2	(Day 84)	$282,200	$20,850	**$303,050**	$23,450	214	16	**230**
3								
4								

PROGRESS EVALUATIONS

Wk#	Eval. Date	A # Days in Sched.	B # Days Lapsed	C=B/A %-Sched Lapsed	D Contract Amount	E T.Amt. Earned	F=E/D %-Contr Earned	Pay every 4 weeks @ $9,200 per wk.
2	(Day 14)	196	14	7%	$257,500	$11,350	4%	
4	(Day 28)	**214**	28	13%	**$282,200**	$32,135	11%	$36,800
6	(Day 42)	214	42	20%	$282,200	$54,450	19%	
8	(Day 56)	214	56	26%	$282,200	$74,625	26%	$73,600
12	(Day 84)	214	84	39%	$282,200	$110,695	39%	$110,400
16	(Day 112)	**230**	112	49%	**$303,050**	$150,605	50%	$147,200
20	(Day 140)	230	140	61%	$303,050	$194,350	64%	$184,000
24	(Day 168)	230	168	73%	$303,050	$224,775	74%	$220,800
28	(Day 196)	230	196	85%	$303,050	$263,400	87%	$257,600
32	(Day 224)	230	224	97%	$303,050	$293,175	97%	$294,400
33	(Day 231)	230	231	100%	$303,050	**$303,050**	100%	**$303,600**

CONTRACTOR PAYMENTS

	A T.Earned to Date	B Minus 10% Retain.	C=A-B Balance #1	D Minus All Prev.Pay'ts	E=C-D Balance #2	F Minus Late Fees	G=E-F AMOUNT PAID	Check Date & Number
DEP	–	–		–		–	$15,000	Week 0 - #
Ck 1	$54,450	$5,445	$49,005	$15,000	$34,005	–	$34,005	Week 6 - #
Ck 2	$74,625	$7,463	$67,163	$49,005	$18,158	–	$18,157	Week 8 - #
Ck 3	$110,695	$11,070	$99,626	$67,163	$32,463	–	$32,463	Week 12 - #
Ck 4	$150,605	$15,061	$135,545	$99,626	$35,919	–	$35,919	Week 16 - #
Ck 5	$194,350	$19,435	$174,915	$135,545	$39,371	–	$39,371	Week 20 - #
Ck 6	$224,775	$22,478	$202,298	$174,916	$27,382	–	$27,382	Week 24 - #
Ck 7	$263,400	$26,340	$237,060	$202,298	$34,763	–	$34,763	Week 28 - #
Ck 8	**$303,050**	–	$303,050	$237,061	$65,990	–	**$65,990**	Week 33 - #
Ck 9								

SUMMARY: COSTS vs. BUDGET

		Budget	Actual
Total Construction Budget	100%	$ 362,778	
(minus) Soft-Costs Allowance	10%	$ 36,278	$ 43,740
(equals) Total Construction Budget	90%	$ 326,500	
Initial Construction Contract Allowance	72%	$ 261,200	$ 303,050
Contingency Fund for Unanticipated Costs	18%	$ 65,300	
Total Expenditures			$ 351,390
SAVINGS			**$ 11,388**

The Grand Tour

You did a great job and have done the final accounting. Now take a tour of the finished house. Take pleasure and have pride in the results and the careful managing you have done of your home renovation. It has all been worth it!

Front porch

Front entry

Back deck 1

Living room entry area

Living room fireplace

Kitchen

Kitchen breakfast room with view of back deck

Formal dining room

Family room behind living room with view of back deck

Master bedroom

Master bath

Back deck 2

The Contract

There is no absolutely perfect construction contract; there are so many things that can go wrong that you couldn't possibly think of them all. This document addresses every problem I've ever encountered, it has held up under the harshest attacks, and it has always kept my clients safe.

However, I am not an attorney, and I suggest that no matter what contract you choose to use, you make sure that it complies with all the laws in your state, that it is to your advantage, and that it is clear and enforceable.

TERMS AND CONDITIONS OF THE CONTRACT FOR THE RENOVATION OF:

_____

(Project Address)

CONTRACTING PARTIES:

PROPERTY OWNER

Name _____

Mailing Address _____

Tel (H) _____ (B) _____

Fax _____ Mobile _____

E-mail _____

OWNER'S AGENT OR PROJECT MANAGER

Firm _____

Contact _____

Mailing Address _____

Tel (B) _____ Mobile _____

Fax _____ Beeper _____

E-mail _____

GENERAL CONTRACTOR

Firm _____

Contact _____

Mailing Address _____

Tel (B) _____ Mobile _____

Fax _____ Beeper _____

E-mail _____

CONTENTS

PART 1: CONTRACT TERMS AND CONDITIONS

GENERAL CONDITIONS

DEFINITION OF THE CONTRACT DOCUMENTS

This contract consists of two parts: Part 1 is this Terms and Conditions Statement and any attachments, addenda, or special conditions statements, and Part 2 is the scope of work as described in the construction drawings and specifications. All attachments to this Terms and Conditions Statement, including the design documents and special conditions statements, are incorporated into this contract by reference.

GENDER REFERENCES

The pronouns he, she, his, hers, him, her, they, them, their (singular and/or plural), etc. are used interchangeably in this document without regard to the actual gender or number of people the sentence refers to. If references are unclear, contracting parties should clarify the wording before beginning work.

PARTIES TO THIS CONTRACT

Property Owner(s): The person(s) whose name(s) appears on the deed of trust for the project property. Agent: The owner may assign an agent to make decisions on his behalf. If an agent is designated, the property owner hereby agrees to abide by their decisions and to pay for the work directed or approved by the agent. A limited power of attorney is attached to this contract and incorporated by reference if the decision maker is not one of the property owners.

Either the property owner or their agent will be the designated decision maker, but not both. In the absence of written and notarized assignment, the property owner shall by default be the sole decision maker. Every reference to the "owner" or "property owner" in these contract documents shall refer to the designated decision maker.

Contractor: The person or firm acting as the general contractor, who has full responsibility for the quality and completion of the job. This person may hire subcontractors as he deems necessary, but anyone engaged by the general contractor shall report to him, shall be governed by the terms and conditions of this contract insofar as it pertains to their work, and shall be held to the same standards as the general contractor.

Further, the general contractor shall be fully and solely responsible for his subcontractors' work and their actions, until the end of the warranty period. This responsibility includes ensuring that they are adequately insured and properly licensed and that they are aware of and act in compliance with the terms and scope of this contract and any laws, ordinances, guidelines, or regulations that may govern their work.

Subcontractor: A tradesman or firm engaged by the general contractor, who is directed by and paid by the general contractor. Subcontractors are not parties to this contract, although the terms and conditions of this contract apply to them in the same way as they apply to the general contractor.

WAIVER OF RIGHTS

Waiver of any default or breach shall not be deemed to be a waiver of any subsequent default or breach. Waiver shall not be construed to be a modification of the terms of the contract unless new terms are put in writing and signed by both parties to the contract.

ASSIGNING THE CONTRACT

The general contractor may not assign this contract to any other contractor without the express permission of the owner.

OWNERSHIP OF THE DESIGN

The drawings, specifications, and other design documents are attached to this Terms and Conditions Statement by reference, and are the property of the designer under copyright law. Such ownership remains in force no matter how these documents are disbursed for the purposes of executing the work.

EXPLICIT AND IMPLIED WORK

The design documents, including drawings, specifications, and special conditions statements, are in outline form for the sake of brevity; stipulations as to details or quality of both materials and workmanship may not be fully explained. However, all work under this contract shall be completed and finished in a workmanlike manner and shall meet the highest standards of professional construction craftsmanship in this area in order to be acceptable.

Materials shall be new, appropriate to their use, of first quality, readily available (not "custom" unless specified to be so), durable in assembly, and installed in accordance with the manufacturer's recommendations.

The drawings or floor plans illustrate the general layout of the structure. They do not show exact dimensions or every construction detail. However, any and all work indicated on or by the drawings, the specifications, or the special conditions statements is included in the project and is conclusively presumed to be included in the contract price.

COMMERCIAL CODE JURISDICTION

It is the responsibility of the contractor to ensure that building codes are met, including determining whether the work on this project is subject to the residential or the commercial building code.

COMPLIANCE WITH HISTORIC GUIDELINES

Properties with historic significance shall be renovated under the guidelines set by either the secretary of the interior or the local historic districts commission or both. If this project requires such compliance, the design documents will clearly indicate what is required.

DAVIS–BACON ACT

If the project is funded with public money, and if the property will contain eight or more dwelling units after the renovation is complete, the contractor is required to comply with conditions set forth in the Federal Fair Labor Standards Provisions (HUD Forms 3200 and 3200-A) including the Davis–Bacon Act. A Fair Labor Standards statement is available upon request from the federal funding agency's compliance officer. Compliance is the obligation of the contractor, and a condition for the release of all payments.

ANTICIPATED HIDDEN CONDITIONS

If the design documents indicate that certain areas must be opened up at the beginning of the job so that the owner and the designer can assess problems that are currently anticipated but hidden from view, the contractor shall open these areas before he does any other work described in this contract. The contractor shall allow ten (10) calendar days in the total contract schedule for the owner to assess any problems and to determine a solution, and shall negotiate a change order in good faith for corrective work.

UNANTICIPATED PROBLEMS

If the contractor uncovers an unanticipated problem, he shall stop work in that area and notify the owner immediately. Once the repair can be defined, the contractor shall negotiate a price for corrective work in good faith.

ALTERNATES

Some of the work indicated in the drawings, the specifications, or the special conditions statements is listed under the heading of "Alternates." Unless otherwise designated, this work is not included in the initial contract. When the owner decides to purchase an Alternate they will do so by executing a change order, and the rules for the use of change orders shall apply.

CHANGING THE CONTRACT

Any change to the contract documents must be described in detail in a change order document. When that document is fully executed (signed by both owner and contractor), the change becomes a part of the contract by reference, and all contract terms and conditions will apply to this new work.

The contractor must provide reasonable proposals to the owner when additional work is requested.

If the contractor does work beyond the scope of the contract documents without authorization of a fully executed change order, he does so entirely at his own risk and expense.

Further, if the contractor does work other than that specified by the contract documents, without a fully executed change order, he may be required by the owner to revise that work and repair any damage in order to restore the area of the repair to good condition.

SITE SAFETY AND SECURITY

When the site is occupied during the construction period, the property owner is responsible for securing the premises every day, and for keeping visitors and trespassers off the site.

When the site is not occupied during the construction period, the contractor has sole responsibility for securing the premises every day, and for keeping visitors and trespassers off the site.

Contractor has sole responsibility for accidents or injuries involving construction workers during work period, under any circumstances.

ABATEMENT OF HAZARDOUS CONDITIONS

If work on this property includes treatment or removal of hazardous materials such as lead-based paint or asbestos, that work will be done in full compliance of all current laws and regulations with jurisdiction.

The finished project shall receive formal clearance from an accredited environmental consultant and a properly licensed laboratory before the project is deemed to have been completed, whether or not remediation activities were required under this contract.

DEMOLITION

When the contract requires the contractor to "demolish" or "remove and discard" (or any similar term) certain items or certain areas of an existing structure, the contractor shall act promptly. Any items removed from the site by order of the contract documents become the property of the contractor once they are off the site.

If the owner wants to salvage any items from this area, they must notify the contractor in writing at least ten (10) days ahead of the day on which the demolition is to take place. The owner (not the contractor) is responsible for removing these items from the property a minimum of twenty-four (24) hours before the time the demolition work is scheduled to begin.

UTILITY USAGE DURING THE RENOVATION

The owner is responsible for providing power and water for the contractor's use. If both water and power are available on the premises, the accounts will be listed in the property owner's name and the property owner will pay these bills directly.

If temporary water or power is required, the contractor's price shall include the cost of setting up the connections, but the owner shall pay the water and power usage bills directly to the suppliers.

SITE INSPECTIONS

Representatives of the owner, the municipal inspections department, and the funding agent will visit the project site periodically to assess work in progress and to ensure that work meets the standards expressed or implied in this contract. Contractor shall ensure that all areas of work are available for inspection at all times.

DISPUTE RESOLUTION

The owner and the contractor hereby agree that if they cannot settle a dispute peaceably between themselves, they will resort first to mediation, and then to binding arbitration. Disputes shall be settled in accordance with the Construction Industry Arbitration Rules as set by the American Arbitration Association, 1633 Broadway, 10th Floor, New York, NY 10019.

PROPERTY OWNER'S RIGHTS AND RESPONSIBILITIES

DESIGNATE THE SOLE DECISION MAKER

Owner shall inform the contractor of the name and contact number for a single individual who shall be the sole decision maker on this project. The contractor shall not take direction from any other person unless he is instructed to, in writing, by the owner.

MAKE TIMELY DECISIONS

Owner must respond to a contractor's request for direction or information within three (3) business days. Failure to give direction or information to the contractor within three (3) business days may result in a delay for which the contractor shall be compensated, either by an extension to the construction schedule, or by financial compensation for his lost time (if there is no other work to be done), or both.

PROTECT MOVABLE PRIVATE PROPERTY

Owner is solely and entirely responsible for storing and protecting any property that they can lift or move. Such items may include (but are not limited to) the contents of closets, cabinets, and other storage areas, wall hangings, tabletop items such as family photographs, jewelry, stereo equipment, pets and pet paraphernalia, decorative accessories, toys, mail, knickknacks such as ashtrays or figurines, site accessories such as exterior in-ground walkway lights, porch, lawn, or patio furniture, garden sculptures, etc., or toys and tools such as bicycles, garden hoses, garbage cans, lawn mowers, etc. If any movable items are damaged during the construction work, the cost of replacing or repairing the items is the responsibility of the owner, not the contractor.

PROVIDE SITE ACCESS

The owner shall provide the contractor and his workers access to the work site during regular working hours—between 8:00 a.m. and 6:00 p.m. Monday through Friday.

CREATE NO CONTRACTUAL CONFLICTS

The owner may not engage any separate or secondary contractor(s), for pay or on a voluntary basis, to do any kind of work on this property during the time the general contractor is in his contract work period, without the express written permission of the general contractor.

SWEAT EQUITY

Property owner may not do any work himself that may be deemed as construction-related work, during the time the work is being done under this primary contract, without a signed sweat-equity agreement, or some other form of express written permission from the general contractor.

CONTRACTOR'S RIGHTS AND RESPONSIBILITIES

KNOWING SITE CONDITIONS AND CONTRACT DOCUMENTS

Contractor hereby attests that he has thoroughly familiarized himself with the existing site conditions and with all the work indicated or implied by the contract documents. It is the contractor's responsibility to check for errors or omissions in the design documents and to bring any such errors or omissions to the attention of the owner prior to the signing of this contract. Once the contract is signed, the owner has the right to refuse to compensate the contractor in time or money for accommodating any design errors or site conditions that were anticipatable, but that were not discussed earlier.

The discovery of a hidden problem on the site does not constitute a design error if that problem was not anticipatable.

SUPERVISION AND CONSTRUCTION PROCEDURES

The contractor shall supervise and direct all work on this site, using his best skills and intentions, and he shall be solely and entirely responsible for, and have control over, construction means, methods, techniques, sequences, and procedures, and for coordinating all portions of the work under the contract, unless the contract documents stipulate otherwise. The contractor, therefore, has responsibility for all work, for all actions of the work crew, and for all subcontractors and vendors that may have access to or provide materials for the work on this site.

PROVIDE ALL REQUIRED TOOLS, ETC.

The contractor shall provide all of his own materials, tools, and equipment, transportation, protective gear or tarps, ladders, miscellaneous materials, drinking water, etc., and may not use any of the owner's personal property for his work.

COMPLY WITH ALL CODES AND STANDARDS

All work under this contract shall comply with building code, with minimum housing code, with all zoning regulations (including those referring to historic preservation requirements), with the National Electrical Code, and with other applicable standards such as ASTM standards for HVAC, lead-paint abatement regulations, etc. References to any codes or standards pertain to the latest issue date of these documents that precedes the date of the signatures on this contract.

SECURE, SCHEDULE, AND PAY FOR ALL PERMITS AND INSPECTIONS

Contractor shall secure and pay for any permits and inspections required by the inspections department with jurisdiction over the project address. Proper sign-offs are required as a condition for interim and final payments;

rough-in inspections must be signed off prior to the 50 percent payment, and final inspections must be signed off, and certificate of occupancy must be secured and given to the owner prior to the release of the final payment.

SECURE AND PROVIDE EVIDENCE OF PROPER LICENSES

If the state where the project is being performed requires that the contractor have any special license(s), then the contractor shall provide a copy of such license to the property owner before signing this contract. It is the responsibility of the general contractor to learn and abide by these state laws. See also: General Contractor–Subcontractor Agreements.

CONTRACTOR INDEMNIFIES OWNER

The contractor hereby agrees to indemnify and hold harmless the owner, the owner's agent, the designer, and their consultants, agents, and employees from and against any claims, damages, losses, and expenses, including but not limited to attorneys' fees, arising out of or resulting from the performance of his work or the work of any person in his employ or under contract to him.

INSURANCE AND/OR BONDS

The contractor is required to provide the owner with an original insurance certificate indicating he has a minimum of $_____ combined general liability coverage currently in force, and that this coverage is written on the occurrence basis. Such coverage shall be maintained for the duration of the contract work period and the duration of the warranty period. A new certificate shall be provided to the owner with each new policy year.

Each insurance certificate must list the property owner as the certificate holder and as "additional insured as their interests may apply," or it will not be acceptable.

In addition, the contractor shall sign a disclosure stating that he is or is not required to carry workers' compensation insurance under prevailing state laws. If he is required to carry such insurance, then proof of such coverage shall be furnished to the property owner before the contract is signed and for every policy year during the contract work period and the warranty period.

If either policy should lapse or be terminated during the course of this contract, no further payments will be issued to this contractor until proof of new or renewed coverage is in the property owner's hands.

If the general liability insurance should lapse or be terminated or if the contractor neglects to provide the owner with current certificates in accordance with the standards stated above, during the warranty period, the owner has the right to seek legal recourse against the contractor at the contractor's expense.

Bonds shall remain in full force and effect throughout the work period and the warranty period. If the bonds should lapse or be terminated during the project work period or during the warranty period, the owner has the right to seek legal recourse against the contractor, at the contractor's expense.

If performance and/or payment bonds are required by the property owner or by state law, it is conclusively presumed that such bonds shall comply in every detail with state and federal statutes. The fully executed bond document shall be in the owner's hands before the contract is signed.

SEQUENCE OF WORK AND DAILY SCHEDULE

Contractor is solely and entirely responsible for the sequence of work and the daily schedule. Owner shall not direct or redirect mechanics, laborers, or subcontractors with regard to task priority or schedule.

THE ROLE OF THE SUPERINTENDENT

If the contractor has employed a superintendent or assistant whose job it is to be present on the site during performance of the work, that person shall represent the contractor, and communications given to that superintendent or assistant shall be as binding as if they had been given to the general contractor directly.

GENERAL CONTRACTOR–SUBCONTRACTOR AGREEMENTS

The relationship between the general contractor and his subs is solely and entirely the general contractor's responsibility. All agreements between the general contractor and his subs are governed by the terms and conditions of this contract. The contractor shall enforce strict discipline and good order among his employees and subcontractors, and shall not employ workers who are unfit or unskilled to do the work assigned to them.

NO KICKBACKS

Contractor and subcontractors shall comply with the Copeland Anti-Kickback Act (18 USC 874), as supplemented in Department of Labor regulations (29 CFR, Part 3), which provides that neither the general contractor nor his subcontractors shall be allowed to induce, by any means, any person employed in the construction, renovation, or repair of this property to give up any part of the compensation to which that worker is otherwise entitled.

SUBCONTRACTOR LICENSES AND PERMITS

General contractor is responsible for ensuring that subcontractors have proper licenses, secure required permits, and pass required inspections.

CONTRACT WORK HOURS AND SAFETY STANDARDS ACT

If this contract is financed in whole or in part by public funds, and if the value of this contract is in excess of $2,000, then the contractor and all subcontractors shall comply with Section 103 and 107 of the Contract Work Hours and Safety Standards Act (40 USC 327–330) as supplemented by the Department of Labor Regulations contained in 29 CFR Parts 3, 4, and 5a, which are briefly summarized below:

Under Section 103 of the act, contractor and subs are required to compute the wages of every mechanic and laborer on the basis of a standard workday of eight hours. A standard workweek is permissible provided the workers are compensated at a rate not less than one and one-half times the basic rate of pay for all hours worked in excess of forty hours in any workweek. Section 5 of the Federal Labor Standards Provisions and HUD form 4010 and 4010.1 set forth in detail the Section 103 requirements.

Section 107 of the act stipulates that no laborer or mechanic shall be required to work in surroundings or under working conditions that are unsanitary, hazardous, or dangerous to the worker's health and safety, as determined under construction, safety, and health standards promulgated by the secretary of labor. An exception is made to this rule where trained workers are doing hazardous materials remediation.

SHOP DRAWINGS

If any part of this work requires off-site fabrication, the contractor shall provide the owner with scaled, dimensioned shop drawings and product data, stamped and signed by the subcontractor who will be fabricating the components.

Owner reserves the right to review such drawings with a consultant or designer, and to return such submittals within fifteen (15) business days marked "approved," "approved as noted," which requires the fabrication to include the noted changes, or "rejected," which requires a redesign and resubmittal of the shop drawing within ten (10) business days of notification of disapproval.

The owner shall not compensate delays or expenses caused by rejection of shop drawings that should have met design specifications. Discretionary changes made by the owner shall be compensated.

SELECTING MATERIALS

All materials shall be free of hazardous substances, harsh chemicals, burred or sharp edges, or other health or safety hazards. All materials shall be new, appropriate to their use, first quality, readily available (not "custom" unless specified as such), durable in assembly, and installed in accordance with the manufacturer's instructions. Fixtures whose primary parts are plastic are unacceptable.

NORMAL WORKING HOURS

Contractor shall restrict his work to normal working hours, between 8 a.m. and 6 p.m. Monday through Friday, except where other arrangements have been made in advance and in writing with the owner.

WEATHER DELAYS

Change orders shall not be issued for time extensions to cover delays caused by weather unless the weather in question is not typical of the average conditions experienced in the project area over the last five (5)-year period. The contractor shall anticipate typical weather patterns and allow for them in the contract schedule.

CONTINUOUS WEATHER PROTECTION

Contractor shall provide continuous protection from weather for all parts of the owner's property that may be opened or in any way exposed as a part of the work under this contract.

KEEP CONTRACT DOCUMENTS ON-SITE

The contractor shall keep a record copy of the contract Terms and Conditions Statement, drawings and specifications, attachments, addenda, change orders, and any other contract modifications on the site at all times for use by the owner, the inspectors, and the lender.

SUBMITTALS AND SAMPLES

The contractor shall furnish the owner with samples of all materials specified by the design documents, for the owner's approval.

In the absence of specific instructions to the contrary, replacement and infill materials shall match as closely as possible the original materials that have been removed, and new materials are to be substantially similar in color and form to other materials in this dwelling, unless otherwise noted. Contractor shall provide owner with samples of finishes and styles that meet the above guidelines.

If the owner changes their materials or finishes, and selects items not available at the contractor's vendor or not within the contract bid allowance, the owner shall bear any additional costs and allow for time delays by executing a change order.

Given the opportunity to choose, the contractor shall make every effort to install fixtures and appliances that will save the property owner on utility and water bills in the future.

MATERIALS SUBSTITUTIONS

The contractor shall not make any substitutions to the materials stipulated in the design documents without the express permission of the owner. Such permission will be indicated by the owner's signature and date on a catalog specifications sheet or physical sample of the substituted material. A copy of the signed sample or spec sheet shall be provided to the owner for his files.

STAGING

During this contract work period, the contractor shall store tools and materials in a location agreed to by the property owner.

PROTECTING IMMOVABLE PRIVATE PROPERTY

Contractor is fully and solely responsible for protecting immovable private property. These items might include (but are not limited to) hardwood floors, fixed carpeting or room-sized rugs, large pieces of furniture such as couches or dining room tables, cabinetry, exterior awnings, heavy porch furniture, gutters, carports, fixed play equipment, driveway or parking pad, lawns, trees, bushes or gardens, etc.

Any damaged immovable items shall be repaired or replaced by the contractor at his own expense.

Before work shall be deemed to be complete, the contractor shall: (1) remove all excess paint from glass and hardware, (2) clean walls, floors, or floor coverings; (3) repair or replace damaged lawn or gardens; (4) snake out all lines and drains to the connection at the street, (5) restore any damaged areas, surfaces, or services to good working condition.

SITE CLEANING

If the site is occupied during the work period, the contractor shall keep the site "broom clean" on a daily basis.

If the site is not occupied, the contractor shall keep the site safe for inspection walk-throughs by removing debris from work areas, and placing it in a covered large waste bin or another covered container, which shall be secured against entry by children, against vandalism, and against weather at all times.

Debris shall be removed from the house daily and from the site at least once a week. If debris is left on the site for more than a week, the owner has the right to have it removed at the contractor's expense by deducting that cost from the contractor's next payment.

ADJACENT PROPERTIES

If adjacent properties or property owners will be affected by work under this contract, it is the contractor's responsibility to notify them of this risk and to protect them from harm.

"Affecting" includes driving over adjacent land to reach a remote destination on the project property; includes dropping trees or tree limbs on adjacent land; includes making noise before 8 a.m. or after 6 p.m. that may disturb the neighbors, and the like.

UNSATISFACTORY WORK

The owner shall notify the contractor in writing of any work that they find unsatisfactory within three (3) business days of identifying such a problem. If the contractor fails to correct the work or consistently fails to carry out work in accordance with the highest standards of the construction industry in the project area, the owner has the right to take remedial action against the contractor.

ACTING IN BAD FAITH

The contractor may be deemed to have acted in bad faith if he does or causes or allows to be done any of the following:
• Acts of deceit, fraud, or willful misrepresentation;
• Covering faulty work or dangerous or deficient existing conditions with new materials;
• Allowing the presence of alcoholic beverages or drugs on the job site; or
• Being or allowing subcontractors or employees to be under the influence of alcohol or drugs while on the job;

- Failing to pay subcontractors, vendors, or employees in a timely fashion, or in any way endangering the completion of work, or the continuity of the warranty;
- Failing to meet the highest standards of the construction industry in the project area; or
- Failing to honor legitimate warranty claims in a timely manner during the warranty period.

ABANDONMENT

If the contractor fails to have workers on the site for more than five (5) consecutive workdays, unless there is a prior written agreement between owner and contractor allowing this, the contractor shall be deemed to have abandoned the site, and the owner may take remedial action.

Change orders shall not be issued for time extensions to cover delays caused by the contractor not manning the site properly.

REMEDIAL ACTION AGAINST THE CONTRACTOR

Remedial action may include (but is not limited to) any of the following:
- Withhold payment for the unsatisfactory work until such work is corrected;
- Withhold payment entirely until the general quality of work meets the standards stipulated by the contract;
- Temporarily stop work in the area of concern;
- Temporarily stop work on the project until the cause for concern has been remedied; or
- Stop work altogether and taking legal remedies to resolve a dispute.

WARRANTY TERMS

The contractor warrants to the owner that materials and equipment furnished under the contract will be of good quality and new unless otherwise required or permitted by the contract documents; that the work will be free from defects not inherent in the quality required or permitted; and that the work will conform to the requirements of the contract documents. Work not conforming to these requirements, including substitutions not properly approved and authorized, may be considered defective or unacceptable or both.

The contractor's warranty specifically excludes remedy for damage or defect caused by abuse, modifications not executed by the contractor, improper or insufficient maintenance, improper operation, or normal use and wear and tear.

WARRANTY PERIODS

The contractor warrants all work on any roof surface for thirty-six (36) months and all other work under this contract for twelve (12) months, beginning from the date of the final payment. There is no limit on the warranty of work governed by law or the building code if that work was not done correctly in the first place.

WARRANTY CLAIMS

If the property owner discovers a deficiency in the contract work after the job is signed off and the contractor has been paid, and if the warranty period stipulated in this contract is still in effect, the property owner shall notify the contractor immediately and in writing of such deficiency, and the contractor shall respond within one (1) week of such notice, and shall complete the repair within thirty (30) days.

If the repair is not completed within thirty (30) days of the first written notice, or in accordance with some other written, agreed-to timeframe, the property owner shall have recourse to the contractor's insurance or bond, or, if these remedies are not useful, the owner has the right to seek a third-party judgment against the contractor through legal action.

If the owner pays another contractor to remedy a problem left behind by the contractor, such action does not relieve this contractor of the full force of his own warranty obligations on all other work.

CONSTRUCTION SCHEDULE AND PAYMENTS

THE CONSTRUCTION SCHEDULE

Time is of the essence. Once the contractor has begun work, he shall pursue the work in a diligent and continuous manner until it is complete.

Failure to work diligently during the contract period shall be grounds for remedial action or for dismissal from the job, and the contractor will forfeit any retainage that has been withheld from his interim payments if that money is required to correct the deficiencies or to finish the job in a way that is satisfactory to the owner. Further, the owner may have recourse to legal action against the contractor if more funds are required to complete the project than remain undisbursed at the time the contractor abandoned the site.

INTERIM PAYMENT REQUIREMENTS

This contract stipulates interim percent-complete benchmarks that must be met before a payment will be released. Contractors shall not be paid for less than that portion of the work. It is the percent of work complete that determines the release of money, not the passage of time.

PROGRESS ASSESSMENTS

If at any time the contractor is 3 percent or more behind schedule, this condition shall be deemed a matter of concern. The contractor shall provide to the owner, upon request, a written plan for catching up, and that proposed accelerated schedule shall be monitored. Continued inability to work in accordance with the construction schedule shall be deemed an act of bad faith on the part of the contractor, and the owner has the right to take remedial action.

Formal progress evaluations shall be conducted by the owner and the contractor together, every second week. Owner and contractor must agree on the percent-complete on every task in the contract, and the value of the payment for that period (if any) shall be calculated based upon the amount the parties agree has been completed, minus a 10 percent retainage and any prior payments.

Interim payments will require appropriate inspections department sign-offs, and final payment requires that the contractor has passed all final inspections and secured and submitted a certificate of occupancy, etc. (see "Completing the Project" below).

If the project property is historically significant, the preservation authority must also approve the completed work prior to the release of the final check. If Davis–Bacon laws apply, payroll submittals must be complete and acceptable to the compliance officer.

If the owner cannot attend a prescheduled progress evaluation walk-through, he shall designate a local, legal representative and shall honor the decisions that representative makes so that the contractor's payments are not delayed.

WITHHOLDING RETAINAGE

The property owner will automatically withhold a standard 10 percent of the amount earned from every interim payment. The final payment will be for 100 percent of the contract value, with no retainage withheld.

PAYING SUBCONTRACTORS AND VENDORS

The contractor is fully and solely responsible for making appropriate and timely payments to subcontractors and vendors.

RELEASING CONTRACTOR PAYMENTS

The contractor shall be paid within _____ business days of the draw walk-through provided the following conditions are met:

• The percent-complete of every task is uncontested,
• The appropriate formal inspections have been passed,
• All applicable regulatory standards and requirements have been met,
• The work in place meets the highest standards of construction craftsmanship, and
• All conditions of the contract have been met for that work period.

    Both the contractor and an impartial witness shall sign and date a lien waiver or a photocopy of the check when he receives the check in hand. Any late fees incurred by the contractor shall be deducted from his final payment. If extensive late fees are anticipated, the owner has the right to withhold additional retainage in the amount equaling the anticipated penalty charges.

COMPLETING THE PROJECT

Contractor shall ensure that proper insurance, workers' compensation coverage, and bond documents are in order prior to sign-off, and that original copies of all documents have been given to the owner before the release of the final payment. In addition, the contractor must complete 100 percent of contract work, which includes (but is not limited to) the following, before final payment will be released:

• Complete all work in the contract documents,
• Complete all punch-list items,
• Pass all inspections,
• Pass a hazardous materials clearance test,
• Secure and submit to the owner an original certificate of occupancy,
• Train owner in the use of all new equipment and appliances,
• Remove all debris and excess materials, and clean the work area so it is ready for occupancy,
• Fill, grade, seed, water, and cover with straw all areas of lawn damaged during the work,
• Repair or replace any surfaces or immovable objects damaged by the workers,
• Clean carpeting of any spots or stains and touch up all paint, and
• Rod out and flush all lines and drains to the connections at the street.

PROVIDE SUBCONTRACTOR LIST TO OWNER

Contractor shall submit to the owner a list of all of his subcontractors and materials vendors, including their tax ID numbers and contractor license numbers, contact name, firm name and address, and contact phone numbers, as a condition of the release of the final payment.

OPERATING AND MAINTENANCE MANUALS

Manuals for all new products, appliances, and machinery shall be given to the owner, and the contractor shall provide complete information about the manufacturer, the vendor, and the make, model, and serial number of each new item.

LATE PENALTIES

There shall be a penalty for not completing the work on time. Money will be withheld from the contractor's final check in the amounts stated below, for every calendar day beyond the completion date that he is still working.

CONTRACT AMOUNT

$0–$30,000	$30,000.01–$50,000	$50,000.01–$75,000	$75,000.01–$100,000	$100K+

First 5 calendar days

$10/day	$50/day	$75/day	$100/day	$120/day

Every day thereafter

$50/day	$100/day	$135/day	$170/day	$250/day

PAYMENT SCHEDULE

The contractor shall satisfactorily complete all work in this contract (including submittal of all required paperwork) in _____ calendar days (_____ 28-day pay periods)

Start Date: _____

_____ percent Complete Target Date: _____

_____ percent Complete Target Date: _____

_____ percent Complete Target Date: _____

_____ percent Complete Target Date: _____

_____ percent Complete Target Date: _____

_____ percent Complete Target Date: _____

_____ percent Complete Target Date: _____

Completion Date: _____

CONTRACT PRICE

The Contractor agrees to complete all work in the base bid for the lump sum of:

$_____ and xx/100

(Write out the price in words here)

($_____.00)

(Write the price in numbers)

Unless otherwise noted, items labeled as "Alternates" in the design documents are not included in this contract.

PART 2: CONSTRUCTION DOCUMENTS

Construction documents, including, but not limited to, drawings, specifications, addenda, and special conditions statements, are attached here and/or are incorporated by reference into this contract agreement.

List of Drawings:
Specifications Dated _____: _____ pages.

List of other attachments:
ALL DOCUMENTS LISTED ABOVE ARE ATTACHED HERE AND INCORPORATED BY REFERENCE INTO THE CONTRACT.

SIGNATURES
Signatures below indicate an agreement to comply with all of the terms and conditions indicated in this contract document. When the contract is fully executed the contractor is authorized to begin work on the start date indicated above, unless he is notified otherwise, in writing, by the property owner.

PROPERTY OWNER:

_____

Print Owner's Name & Complete, Permanent Address

_____   _____

Property Owner's Signature   *Date*

_____

Print Owner's Legal Agent's Name & Complete, Permanent Address

_____   _____

Signature of Legal Agent   *Date*

CONTRACTOR:

_____

Print Contracting Firm Name & Complete Address

_____

Print Company Owner's Name

_____   _____

Signature of Owner of General Contracting Firm   *Date:*

INDEX